ENGINEERING PITTSBURGH

ENGINEERING PITTSBURGH

A History of Roads, Rails, Canals, Bridges & More

ASCE Pittsburgh Section
100th Anniversary Publication Committee

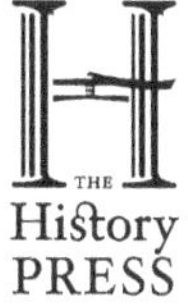

Published by The History Press
Charleston, SC
www.historypress.com

Copyright © 2018 by American Society of Civil Engineers Pittsburgh Section
All rights reserved

Back cover, bottom image courtesy of the Carnegie Library of Pittsburgh.

First published 2018

Manufactured in the United States

ISBN 9781625859693

Library of Congress Control Number: 2018942435

Notice: The information in this book is true and complete to the best of our knowledge. It is offered without guarantee on the part of the authors or The History Press. The authors and The History Press disclaim all liability in connection with the use of this book.

All rights reserved. No part of this book may be reproduced or transmitted in any form whatsoever without prior written permission from the publisher except in the case of brief quotations embodied in critical articles and reviews.

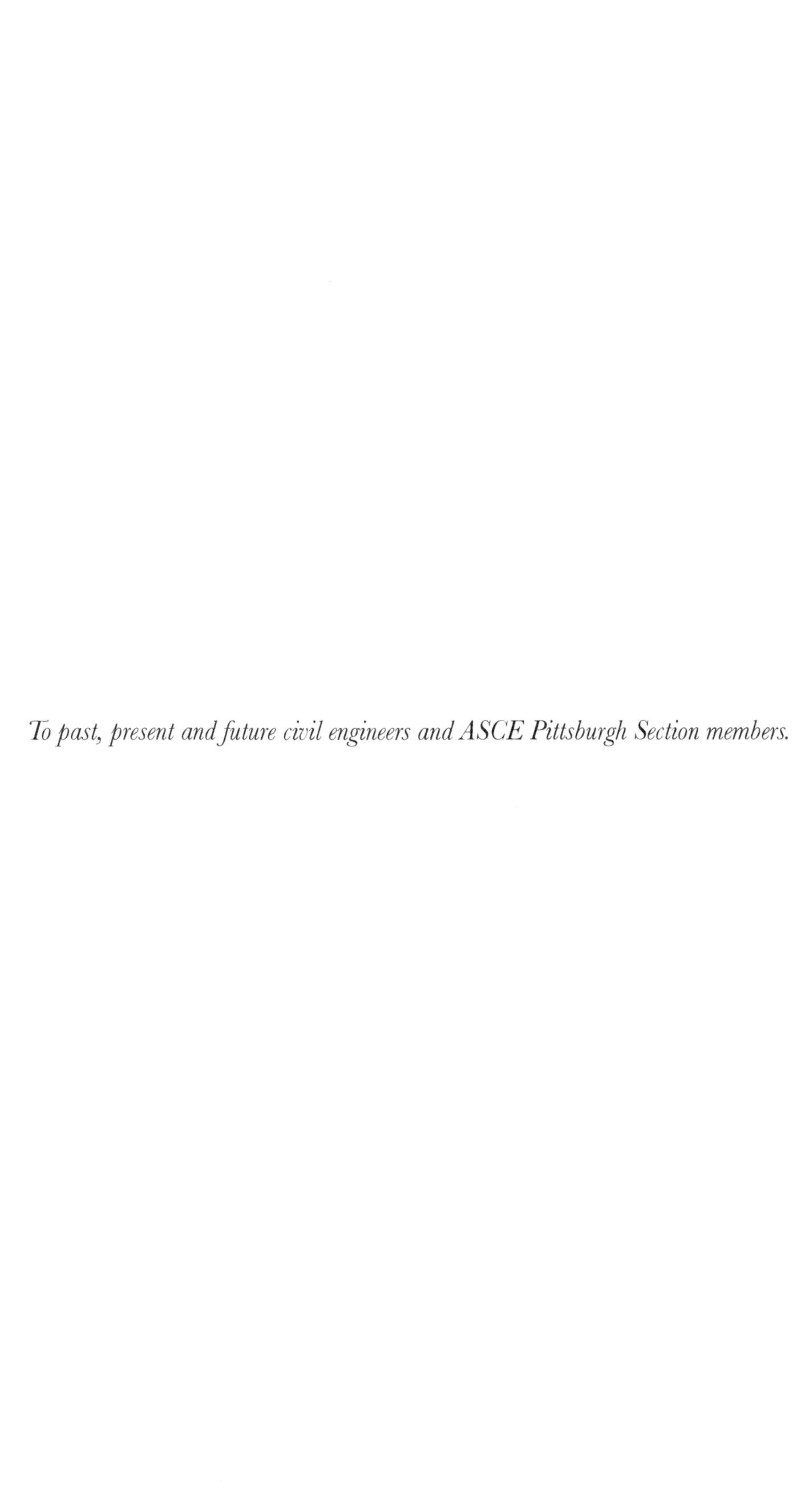

To past, present and future civil engineers and ASCE Pittsburgh Section members.

CONTENTS

ACKNOWLEDGEMENTS

This publication is part of the centennial celebration of the American Society of Civil Engineers (ASCE) Pittsburgh Section. We gratefully recognize the legacy of past and current Section leaders and members who, since its founding in 1918, have supported the Section's purpose of "providing opportunities to improve and develop technical and professional skills of civil engineers, and provide accurate information to support responsible development of public policy that governs and affects the profession of civil engineering."

The authors recognize our local academic institutions for shaping the highest quality of civil engineers for society's benefit. These institutions have advanced our profession through theoretical and applied research, educational training, collaborations with local industry and government and by maintaining a wealth of accessible technical resources and professional outreach. We convey our deepest appreciation for the innumerable contributions to civil engineering, and thus to this publication, from Carnegie Mellon University, Geneva College, Point Park University and the University of Pittsburgh.

To our families, friends, colleagues, mentors, collaborators and employers who provided research, editorial content, knowledge, resources, understanding and—foremost—patience and support: you have our deepest gratitude and lasting appreciation.

The content of this publication was enriched by the selfless third-party reviews provided by Thomas G. Leech, PE, and James L. Withiam, PhD, PE. Tom and Jim, we heartily thank you for your valuable contributions.

Special gratitude for their collaboration goes to David A. Dzombak, Ralph W. Gilbert Jr., Radisav D. Vidic, Jelani J. Virgo, Helen Wilson, Lauren Winkler and David E. Wohlwill.

Written on behalf of the editorial team of *Engineering Pittsburgh: A History of Roads, Rails, Canals, Bridges and More.*

N. CATHERINE BAZÁN-ARIAS, PhD, PE, D.GE, PMP, F.ASCE
Publication Coordinator

GREGORY F. SCOTT, PE, M.ASCE
TODD M. WILSON, MBA, PE, M.ASCE
Publication Facilitators

Prologue

CIVIL ENGINEERS, ASCE AND THE PITTSBURGH REGION

[A]nd upon whom will rest the responsibility for getting us out of this predicament if not upon the engineer—the final repository of all the toughest problems of humanity?
—Winters Haydock, chief engineer, Citizens Committee on City Plan of Pittsburgh, November 22, 1921

By N. Catherine Bazán-Arias, PhD, PE

In 2018, the American Society of Civil Engineers (ASCE) Pittsburgh Section celebrates its 100th anniversary. But for more than a century, civil engineers have been part of Pittsburgh's development and resilience, as well as its transformation from a military fort to a vibrant, forward-thinking city. For the past century, the ASCE Pittsburgh Section has proudly been part of the support system of our local civil engineers. This first centennial publication aims to highlight some of the civil engineering achievements in Pittsburgh and its surrounding regions—the works that link our city and its environs to our nation.

To begin this journey, let us establish our framework. Founded in 1852, ASCE is the nation's oldest engineering society. Its mission is "to deliver value to our members, advance civil engineering, and protect the public health, safety, and welfare." As described by ASCE, "Civil engineers design, build, and maintain the foundation for our modern society—our roads and bridges, drinking water and energy systems, sea ports and airports, and the infrastructure for a cleaner environment, to name just a few." In Pittsburgh, civil engineers are responsible for our roads, rails, bridges, tunnels, waterways and highways. The design of canals, locks and dams and water and wastewater systems is the work of civil engineers. These civil engineering works provide clean water, control flooding, harness hydraulic power and typically are part of the critical infrastructure that sustains our socioeconomic resilience. Through instruction at our local universities and colleges, Pittsburgh's civil engineers have transformed a once roughened terrain prone to landslide and floods into one of the most livable cities in the country.

DID YOU KNOW?

The Pittsburgh Section was initiated in 1917 but was not ratified until 1918. It is theorized that the onset of the influenza pandemic of 1918–19 caused the delay.

How did present-day Pittsburgh develop? To answer that question, we step back to the time when the first Native Americans arrived in the region. As attested by sites such as the Meadowcroft Rockshelter, located about thirty miles southwest of Pittsburgh, people have lived in our region for at least sixteen thousand years. As the first settlers looked for shelter and food, they had to rely on innovation, ingenuity and resourcefulness to establish water collection systems, trade routes and settlements that would weather seasonal changes and provide protection. These settlers realized that the Monongahela, Allegheny and Ohio Rivers were sources of food, water, transportation and, alas, floods. Thus, the need to design, build and maintain infrastructure in our region—and the need for civil engineers—was born out of the need to coexist with topographic and climatic benefits and challenges.

In this book, we journey back to the 1600s, when the city of Pittsburgh and the Commonwealth of Pennsylvania were yet to be born. From descriptive, phonetic Native American names such as Monongahela ("falling banks"), Youghiogheny ("contrary stream") and Punxsutawney ("town of the mosquitoes") to our present-day state borders, the "Pennsylvania's Borders" chapter allows us to witness charters, land disputes and reconciling agreements enacted by our young United States government. We will traverse the Allegheny Mountain by the Allegheny Portage Railroad, crossing incline planes for the first time, using wooden ties instead of stone sleepers and constructing reservoirs on the east and west side of the Allegheny ridge to supply water for canals. The canals that made the navigation of our river network feasible are vividly described in our "Canals" chapter. The daunting history that made the Pennsylvania, Beaver Division, Erie Extension and Lake Erie to the Ohio Canals realities comes to life working around budding towns with limiting construction equipment and transportation and scarce budgets, as well as how these were overcome.

Our "Railroads" chapter brings to life the events that generated the image of the railroad engineer, transit in tow, in search of feasible layout to connect villages, towns and cities. From plans in 1830 to link Washington, Pennsylvania and Pittsburgh to the then-new National Road through legendary constructions and visionaries such as Charles De Hass, J.P. Morgan and George Jay Gould, we follow the desires and decisions that enabled the industrial and commercial development of Western Pennsylvania. We step behind the history of the Chartiers Valley Railroad, the Horseshoe Curve, the Gallitzin Tunnel, the Wabash and Montour Railroads and our present-day Hot Metal Bridge, to name a few.

We then segue into the "Roads and Highways" chapter, delving into the transformation from Native American trade routes and packhorse roads, such as Braddock's and Forbes' Roads, to the birth of the nation's first highways and the Pennsylvania Turnpike. Along the way, we witness the challenges in planning, constructing and maintaining roads and the delicate balance between local, regional and national interests in funding some of our now well-known highways. Speaking of transformations, one of the city's most notable landmarks, the juncture of our three rivers locally known as "the Point," is surrounded by arguably Pittsburgh's most notable constructions: bridges. And while the specific number of bridges may be debatable, it is certainly without a doubt notable. It has taken hundreds of bridges to traverse our deep valleys, creeks, rivers and hilly terrain. Distinguished engineers such as John A. Roebling (wire rope), Gustav Lindenthal (Smithfield Bridge) and George S. Richardson (Fort Pitt and Liberty Bridges, among others), optimized materials and construction techniques and even revolutionized bridge elements to render our city's numerous passages over water and land. Our "Bridges" chapter provides a succinct account of the need, creativity and civil engineering expertise that has been required for some of Pittsburgh's most distinguished constructed features to persevere through population expansion and extensive use.

One of the main purposes of the infrastructure achievements is to provide people the means to quickly and safely traverse distances through the area's irregular terrain. The "Public Transportation" chapter begins with our most

> It wriggles in and it wriggles out
> And leaves the traveler still in doubt
> Whether the snake who made the track
> Was going south or coming back.
>
> *—unknown nineteenth-century poet describing the Waynesburg and Washington Railroad*

basic way to travel: walking. Pittsburgh's legendary public steps—maintained by our city—once upon a time were the only connection for many homes located across our many impressive hills. An alternative to these challenging cardiovascular throughways came along when our "inclines" were built, of which two remain: the Duquesne and the Mount Washington. Follow along the history of our public ways and transportation as steps and inclines gave way to horsecar lines, cable cars, electric streetcars, trolleys and Light Rail Transit. From downtown's underground subway to the pioneer development of our busway and technology that is making self-driving vehicles a reality—all are presented alongside Pittsburgh's growth.

Speaking of technology, our next chapter takes us through the history of one of the most revolutionary modes of transportation: aviation. From Brunot's Island and Mayer Air Field to our international presence, our "Airports and Aviation" chapter narrates the story of the pioneering days of aviation, highlighting the contributions of the early airfields, aircraft and personalities that emerged from Western Pennsylvania. Did you know that Samuel Pierpont Langley, a director of the Allegheny Observatory, attempted manned flying less than ten years before the Wright brothers' historic flight in 1903? Or that Amelia Earhart once landed in Rodgers Field? Fly alongside the anecdotes in this chapter as it unveils how community airfields that hosted notable achievements, aircraft and celebrities became modern-day airports that support our region's growing economy.

For all of the aforementioned achievements, what would our city and region be without drinking water or proper control of our wastewater and floods? The chapters on "Drinking Water," "Wastewater" and flood risk management aim to address a cherished element and prominent resource, water, as well as its impact and contributions to our city and our region. This triad of journeys begins with a presentation on the time when rivers and wells were sufficient to provide for early settlers and young communities. However, this proved insufficient as population and basic needs grew. The chapter continues through the early attempts to store drinking water in untreated, uncontrolled reservoirs to modern-day, environmentally regulated facilities that provide the once-upon-a-time luxury of safe, reliable drinking water. Follow along the transformation of our first public water system, servicing about 1,600 people, to the modern-day reservoirs that fulfill state and federal quality requirements to provide drinking water to nearly eighty-three thousand customers.

Our historical journey proceeds with our next chapter and the first sand filtration and chlorination of Pittsburgh's water supplies. These methods were implemented to address the heavy pollution that our rivers were experiencing from untreated sewage and industrial waste, including acid mine drainage and mill effluent. The "Wastewater" chapter delves into the partnerships that evolved after World War II between elected officials and corporations to address smoke abatement, flood control and regional sanitation, culminating (after overcoming significant challenges) in an award-winning collection and wastewater treatment system.

DID YOU KNOW?

Emerald Park was built from a Native American trail that once traversed "Coal Hill," as Mount Washington and Duquesne Heights were known.

As much as water is essential to our well-being, it can also be a threat when uncontrolled; massive quantities flow into regional streams and rivers within a relatively short period of time. Our flood risk management chapter, "Navigation and Flood Control on the Three Rivers," takes us through the often-turbulent events that demanded the construction of dams and their appurtenances to prevent loss of life and damage to property and infrastructure. Using lessons learned from the various flood events through the latest constructions of the twentieth century, this chapter vividly describes how small creeks became agents of disaster and how seemingly calm rivers swelled to overwhelm downtown Pittsburgh and surrounding neighborhoods, prompting federal legislation aptly named the "Flood Control Act." The development and construction of cofferdams, float-in dams, slackwater lakes and lock and dam systems is presented through a series of regional case histories and interweaved in a discussion of the future of river navigation on the Three Rivers.

Culminating our journey, we travel to the height of Pittsburgh's steel industry and the construction of some of the most iconic buildings of the late nineteenth and early twentieth centuries: the Carnegie Steel, the Park and the Frick Buildings. Shortly thereafter, the Pennsylvania Chocolate Company Building, now known as the Penn Rose Building, became the first all-concrete building in Pittsburgh. But one of the most emblematic structures still standing came from a visionary chancellor, John Bowman, the driving force behind the Cathedral of Learning, one of the structural designs of Homer S. Balcom (of Empire State Building fame). Although classes were held in 1931, the construction phase was not considered complete until 1937. Through some other notable works, it was not until 1971 that Pittsburgh's tallest building to date was completed. The U.S. Steel Building, at sixty-four stories and 841 feet, was at the time the tallest building in the world outside New York and Chicago. Structural designer Leslie E. Robertson incorporated a then-new weathering constructional steel formulated to resist corrosion despite remaining unpainted. The massive columns are exposed on the exterior, resulting in the distinctive dark-brown oxide coating, which requires minimum maintenance, that we can see today. The hollow columns are filled with water and a rust inhibitor to provide fire protection. This last chapter covers these and many more notable buildings that grace our city.

Did You Know?

As many as ninety-seven thousand local children donated a dime apiece in the famous "Buy a Brick" campaign to help fund the Cathedral of Learning's construction. Each child received a certificate testifying that he or she was a member of the "fellowship of builders of the Cathedral of Learning."

Pittsburgh's resiliency and resourcefulness in shifting from an industrial economy to one presently based on healthcare, research and tourism are significantly founded on strong academic formations. Our local colleges and universities have forged legions of civil engineers—several of whom are ASCE Pittsburgh Section members—who strived to build a better quality of life for their communities and surrounding environs. Our oldest and most prolific institution, in terms of number of alumni, was founded in a log cabin in 1787 as the Pittsburgh Academy. Developing rapidly, it had grown into the Western Pennsylvania University (WPU) by 1819 and, by 1883, had graduated thirteen engineers. That same year, WPU graduated its first official civil engineer, William Carey Coffin Jr., and ten years later, it graduated its first African American civil engineer, William Hunter Dammond. WPU was graduating about a dozen civil engineers annually when its name was changed to the University of Pittsburgh (Pitt) in 1908.

Following World War I, the Civil Engineering Department was graduating about 20 students per year. One of its 1930 graduates, Michael A. Gross, PE, was recognized for his lifetime of service to the ASCE Pittsburgh Section through its most prestigious award, named in his honor. The civil engineering major has been continuously accredited by ABET since its inception in 1936. By the time the new Engineering Hall was constructed in 1952, Pitt was graduating about 35 civil engineers. Its first PhD graduate was James V. Hamel in 1970. Today, the Department of Civil and Environmental Engineering at the University of Pittsburgh is proud of its civil engineering heritage and its joint role of educating undergraduate (currently 290 enrolled) and graduate (currently 140 enrolled) students and advancing technology through theoretical and applied research. The Pitt ASCE Student Chapter has been a strong supporter of the ASCE Pittsburgh

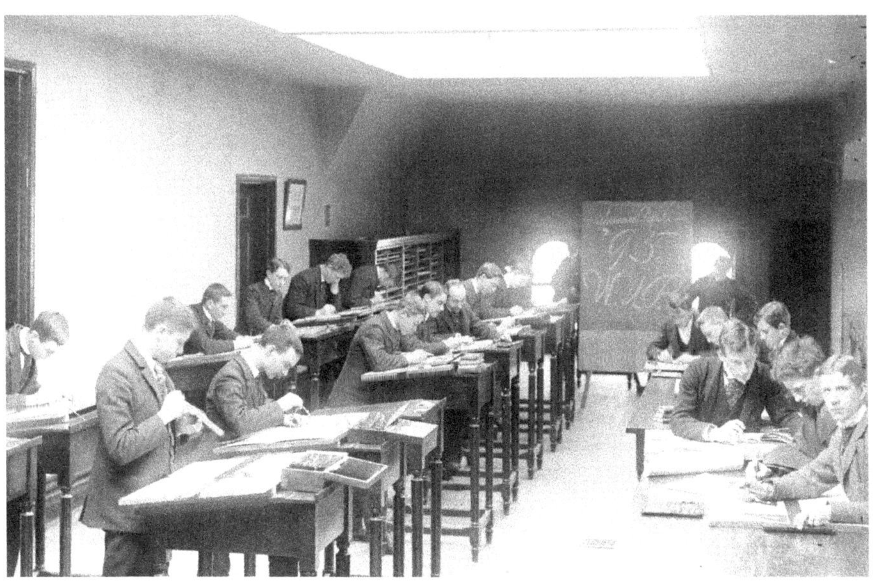

Drafting class in the engineering classroom at the Western University of Pennsylvania, circa 1895. *Archives & Special Collections, University of Pittsburgh Library System.*

Section since their joint inception with the Section in 1918. The influence of the nearly 6,000 Pitt civil engineering alumni on the infrastructure and natural environment in Western Pennsylvania is an outstanding legacy.

Another prestigious local department of civil engineering was initiated as the Study of Civil Practice (SCP) under the School of Applied Science in 1905. Part of the Carnegie Institute of Technology (CIT), the new SCP offered courses in structural design, railroad construction and municipal engineering. In 1908, the SPC became the Department of Civil Engineering, and by 1924, an ASCE student chapter had been formed. The Bachelor of Science in civil engineering at CIT was first accredited in 1936 by the Engineers Council for Professional Development (ECPD), the forerunner of ABET, and the first PhD was awarded to Yisheng Mao in 1921. Graduate education increased significantly after World War II, when research received greater emphasis nationwide. In 1967, CIT merged with the Mellon Institute, a science and industrial research center, to form Carnegie Mellon University (CMU). A research program in field robotics initiated in the early 1980s grew

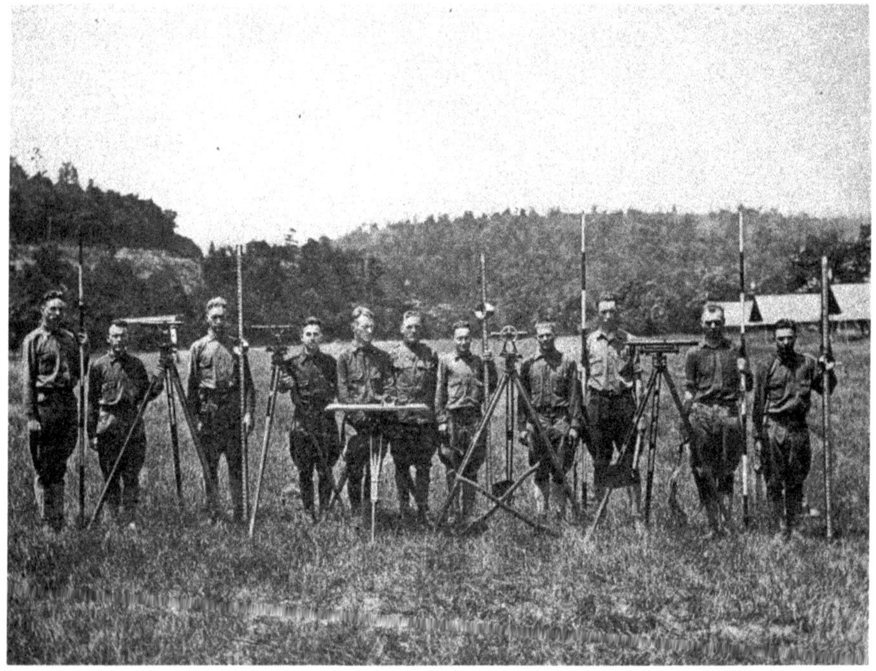

Surveying class at Camp Hamilton, circa 1917–30. After World War I, training focused less on military preparation and more on engineering. *Archives & Special Collections, University of Pittsburgh Library System.*

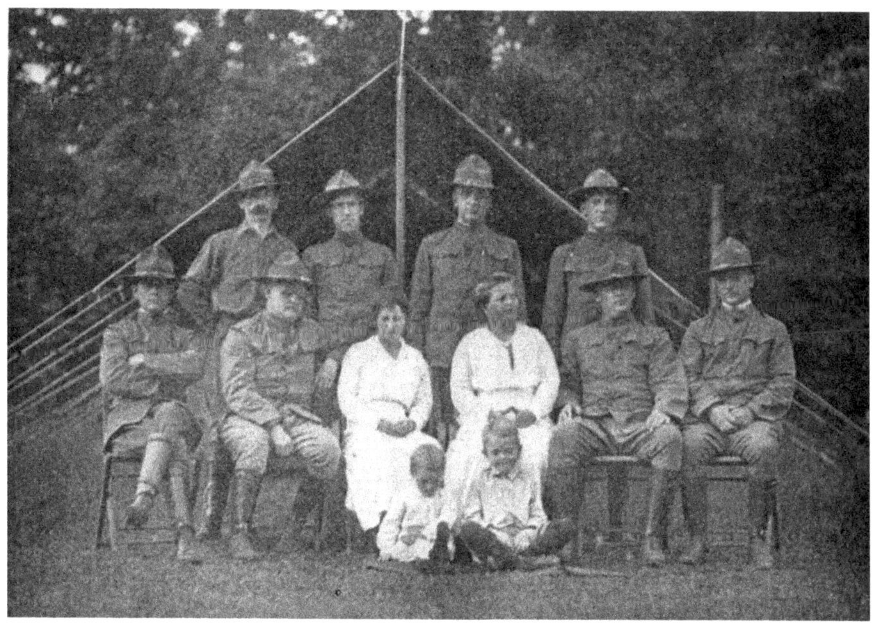

Engineering faculty at Camp Hamilton in Windber, Pennsylvania, circa 1917–30. Faculty provided classroom and field instruction in surveying, hydraulics and sanitation. *Archives & Special Collections, University of Pittsburgh Library System.*

rapidly and became the Carnegie Mellon Field Robotics Center, now part of the distinguished Robotics Institute. In 1994, the department changed its name to the Department of Civil and Environmental Engineering, reflecting a growing education and research field. Today, CMU is renowned internationally and continues its efforts to innovate and help advance the field in the twenty-first century.

Over the decades, additional academic programs providing civil engineering degrees, or degrees that support civil engineers, have developed in the region. Some of these institutions include Point Park University, Geneva College and the Community College of Allegheny County. Thus, academia continues to forge professionals who contribute to the progressive development of our city and its surrounding areas.

This publication recognizing the 100th anniversary of the founding of the Pittsburgh Section of ASCE is a brief testament to the commitment and dedication of the men and women who relentlessly strived—and those who continue to strive—toward the vision of "building a better quality of life" by creating and sustaining our local and regional infrastructure. Several of its members have been recognized by awards of merit and

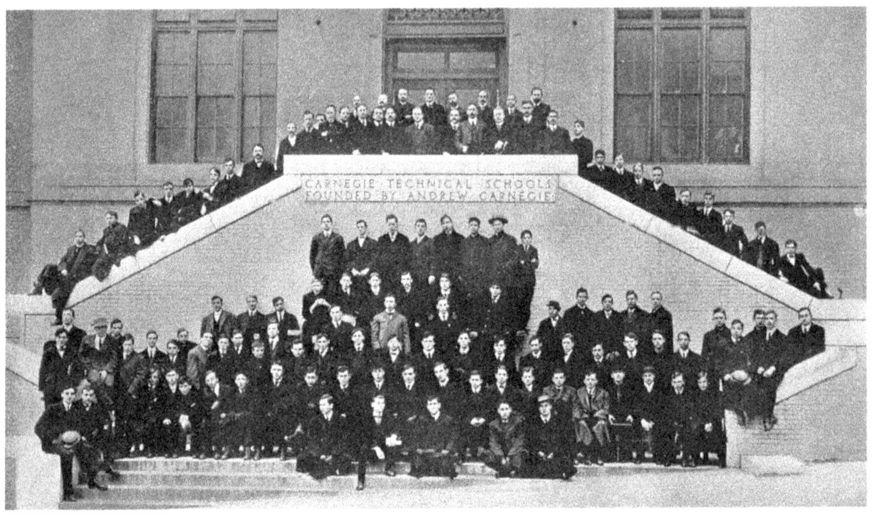

First class and faculty of the "Study of Civil Practice" under the School of Applied Sciences, circa 1906. *Carnegie Mellon University Archives.*

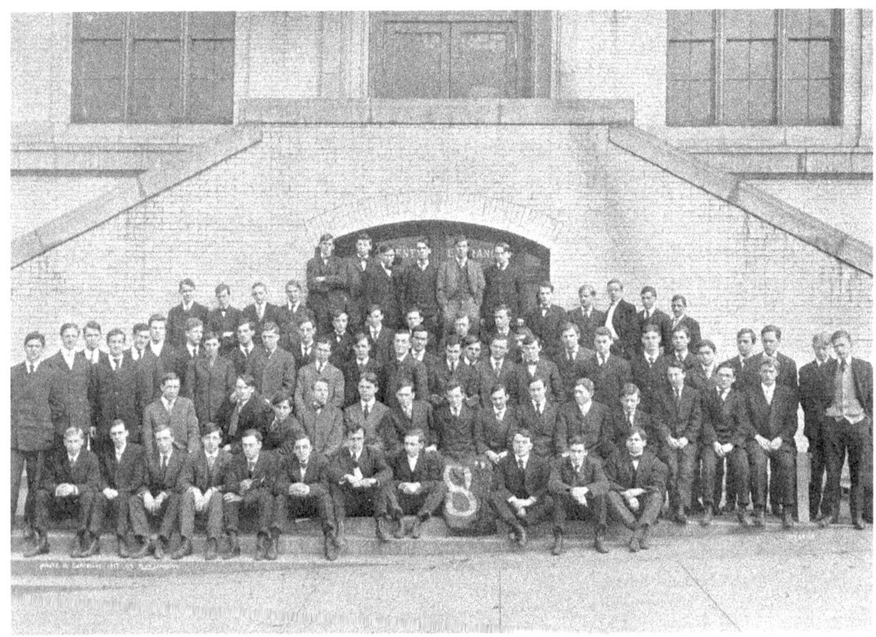

First "Study of Civil Practice" graduating class under the School of Applied Science, circa 1908. *Carnegie Mellon University Archives.*

achievement; all have been civil engineers working to contribute their skills and knowledge to our profession. The chapters herein present a glimpse of some of the region's and city's civil engineering achievements generated from collaborations between academia, industry and research. And while the chapters' contents are not exhaustive, the authors writing them have aimed to be representative. Join us in this journey into civil engineering in Pittsburgh and its surrounding regions!

PENNSYLVANIA'S BORDERS

How They Got that Way

By Gregory F. Scott, PE, and Jodi S. Klebick

First Peoples

The establishment of what is we now recognize as the Commonwealth of Pennsylvania began in 1681, although this land was inhabited long before that date by Native Americans. As evidenced by artifacts from the Meadowcroft Rockshelter in Washington County, Pennsylvania, the area may have been continually inhabited for more than nineteen thousand years, since Paleo-Indian times. At the time of William Penn's arrival, there were about twenty thousand Native Americans living in what is now Pennsylvania. These people collectively belonged to two groups made up of many tribes, based on the languages they spoke: the Algonquin and the Haudenosaunee—more commonly called the Iroquois Confederacy of tribes. The Lenape and the Munsee tribes were offshoots of the Leni-Lenape (meaning "True People") tribe of the Algonquins who inhabited the eastern portions of current-day Pennsylvania along the Delaware River and were therefore commonly known by settlers as the Delaware Indians. The Susquehannock tribe lived along the Susquehanna River to which they gave its name. Northern portions of modern Pennsylvania overlapped the southern boundaries of the Iroquois Confederacy, with the Oneida and Seneca tribes being the largest groups in this region. The far northwest was once occupied by the Erie tribe. The

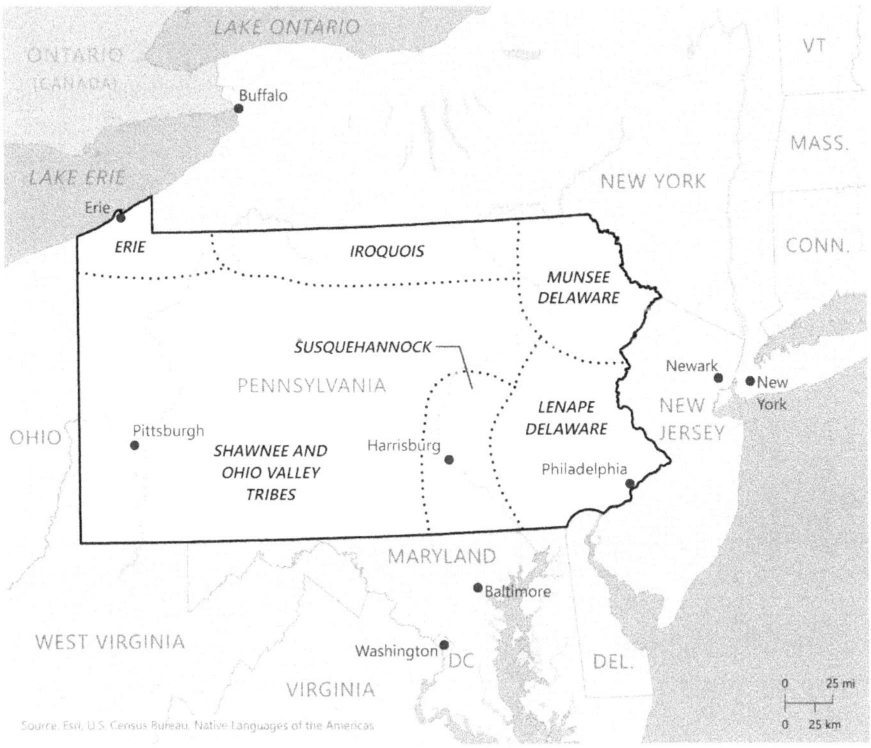

Native American tribes of Pennsylvania. *Lauren Winkler.*

balance of what is now central and Western Pennsylvania was inhabited by the Shawnee peoples, who were also in the Algonquian language group. The boundaries of the land controlled by Native American peoples were never formally established by survey for "landownership" as understood by colonizing western Europeans.

Throughout the course of their history, Native American cultures rose and fell due to variations of food availability, tribal warfare and cultural assimilation. The Monongahela culture was one such people whose presence gave its name to a significant river in Western Pennsylvania, but that culture had vanished by the beginning of the 1600s. Also affecting Native American peoples and the extent of their occupation of this region was the introduction and spread of European diseases. Long before Europeans penetrated into what is now Pennsylvania, infectious diseases were being transmitted via indigenous peoples themselves via trade routes from the coastal plains inland.

While these tribes are almost wholly extinguished from what is now Pennsylvania, their presence is still felt in the names of many rivers and places in the region. Names such as Youghiogheny, Allegheny, Aliquippa and Punxsutawney are their lasting reminders. It is important to remember that these original "Pennsylvanians" were the first to navigate the state's streams and rivers, build settlements that later turned into towns and cities and blaze the pathways that were the first overland transportation links, many of which were later established as the state's first roads.

PENN'S WOODS

Pennsylvania, meaning "Penn's Woods," formally came into being in 1681, when King Charles II of England used a grant of land to settle debts with William Penn that he had inherited from his father, Admiral Sir William Penn. By the late 1600s, the only available tract of land controlled by the English in eastern North America was south of New York, west of New Jersey and north of Maryland. On March 4, 1681, His Majesty King Charles II signed the Pennsylvania Charter, which states:

> *Doe give and grant unto the said William Penn, his heires and assignes all that tract or parte of land in America, with all the Islands therein conteyned, as the same is bounded on the East by Delaware River, from twelve miles distance, Northwarde of New Castle Towne unto the three and fortieth degree of Northern latitude if the said River doeth extend soe farre Northwards; but if the said River shall not extend soe farre Northward, then by the said River soe farr as it doth extend, and from the head of the said River the Easterne bounds are to bee determined by a meridian line, to bee drawn from the head of the said River vnto the said three and fortieth degree, the said lands to extend Westwards, five degrees in longitude, to bee computed from the said Easterne Bounds, and the said lands to bee bounded on the North, by the beginning of the three and fortieth degree of Northern latitude, and on the south, by a circle drawne at twelve miles, distance from New Castle Northwards, and Westwards vnto the beginning of the fortieth degree of Northerne Latitude; and then by a straight line Westwards, to the limit of Longitude above menconed.*

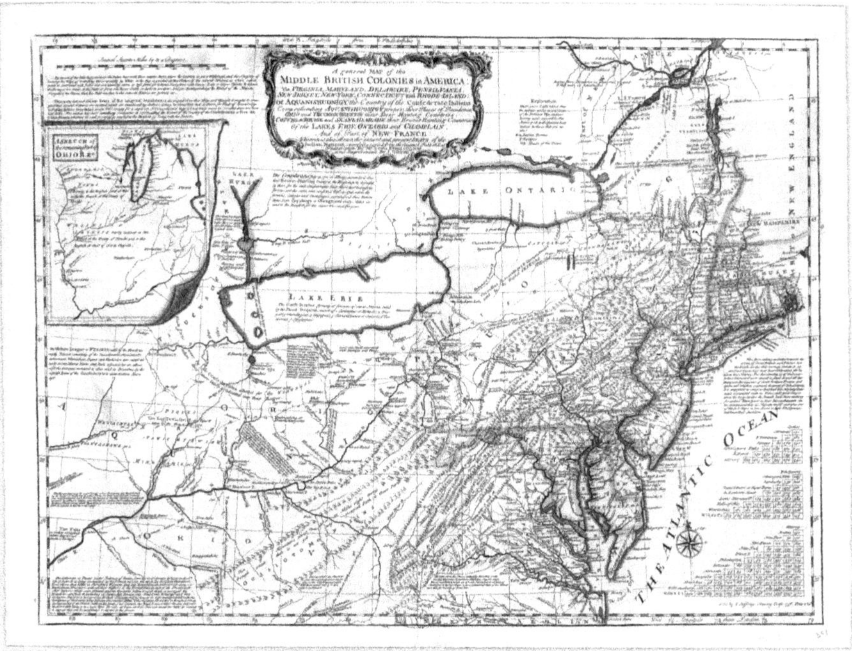

Map of middle British colonies in America. *MG-11.1, map no. 874, Record Group 10, Office of Governor Robert P. Casey, proclamations (series#10.3). Pennsylvania Historical and Museum Commission, Pennsylvania State Archives.*

The eastern boundary of the Delaware River was clearly established, as it sat on a geographical feature. But the western boundary, according to the charter, was to be five degrees in longitude west of the eastern boundary, thereby giving the colony somewhat parallel boundaries on its east and west extents. More troublesome were the northern and southern boundaries.

The Pennsylvania Charter determined the northern border to be the forty-third degree of latitude (just above present-day Buffalo, New York), well within the borders of the Dutch Province of New Netherland, which was ceded to England in 1667. The southern boundary was even more difficult to establish, as the point of beginning for its southeastern boundary did not even exist. The charter started with the intersection of a circle twelve miles from New Castle (now located in Delaware) and the beginning of the fortieth degree of latitude; however, the fortieth degree is so far north of New Castle that the lines never intersect. The fundamental problem was a poor understanding at that time of where the fortieth degree of latitude actually lay. Dating back to the first maps from the settlement of the Virginia Colony,

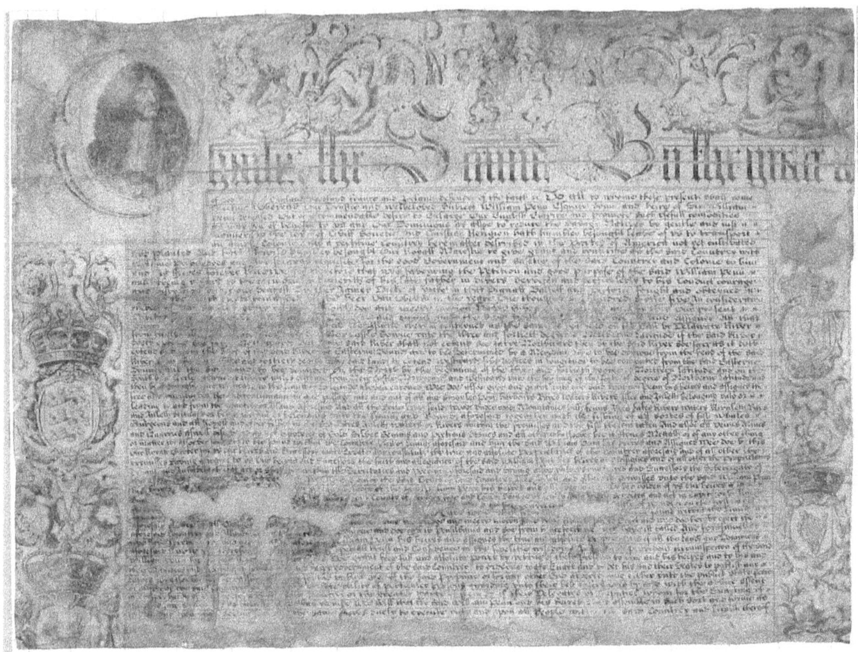

First page of the 1681 Pennsylvania Charter. *RG-26.2, 1681 PA Charter, page 1, Record Group 10, Office of Governor Robert P. Casey, proclamations (series#10.3). Pennsylvania Historical and Museum Commission, Pennsylvania State Archives.*

the head of the Chesapeake Bay was thought to be just below the fortieth degree, but the fortieth degree actually falls well north of Philadelphia. The Maryland Colony was carved out of the Virginia Colony for Lord Calvert but had an undefined western limit (which wasn't set until 1897, and its southern border with West Virginia wasn't settled until 1912 by the U.S. Supreme Court, but that's another story). Beyond that, Virginia had a claim to the fortieth degree of latitude as well, and the vagaries of the royal charters even gave rise to claims on the land north and west to the Mississippi River.

These claims were mostly moot at the time because they gave no consideration to the claims by the French Crown to land beyond the Appalachian Mountains or to the Native Americans who inhabited these lands. A desire to compensate the Native Americans for their land, along with Quaker pacifism espoused by the Penn family, enabled Pennsylvania to settle the southeast region of what is now Pennsylvania during the "long peace" under Indian-brokered alliances.

Borders with neighboring colonies had not yet become important enough to be determined when continual western expansion of settlers in the first half of the 1700s, aided by the Iroquois Confederation "permission," resulted in expropriation of lands under control of the Lenape and Shawnee peoples. These conflicting land claims played a large part in sparking the Seven Years' War, which lasted from 1756 to 1763. The 1763 Treaty of Paris, which ended the war, removed the French claims on North America and for the first time made relevant the question regarding what the western borders of the colonies were. On October 7, 1763, King George III of England issued the Royal Proclamation of 1763 forbidding colonial settlement west of the Appalachian Mountains, effectively determining these boundaries by royal decree and thus voiding grants of lands farther west made earlier.

Adjustments were made to the 1763 line in the 1768 Treaty of Fort Stanwix and the Treaty of Hard Labor, as well as again in 1770 in the Treaty of Lochaber. However, resentment of England by the colonies, especially the restrictions on new land, continued to grow, resulting in the American

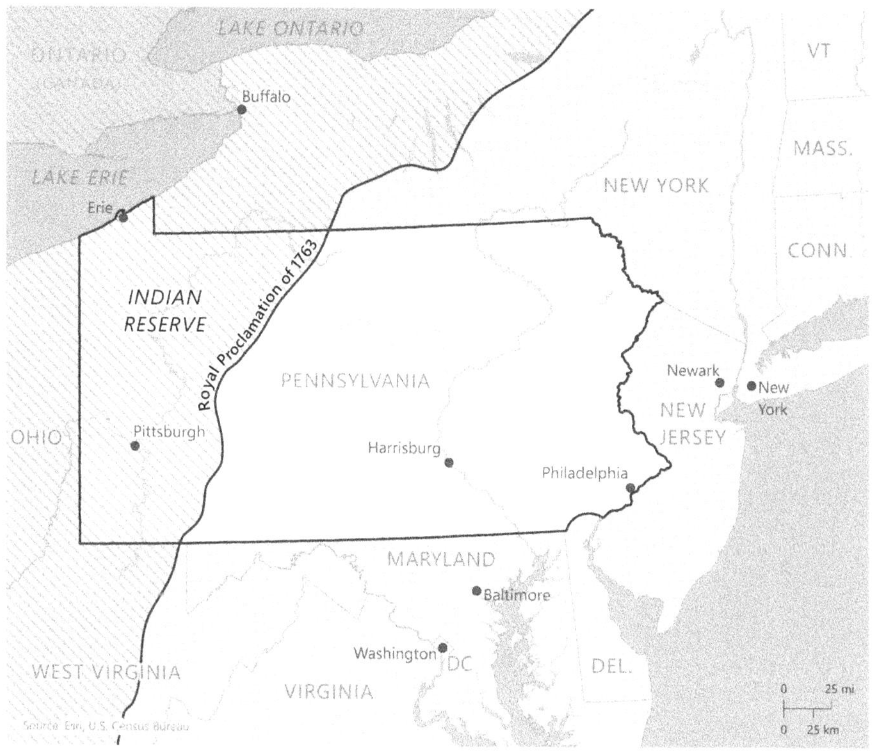

Royal proclamation of 1763. *Lauren Winkler.*

Revolution. Upon signing the Treaty of Paris ending the Revolutionary War in 1783, the United States would become the final arbiter of the official borders of Pennsylvania.

SURVEYORS TOOLS

One of the earliest written descriptions of a surveyor is contained in Master John Fitzherbert's *The Art of Husbandry*, published in 1523. In it, the surveyor's feudal role was that of executive officer for a landed nobleman. The French words of *sur* (over) and *voir* (see) described the surveyor's duty to oversee the nobleman's estate. When the English landed gentry began enclosing land during the reign of the Tudors, the visual inspection of the estate and the written report describing the "buttes and bounds" and the rent or service due from the land's tenants grew in importance. The need to measure and map the holdings fell on the surveyor to determine where

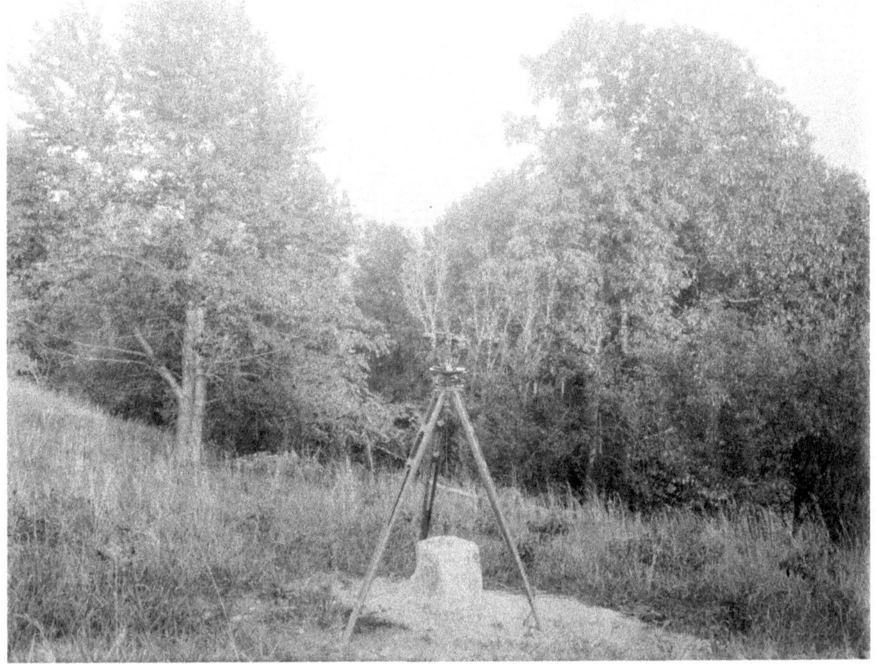

Early surveying equipment. *RG-17.394, Box 4, image no. 5078, Record Group 10, Office of Governor Robert P. Casey, proclamations (series#10.3). Pennsylvania Historical and Museum Commission, Pennsylvania State Archives.*

the estate's boundaries abut (or, to use another French word, *mete*) other boundaries, hence the work of the surveyor was to produce the "metes and bounds" of a property.

Standardized topographical surveying was made possible by the inventions of a seventeenth-century English mathematician Edmund Gunter. In 1624, Gunther published *The Description and Use of the Sector, the Cross-Staffe, and Other Instruments for Such Studious of Mathematical Practise.* In his book, Gunter described a chain four perches in length made up of one hundred links. A perch was sixteen and a half feet, and Gunter's chain therefore measured sixty-six feet in length. His one hundred links allowed the easy conversion of a measurement system based on four to the new decimal system based on ten. The introduction of the precision Theodolite in the early 1700s combined with trigonometry would be the tools used by surveyors until the advent of electronic distance measurement in the 1950s, total stations in the 1970s and the widespread adoption of Real Time Kinematic surveying using Global Positioning Systems in the 1980s.

SETTLING PENNSYLVANIA'S BORDERS

Geographic inaccuracies contained in Pennsylvania's 1681 charter and the other colonies' vague borders created great confusion between the Penns of Pennsylvania, the Calverts of Maryland and even the landed gentry of New York and Virginia. Disputes over property rights and jurisdictional enforcement caused by these competing land claims even resulted in violence. Cresap's War broke out in 1730 over conflicting land claims from Thomas Cresap, a Marylander, and Quaker minister John Wright, a Pennsylvanian in the region that is now York County, Pennsylvania. The colony of Maryland deployed its militia in 1736, and Pennsylvania responded in kind in 1737. Only intervention by King George III of England in 1738 prompted a cease-fire and established a compromise boundary between the two conflicting claims. The border between Pennsylvania and Maryland was agreed to as the line of latitude fifteen miles south of the then southernmost house in Philadelphia.

In 1763, the Penns and Calverts commissioned two highly skilled Englishmen, astronomer Charles Mason and surveyor Jeremiah Dixon, to accurately establish the Pennsylvania-Maryland border, as well as the Delaware Colony's borders with both Pennsylvania and Maryland. In

April 1765, Mason and Dixon began work on the Pennsylvania–Maryland survey, which was fixed as the 39° 43' N parallel. The boundary was marked by stones every mile (milestones) and crownstones every five miles. The four-sided stone obelisks were shipped from England expressly for these purposes. Milestones had the letter *M* carved on the side facing Maryland and the letter *P* carved on the side facing Pennsylvania. Crownstones also included the coat of arms for the Calverts and Penns. Many of these stones are still visible today. Mason and Dixon extended the boundary survey 232 miles west until October 8, 1767, to near present-day Mount Morris, Pennsylvania.

Having crossed a war path just east of Dunkard Creek, they were informed by their Iroquois guides that they could not continue. Mason recorded in his journal, "This day the chief of the Indians which joined us in the 16th day of July informed us that the above-mentioned war path was the extent of his commission from the chiefs of the six nations that he should go with us, with the line: and that he would not proceed one step farther westward." The termination of the survey in 1767 was 21.65 miles short of Pennsylvania's western boundary. The methodology developed by Mason and Dixon for the survey utilized the most precise portable astronomical telescope of the time, an astronomical clock, tables of star positions, a Hadley's quadrant, a transit, spirit levels, surveyor's chains and wooden rods. Its accuracy was within inches of the best techniques available into the twentieth century before the advent of Global Positioning Satellites (GPS). The technique used by Mason and Dixon, known as the "secant method," was the basis for subsequent large-scale precise boundary surveys in the United States.

After the Treaty of Paris in 1783 ended the Revolutionary War, the now independent states attempted to reassert their boundary claims from their original charters—even Connecticut, citing its 1662 charter that granted it rights to all lands to the west of the colony to the Pacific Ocean, unless they were owned by another "Christian prince or state." Taking this to exempt New York, which was a Dutch colony at the time, Connecticut claimed the northern third of what is now Pennsylvania. Connecticut even organized settlement efforts resulting in the Yankee-Pennamite Wars with Pennsylvania settlers. The war, which flared up in the Wyoming Valley between 1769 and 1775, only ceased with the beginning of the Revolutionary War.

It was Virginian Thomas Jefferson who recognized that the new American government required funds and that the sale of public lands could provide them. Virginia's own claims to the Forks of the Ohio could

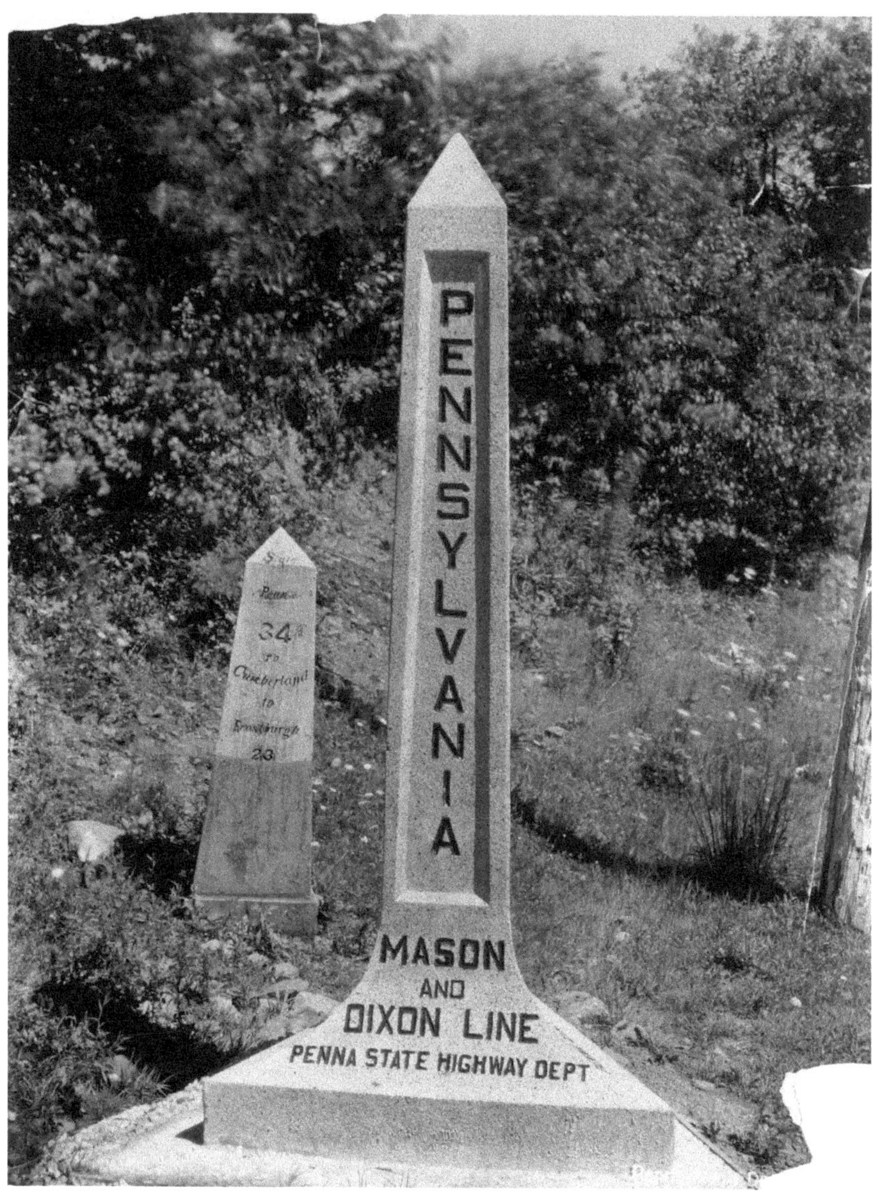

Pennsylvania Mason-Dixon line historical marker. *RG-12.14, image no. 249, Record Group 10, Office of Governor Robert P. Casey, proclamations (series#10.3). Pennsylvania Historical and Museum Commission, Pennsylvania State Archives.*

be argued by its charter and made legitimate by its original construction of Fort Prince George in 1754 (the Virginians were subsequently chased out by the French, who demolished the English fort and erected Fort Duquesne in its place) and the seizure by force from the Native Americans of what became Pittsburgh in Lord Dunmore's War in 1774. Facing a national debt estimated to be over $40 million at the time (about $1 billion in 2018) and having no means to impose tariffs or taxes over the objection of the states, on March 1, 1784, Congress approved Jefferson's proposal that Virginia cede all claims to the land west of Pennsylvania as originally established in its charter (five degrees in longitude from its eastern border), and the other states did likewise. There remained joint commissions in 1786 and 1782 to settle the issue of the rights of settlers from other states within Pennsylvania—this being a time when the concept of being an American was secondary to one's state allegiance. However, there remained the question of where exactly the western border of Pennsylvania fell.

In 1784, surveyors Andrew Ellicott, from Maryland, and David Rittenhouse, from Pennsylvania, were tasked with completing the survey of the Mason-Dixon line that had been abandoned seventeen years earlier. Upon completion of this task, Ellicott and Rittenhouse were appointed in 1786 to lead a boundary commission to conduct a survey to define the western border of Pennsylvania and the Ohio Country. The survey team that headed out to the then-rugged frontier was headed up by Thomas Hutchins, and the border they determined was called the Ellicott Line. Evidence of their work can be seen today where Pennsylvania Route 68 becomes Ohio Route 38 just east of East Liverpool, Ohio, as it traces the northern shore of the Ohio River and crosses from Pennsylvania to Ohio. Standing alongside the highway sits a barely noticed but significant stone obelisk. The "Point of Beginning" marks the western boundary of the Commonwealth of Pennsylvania. The monument carries an inscription that reads, "The Point of Beginning. 1112 feet south of this spot was the point of beginning for surveying the public lands of the United States. There on September 30, 1785, Thomas Hutchins, first Geographer of the United States, began the Geographer's Line of the Seven Ranges."

The importance of the Ellicott Line (running south–north at longitude 80° 31′ 12″) was that it was to become the first principal meridian used in the Public Land Survey System, created by the Land Ordinance of 1785 to survey the Seven Ranges in eastern Ohio under the oversight of the Surveyor General's Office. This survey system was then used to survey the majority of the United States. The surveyor general eventually became part

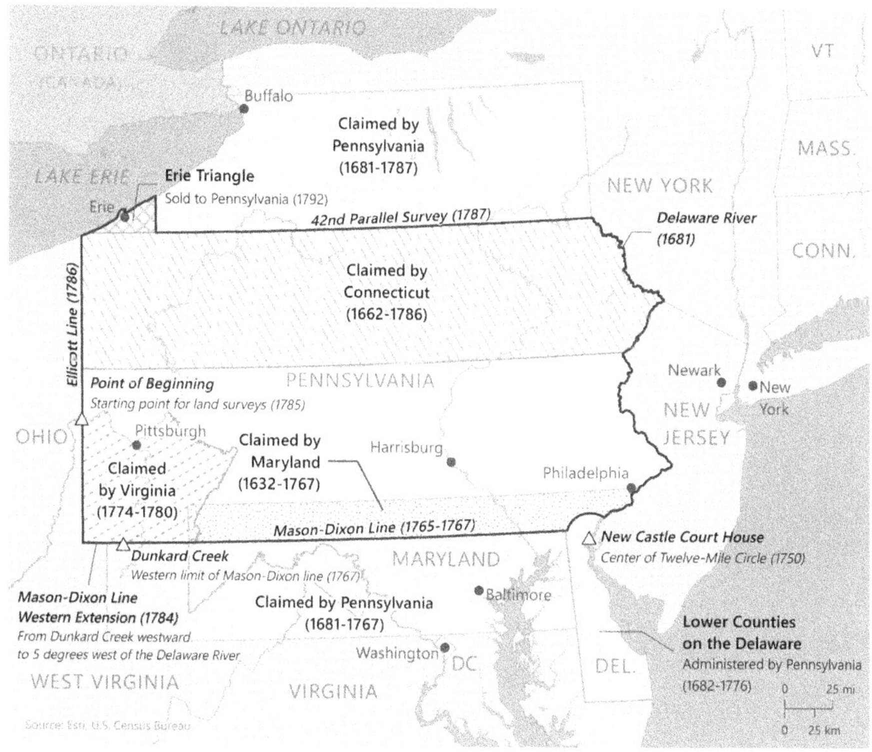

Pennsylvania borders and historical land claims. *Lauren Winkler.*

of the General Land Office, which later became part of the U.S. Bureau of Land Management. Until this day, the U.S. Bureau of Land Management still manages the State Plane Coordinate System.

The conflicting claims for Pennsylvania's northern border began to be settled in 1785. A compromise was reached between Pennsylvania and New York that their shared border would be set at the forty-second parallel, versus the forty-third parallel as described in Pennsylvania's original charter. The survey was completed in 1786 by Andrew Ellicott, representing Pennsylvania based on the state's satisfaction with his earlier surveys, and with Revolutionary War general James Clinton and Surveyor General of New York Simeon DeWitt representing New York. The western edge of New York was established twenty miles east of the peninsula jutting into Lake Erie, called Presque Isle ("almost an island" in French). This survey was approved by Pennsylvania and New York in 1787, but it left a remaining three-hundred-square-mile triangle of land claimed by Pennsylvania, New York, Connecticut and Massachusetts. This area became known as the "Erie Triangle." As Pennsylvania was landlocked, the new federal government pressured all four states to surrender their claims and subsequently sold the land to Pennsylvania on March 3, 1792, for $0.75 per acre, for a total value of $151,640.25.

CANALS

By David L. Wright, PE

Early Transportation: Slow, Expensive and Hazardous

As early as 1768, a few daring pioneer families with their household goods passed Pittsburgh on their way westward down the Ohio River to new settlements. By building covers, rafts became houseboats to be floated downriver and then broken up for materials at the end of the trip. Keelboats were built with design similar to the eastern Durham boat. The boats were rowed, poled from the sides or pulled from the bank upstream after a relatively easy trip downstream. Trips began in the late fall and early spring, when the water was high enough. In addition to low water in the summer, river hazards included rapid waterfalls (called riffles), gravel bars, floating trees and snags hidden under the water.

Robert Fulton and Nicholas Roosevelt built the *New Orleans*, the first steamboat on the western rivers, featured at Pittsburgh in 1811. Captain Henry Shreve of Brownsville developed a shallow-draft, light engine boat that served as the prototype for all riverboats to be built in the next hundred years. He also broke the Fulton monopoly on the western rivers. Shreve used double-hull boats to remove river snags. By 1835, 304 steamboats had been built in Pittsburgh, 221 in Cincinnati, 103 in Louisville and the remaining 56 in other towns along the rivers. Pittsburgh also became the center of manufacturing steam engines that were installed in boats up and down the rivers.

Pioneers could use Forbes' Road and Kittanning Path over the mountains from the east. Movement on roads was slow and expensive. One writer in 1812 stated, "It requires a good team of five or six horses from 18 to 35 days to transport 2500 to 3500 pounds of goods from Philadelphia to Pittsburgh."

ENGINEERING THE SOLUTION

Canal transportation made Britain's English Midlands the center of the Industrial Revolution between the 1760s and 1800. Raw materials imported from the colonies could be transported to the factories of Manchester and Birmingham and then carried out as finished products to the port cities to be shipped all over the world. The British also built primitive railroads to carry minerals from mines. Timber rails were fastened to wood or stone sleepers, with metal bars spiked in on top to reduce wear. Trains were powered by animals and locomotives pulling on level track, utilizing the force of gravity to coast down hills and steam-driven stationary engines to pull up hills.

The American canal "boom" started in New England in 1802, using British technology, with the opening of the Middlesex Canal. In 1810, New York State laid out plans for a canal from the Hudson River, near Albany, across the state to Lake Erie. The Mohawk River had sliced a gorge through the Allegheny Ridge at Little Falls, making an all-water route feasible, and the Hudson River, tidal all the way to Albany, provided easy steamboat navigation to New York City.

The Erie Canal was an instant success. Time to travel from Albany to Buffalo was reduced from thirty-two days to five days. Canalboats, pulled by a team of mules or horses, could carry about seventy tons of cargo compared to a wagon, which could maybe carry about two tons. A year after it opened in 1826, about seven thousand boats were operating on the canal. The canal commissioners collected tolls of $500,000, five times the interest due on the canal's outstanding bonds. In 1837, the commissioners reported that the entire debt had been repaid. In the eleven years after the Erie Canal opened, the value of New York City real estate tripled, and its population had quadrupled by 1850.

THE PUSH FOR CANAL DEVELOPMENT IN PENNSYLVANIA

As early as 1762, in order to develop trade, Philadelphia merchants requested that a board be appointed to explore the possibility of connecting the West Branch of the Susquehanna River with a tributary of the Ohio River. Philadelphians finally initiated canal legislation after the Erie Canal became a reality. They sent leading Greek Revival architect William Strickland and his assistant, Samuel Honeyman Kneass, to England to study canals and make drawings.

The legislature appointed a three-man commission to survey a route to connect the Susquehanna and the Allegheny Rivers. On February 2, 1825, it proposed a continuous waterway by constructing a four-and-a-half-mile-long tunnel under Allegheny Mountain between what is now Lilly and a point in Blair's Gap above what is now Hollidaysburg. This seemed possible because the British had already constructed more than forty miles of canal tunnels at that time, the longest being the three-mile-long Standege Tunnel, which opened in 1811 on the Huddersfield Narrow Canal in northern England. However, in his minority report, Charles Trcziyulny doubted the practicality of such a long tunnel. Not only was it too costly and time-consuming to construct, but the mountain also did not provide an adequate water supply to operate the numerous canal locks required to reach the tunnel.

Because many of Philadelphia's financial institutions had gone bankrupt as a result of the completion of the Erie Canal, commonwealth legislators quickly approved an act on February 26, 1826, authorizing an uninterrupted waterway between Philadelphia and Pittsburgh. Not only was the canal building program undertaken without a plan, but the program also advanced with borrowed money on the assumption that tolls would be collected to pay off the debt. The Erie Canal had been partially financed by a tax on the land along the route, which was predicted to increase in value as trade developed.

CONSTRUCTING THE WESTERN DIVISION CANAL BETWEEN PITTSBURGH AND JOHNSTOWN

Nathan S. Roberts, an experienced engineer who served as first assistant engineer of the Rome–Rochester stretch of the Erie Canal, was appointed engineer for the Western Division on April 5, 1826. He promptly started a survey line from the foot of Liberty Avenue in Pittsburgh up the south side of the Allegheny River to the Kiskiminetas River. However, when he reached the steep, unstable slopes coming directly down to the river's edge upstream of where the Highland Park Bridge is located, where no room was available to construct a canal, he started a second survey line up the north side.

When Roberts submitted his report favoring the village of Allegheny (today the North Side of Pittsburgh) along the north side of the river to the canal board, "two gentlemen appeared as representatives of the citizens of Pittsburgh." They insisted that under the terms of the law, the canal must start in Pittsburgh. The commissioners authorized construction to start outside Allegheny, from Pine Creek, northward to the Kiskiminetas in the fall of 1826, to provide time to settle the disagreement.

In 1827, the commonwealth legislature authorized construction of 44 miles of canal from the Allegheny River along the Kiskiminetas River and the Conemaugh River to Blairsville. Further extension another 30 miles up to Johnstown at the bottom of Allegheny Mountain was approved the next year. The entire 103½-mile Western Division between Pittsburgh and Johnstown included sixty locks plus the four on the Allegheny Branch and the four between the Pittsburgh Basin and the Monongahela River. It also had sixteen aqueducts across rivers and streams, sixty-four culverts, thirty-nine waste weirs, 152 bridges and two tunnels.

An aqueduct carried the canal across the Conemaugh River into the one-thousand-foot Bow Ridge Tunnel cut through a sharp bend in the river below Blairsville. It was the third canal tunnel built in the United States; the first was at Auburn on the Schuylkill Canal and the second near Lebanon on the Union Canal. This tunnel was plugged to construct the Conemaugh Reservoir to control floods after the 1936 flood. A corrugated metal pipe that drains the tunnel downstream of the plug marks its location.

The route also included ten river dams to create twenty-seven miles of slackwater canal. The first dam, at Leechburg, was 27 feet high and 574 feet long. It backed up the river water to Apollo and supplied water to the canal down to Pittsburgh. Additional dams upriver created slackwater navigation for sections of river valleys too narrow to provide room for a canal out of the river. The canal ran in slack water in Packsaddle Gap through Chestnut Ridge between Torrance and Bolivar, as well as in the Conemaugh Gorge through Laurel Ridge between Seward and Johnstown.

The village of Allegheny became a borough during canal development on April 14, 1828. Streets and lots for Sharpsburg and Tarentum were laid out along the canal when it opened.

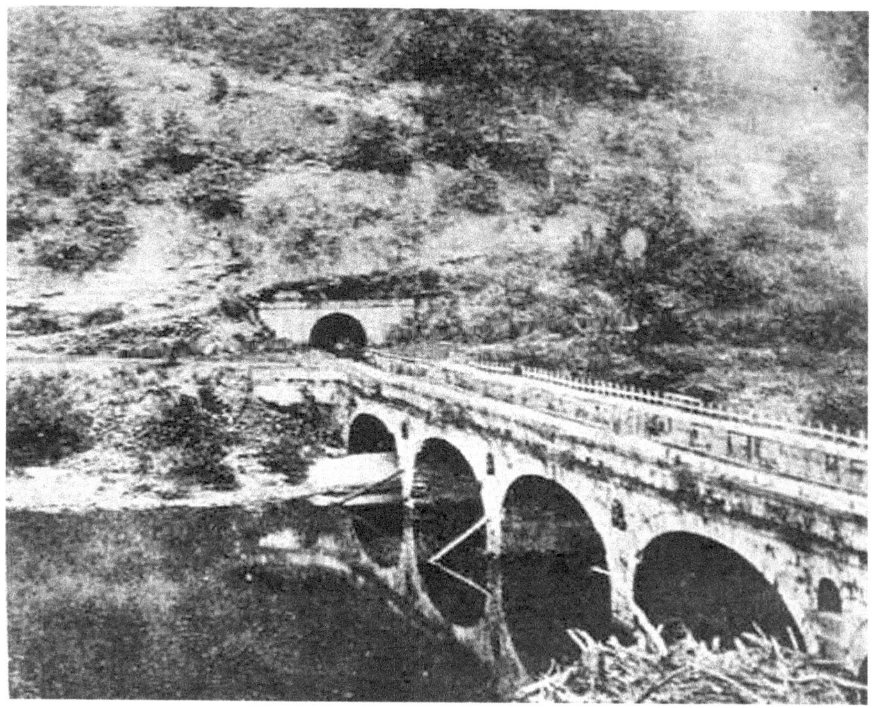

A stone arch bridge carried the canal across the Conemaugh River and into a tunnel that is now plugged for the Conemaugh Reservoir. A corrugated metal pipe, which drains the tunnel below the plug, now marks its location. *Ms. Nancy O'Dell.*

CONNECTING PITTSBURGH TO THE CANAL

Meanwhile, during the winter of 1826, the people of Allegheny and Pittsburgh whipped themselves into a frenzy about the problem of these five miles below Pine Creek. The citizens of Allegheny offered to construct a large canal basin with warehouses and wharves from which freight could be taken by wagon to Pittsburgh across the St. Clair Bridge, now the Sixth Street Bridge, over the Allegheny River. But Pittsburghers had agitated for ten years for a canal and did not want to lose it to the rival town across the river. After sending a committee to the state capital to lobby, the canal commissioners adopted a plan to bring the canal into the village of Allegheny and turn left at a basin to outlet into the river at a location about seven hundred feet downstream of the Sixth Street Bridge. To avoid the toll for wagons crossing the Allegheny River Bridge, the canal commission awarded a contract for a canal aqueduct over the Allegheny River to William LeBaron and Sylvanus Lothrop on June 3, 1827. With seven spans each 160 feet long, the aqueduct was constructed across the Allegheny River along what is now the upstream side of the Norfolk Southern bridge into Eleventh Street. The aqueduct had a wooden trough with heavy, two-and-a-half-inch-thick white pine planks that were laid diagonally in two courses to hold the water. A sidewalk was located along one edge of the aqueduct, and a towpath was located along the other. A roof protected the trusses from the weather.

The canal continued on Eleventh Street with a basin on its east side between Penn and Liberty Avenues. An 1852 map also shows a smaller basin built on the west side. The canal ran along the east side of Grant Street. It then curved to the left under what is now the U.S. Steel Building to enter a tunnel under Grant's Hill. The hill was named for British major general James Grant, who was defeated by the French at that location during the French and Indian War.

Pittsburgh City Council guaranteed to pay the extra cost of the tunnel route to avoid a cheaper route using Smithfield Street or Liberty Avenue, which would have interfered with the free growth of the city. The tunnel was built by cut and cover. This was confirmed when engineers for the Allegheny County Port Authority drilled exploratory core holes in the 1980s for design of the Light Rail Transit line to the south of Pittsburgh.

The canal exited from the tunnel at Forbes Avenue, where water flow was lowered by locks through Suke's Run into the Monongahela River, and

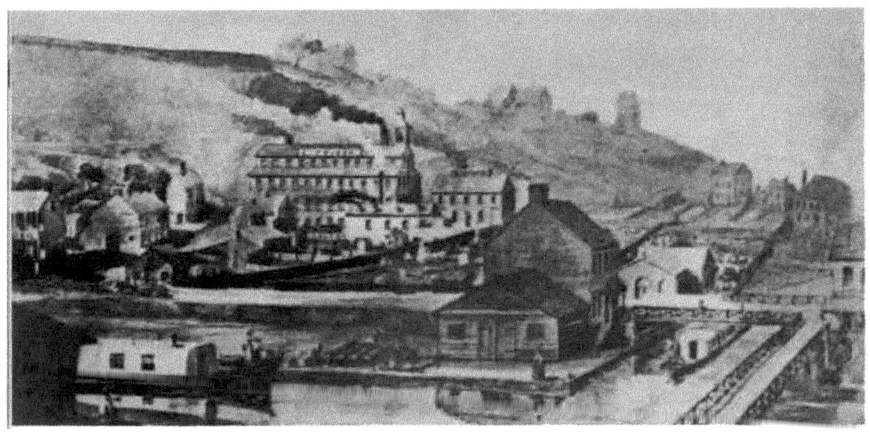

A cross-section drawing of the Allegheny River Aqueduct shows the wood trough, towpath and roof to protect the trusses from the weather. *Ms. Nancy O'Dell.*

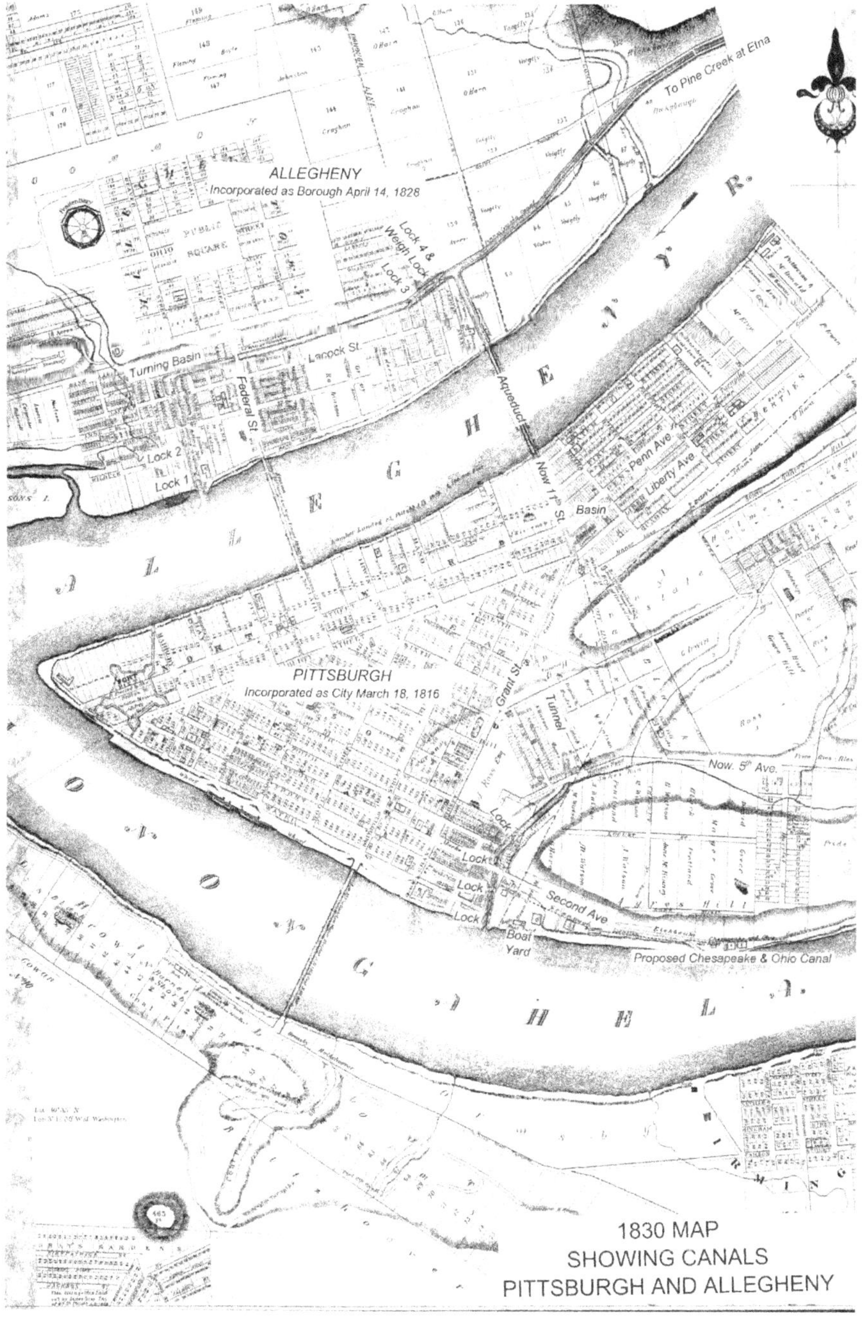

This 1830 map of Pittsburgh and Allegheny shows the canal locks, canal basin, aqueduct across the Allegheny River and tunnel under Grant's Hill. Note the proposed Chesapeake and Ohio Canal shown along the Monongahela River. *The Gateway Engineers.*

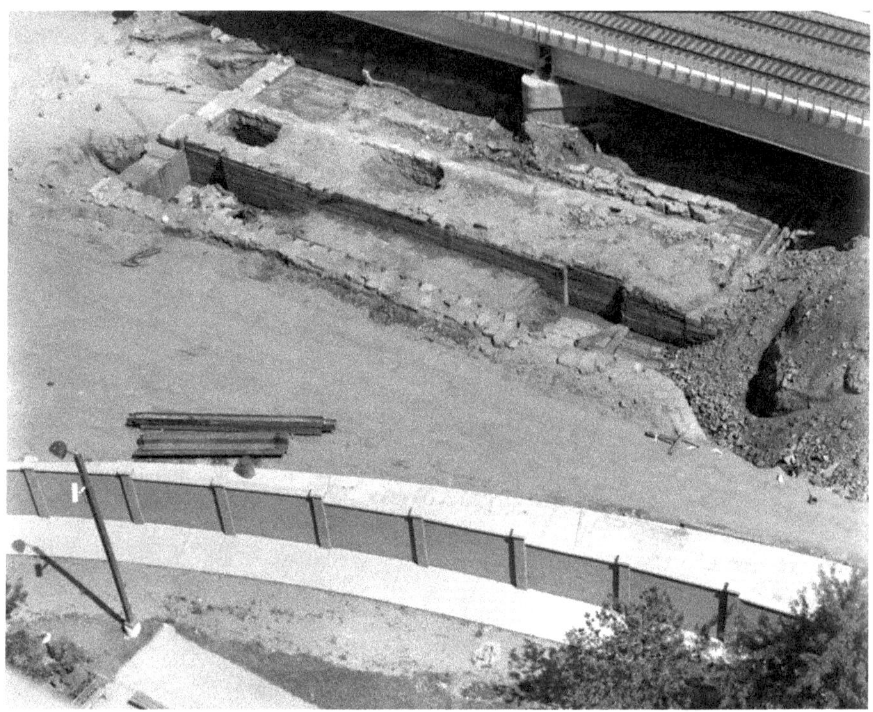

Lift Lock No. 4 and the Pittsburgh Weigh Lock were excavated and recorded by GAI Consultants for the I-279 construction project on Pittsburgh's North Side. *Library of Congress HAER Collection.*

the projected extension of the Chesapeake and Ohio Canal. The C&O Canal ended at Cumberland, Maryland, so the tunnel was not used and was allowed to collect silt. It did serve as an overflow channel to carry excess water away from the Pittsburgh basin.

When the canal could first hold water, the passenger boat *General Lacock* made the first trip into Pittsburgh in 1829. However, parts of the Western Division had their problems. A landslide in Sharpsburg filled up the canal as it was being completed, so it had to be cleared out. The aqueduct across the Allegheny River at the Kiskiminetas River had to be rebuilt twice after floods in 1831 and 1832 badly damaged both the high dam and its lock at Leechburg. Another problem was falling rock fragments from the tunnel at the loop of the Conemaugh River. The problem was repaired between 1830 and 1831 by installing a brick liner for most of its length. It was not until 1834, when the through route from the east opened, that passenger packets and freight boats could maintain a regular schedule.

OVER THE MOUNTAIN ON THE ALLEGHENY PORTAGE RAILROAD

The Board of Canal Commissioners had been appointed in 1824 and prepared several surveys for various routes between Harrisburg and Pittsburgh. On March 21, 1831, the commonwealth passed a law authorizing the Board of Canal Commissioners to commence the construction of the Portage Railroad over the Allegheny Mountain. The board appointed Sylvester Welch, the principal engineer of the recently completed Western Division of the Pennsylvania Canal, to the same position in the building of the Portage Railroad. He nominated, and the Board of Canal Commissioners appointed, twenty-year-old Solomon W. Roberts as his assistant. Roberts had been trained by Josiah White, who was his uncle and manager of the Lehigh Coal and Navigation Company. Young Roberts had been a rod man and leveler on fifteen miles of the Lehigh Canal. Moncure Robinson, retained as a consultant engineer for the Portage Railroad, had participated in its previous surveys.

The thirty-six-mile-long Portage Railway was designed with five inclined planes and six levels on both sides of Allegheny Mountain and numbered eastward from Johnstown to Hollidaysburg. The inclines were needed because railroad locomotives, when work began, could not transport passengers and goods along the steep grades over the Allegheny Mountain. Only eighteen months before, the little engine, called "the rocket," was first demonstrated for the Liverpool and Manchester Railroad. The combination of the tubular boiler with the blast-pipe to force air through the fire was the cause of its success.

The whole total length of the inclines was 4.4 miles, with an aggregate elevation differential of 2,007 feet. Their angles of inclination ranged from 4.15 degrees to 5.85 degrees. The railroad levels between planes were located with moderate grades, and the sharpest curve had a 442-foot radius. The track gauge was 4 feet, 9 inches. Leveling instruments used for the canal were similar to those for the canal, but instruments to lay out curves were poor because a surveyor's compass was mostly used.

When the surveyors locating the railroad reached the horseshoe bend of the Conemaugh River, about eight miles from Johnstown, Solomon W. Roberts was in charge. A decision was made to cross the stream on a high bridge to avoid two miles of track. The Conemaugh Viaduct, with its seventy-foot-high, single eighty-foot arch span, was later used by the New Portage Railroad and the Pennsylvania Railroad until it

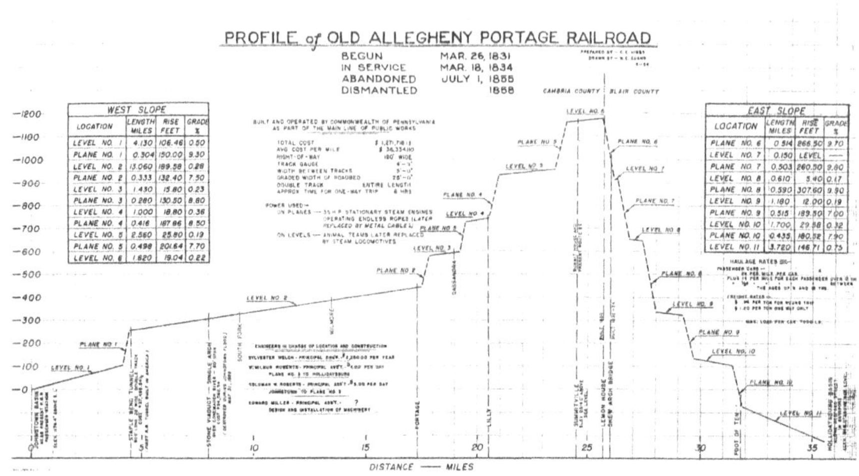

WEST SLOPE			
LOCATION	LENGTH MILES	RISE FEET	GRADE %
LEVEL NO. 1	4.130	106.46	0.50
PLANE NO. 1	0.304	150.00	9.30
LEVEL NO. 2	13.060	189.58	0.28
PLANE NO. 2	0.333	132.40	7.50
LEVEL NO. 3	1.430	15.80	0.23
PLANE NO. 3	0.280	130.50	8.80
LEVEL NO. 4	1.000	18.80	0.36
PLANE NO. 4	0.416	187.86	8.50
LEVEL NO. 5	2.560	25.80	0.19
PLANE NO. 5	0.498	201.64	7.70
LEVEL NO. 6	1.620	19.04	0.22

EAST SLOPE			
LOCATION	LENGTH MILES	RISE FEET	GRADE %
PLANE NO. 6	0.514	266.50	9.70
LEVEL NO. 7	0.150	LEVEL	——
PLANE NO. 7	0.503	260.50	9.80
LEVEL NO. 8	0.610	5.40	0.17
PLANE NO. 8	0.590	307.60	9.90
LEVEL NO. 9	1.180	12.00	0.19
PLANE NO. 9	0.515	189.50	7.00
LEVEL NO. 10	1.700	29.58	0.32
PLANE NO. 10	0.435	180.52	7.90
LEVEL NO. 11	3.720	146.71	0.75

was destroyed by the Johnstown Flood in 1889. Bridge construction was directed by Scottish stonemason John Durno. The sandstone used for construction was split from the erratic blocks, often of great size, found lying in the nearby woods. The facing stones were laid in mortar made from silicious limestone found near the spot, without the addition of any sand, and backed by the silicious limestone.

At the Staple Bend of the Conemaugh River, four miles east of Johnstown, a 901-foot-long tunnel was cut through a spur of the Allegheny Mountain to avoid a bend that would have necessitated two and a half additional miles of track. Recognized as the first railroad tunnel constructed in the United States, it was cut through rock to form a 20-foot-high and 19-foot-wide opening. The eastern, sixteen-mile-long section of the Portage Railroad from the summit down to Hollidaysburg was located by W. Milnor Roberts, who joined the engineer corps in as principal assistant. He and Solomon Roberts had worked together on the Lehigh Canal in 1827. The commissioners awarded contracts in Ebensburg for railroad construction between Johnstown and the summit on May 25, 1831, and from the summit to Hollidaysburg on July 29, 1831. A 120-foot width was cleared the full length of the railroad through the forest of heavy spruce and hemlock timber, many of the trees being more than 100 feet tall. A workforce of about two thousand men was employed at one time for the grading and installation of the 159 stone bridges and culverts.

In 1831, Edward Miller returned from England, where he studied the most recent railroad technology. As principal assistant engineer, he specified two thirty-five-horsepower steam engines at the head of each plane. Hemp ropes

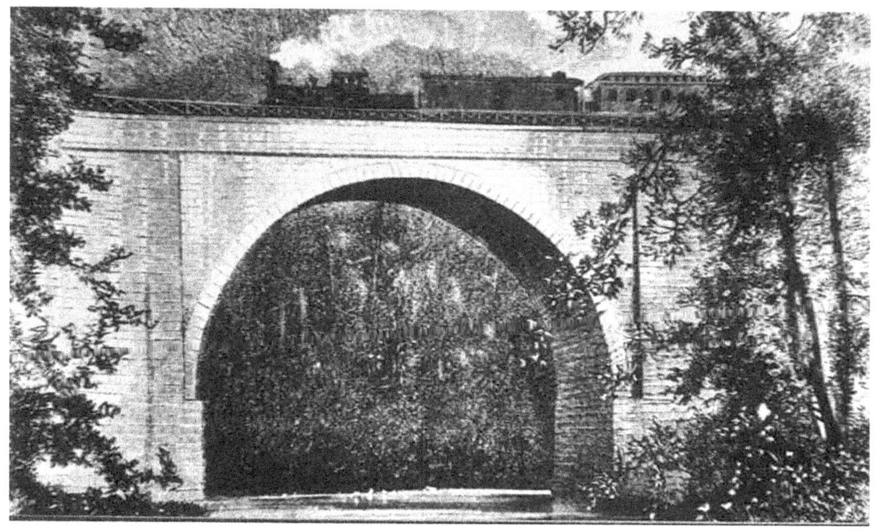

Conemaugh Viaduct carried the Old Portage Railroad, New Portage Railroad and Pennsylvania Railroad until the Johnstown Flood destroyed it in 1889. *Ms. Nancy O'Dell.*

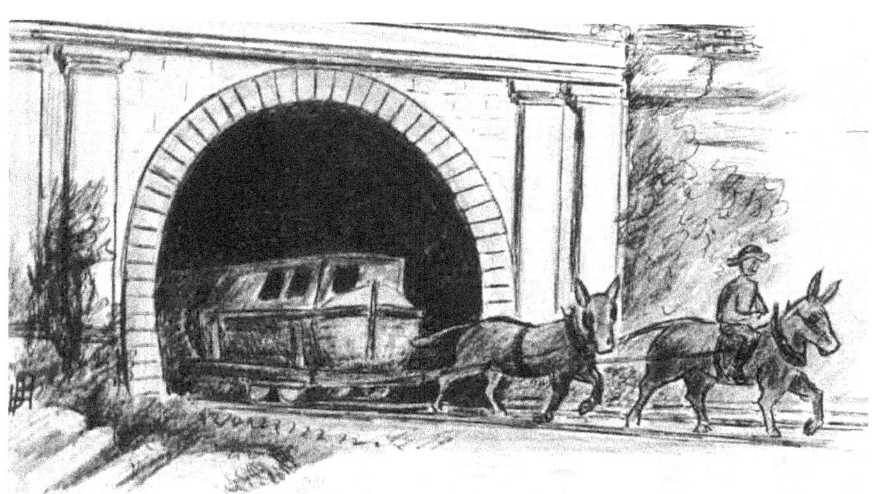

Phill Hoffman's painting depicts horses/mules pulling a section boat out of the Staple Bend Tunnel west of Mineral Point. *Ms. Nancy O'Dell.*

were first used and gave much trouble, as they wore out and broke after a few years of service and varied greatly in length with changes in the weather, although sliding carriages were prepared to keep them stretched without too much strain. John Roebling, a recent German immigrant who had served as a surveyor on the Portage Railroad, saw the problem and developed wire rope that replaced the hemp rope, which was a great improvement.

The laying of the first track and turnouts, with a double track on the inclines, was contracted for on April 11, 1832. The rails weighed about forty pounds per yard and were rolled in Great Britain. Hauling them from the canal at Huntington by wagon was laborious work. Thirteen-pound cast-iron chairs spaced at three feet supported the rails. In most cases, the chairs were bolted to three-and-a-half-cubic-foot blocks of sandstone imbedded in broken stone. These stone blocks were required to be two feet long, twenty-one inches wide and twelve inches deep. A timber foundation with crossties and mud sills, which stood much better than the stone blocks, was used on high embankments. On the inclined planes, flat bar rails were laid on timber rails fastened to the wood crossties.

It was thought that stone sleepers would be better than wood because they do not deteriorate in the weather. However, the attempt to construct track with nonperishable materials failed because the rails spread apart. Many wood crossties were added between the stone sleepers to prevent this. While the engineers strived to build a great public work to endure for generations, the Portage Railroad was replaced by something better about twenty years later. Powered by animals, the first car passed over the road on November 26, 1833, about two and a half years from the beginning of work. By the time the canal navigation opened for the season on March 20, 1835, the second track had been completed.

The Portage Railroad first operated as a public highway, with teamsters driving as they wished, unable to pass in opposite directions on the single track. Soon after opening, the commonwealth authorized the canal commissioners to purchase locomotives to be operated by state employees on a schedule. The first locomotive, named the "Boston" because it had been made in that city in 1834, was put into operation on the longest level, the thirteen-mile section between Johnstown and Plane No. 1. To avoid the cost and delay of unloading and loading freight between canalboats and railroad cars, at each end of the Portage Railroad the shipping companies ran sectional boats that, like modern shipping containers, could be loaded onto railroad cars for the ride over the mountain. After more powerful locomotives made the inclines obsolete, the state constructed the New Portage Railroad to replace the

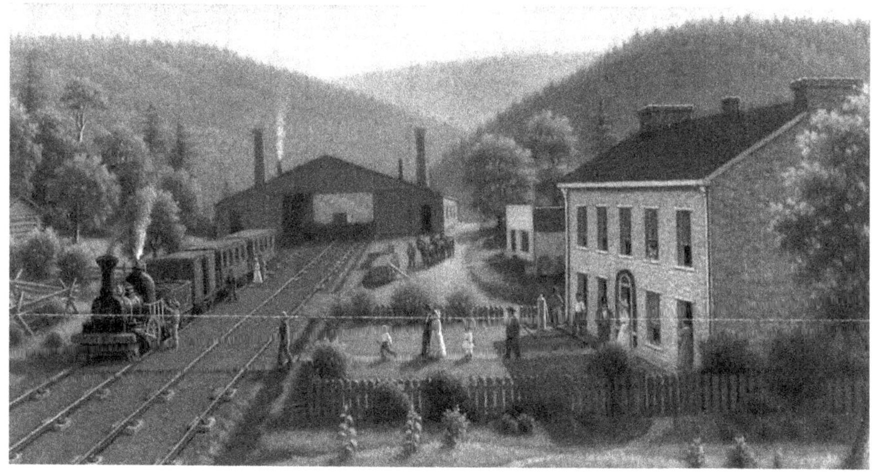

The Allegheny Portage Railroad National Historic Site preserves the Lemon House Tavern and replicas of the Plane 6 Engine House, locomotive and track. *Ms. Nancy O'Dell.*

inclines. The railroad was routed up from Hollidaysburg through the Mule Shoe Curve in Blair's Gap and climbed up the east side of the mountain through a tunnel at the summit. Other sections of the New Portage Railroad bypassed the five planes heading down to Johnstown.

The Pennsylvania Railroad Company used part of the New Portage Railroad to build its continuous railroad line across the state between Philadelphia and Pittsburgh. Opening the Pennsylvania Railroad across the state in 1852 ended most of the canal traffic. The Pennsylvania Railroad Company bought the Main Line of Pennsylvania canals and railroads across the state in 1857. The Pennsylvania Railroad closed the New Portage Railroad and salvaged its rails to construct its own expansion. The Western Pennsylvania Railroad built its tracks over part of the western division canal after abandonment in 1864.

The National Park Service now offers van tours of the Allegheny Portage railroad from its National Portage Railroad National Historic Site near Cresson. Visitors can view the historic Lemon House Tavern, which served thirsty travelers; a reproduction of the Plane No. 6 Engine House and locomotive; and the skew stone arch bridge, which carried the turnpike road over Plane No. 6. Hikers can walk down the 6 to 10 Trail along the route of the Old and New Portage Railroads from Plane No. 6 to Plane No. 10. Hikers can also use the Portage Railroad from Mineral Point to the Staple Bend Tunnel and Plane No. 1.

BEAVER DIVISION AND ERIE EXTENSION CANAL CONNECTS TO THE WEST

The February 26, 1826 canal act authorized surveying several routes to extend the planned system of canals, river navigations and railroads across the state to Erie and to construct a navigable feeder canal between French Creek and the summit level at Conneaut Lake. In an act passed on January 10, 1827, Ohio incorporated the Pennsylvania and Ohio Canal Company in Ohio to connect a Cross Cut Canal, along the Mahoning River, to a canal planned in Pennsylvania. Pennsylvania followed Ohio with its act to incorporate the Pennsylvania and Ohio Canal Company in Pennsylvania.

In 1828, work started on the French Creek Feeder. The commissioners studied to route a canal from the Allegheny River up French Creek to near Meadville and then on a feeder canal running down along the north side of Conneaut Marsh to the summit level. However, Pittsburgh's political leaders favored a water route from Pittsburgh to Erie along the Ohio River to Beaver and, from there, up the Beaver and Shenango Rivers to the summit level, connecting with the Cross Cut. Canal near New Castle. As a result, the commonwealth signed the March 31, 1831 act to authorize the Beaver and Shenango Rivers route.

The canal's principal engineer, Dr. Charles T. Whippo, a former medical doctor who turned engineer for the Erie Canal in New York, submitted his first report, which included a profile map, in July 1831. Because Whippo feared that damming the river would flood the adjacent land, he proposed a canal from a dam to feed from Neshannock Creek, at New Castle, to a point 5.77 miles south at Clarke's Mills. From there, he proposed slackwater navigation, with a towing path along the east side of the river, southward 14.44 miles as far as Brighton (now New Brighton). He located a canal 1.31 miles through Brighton down to Fallston to avoid damaging the milldams that were in the river. The canal continued as slack water the last 2.72 miles from Fallston to the Ohio River at Rochester.

The canal commissioners accepted his report, and the canal construction work was completed from the Ohio River to Western Reserve Harbor, now called Harbor Bridge, five miles north of New Castle, in 1833. The harbor served as a shipping point for freight and passengers into the Western Reserve area of northeastern Ohio. The last lock on the Ohio River was built extra-large to handle small steamboats. The Cross Cut Canal was completed from its connection at Mahoningtown to Akron, Ohio, in 1838.

W. Milnor Roberts made a thorough inspection and found the canal in poor condition due to flood damage. The cost of repairs far exceeded the income from tolls. After spending $4 million ($126 million in 2017) to extend the canal to Lake Erie, the commonwealth sold the entire Beaver and Erie project to the Erie Canal Company in 1843. Erie business people formed the private company and elected Rufus Reed as president. Reed owned a fleet of sailing ships on the Great Lakes.

The new company spent another $500,000 and completed the canal in 1844. The work included finishing the forty-four-lock, sixty-one-mile Shenango Division to Conneaut Lake, raising the lake level 11 feet to supply water to the summit level and cutting the two-and-a-half-mile summit level 10 to 27 feet deep between the Shenango River and Conneaut Creek. The forty-five-and-a-half-mile Conneaut Division dropped 510 feet from the summit level through composite wood and stone locks to terminate in Erie Harbor at Navy Yard Run below Reed's Pier. The canal crossed Elk Creek by a gigantic, 400-foot-long and 84-foot-high aqueduct and Walnut Creek

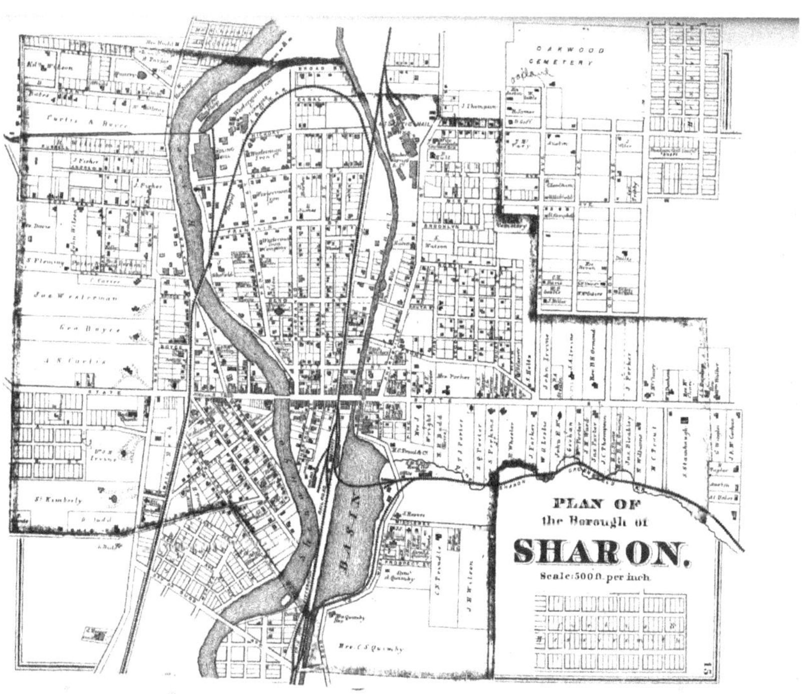

Quaker Steak and Lube Restaurant is located in what used to be Sharon's canal basin. *From the* Mercer County 1873 Atlas.

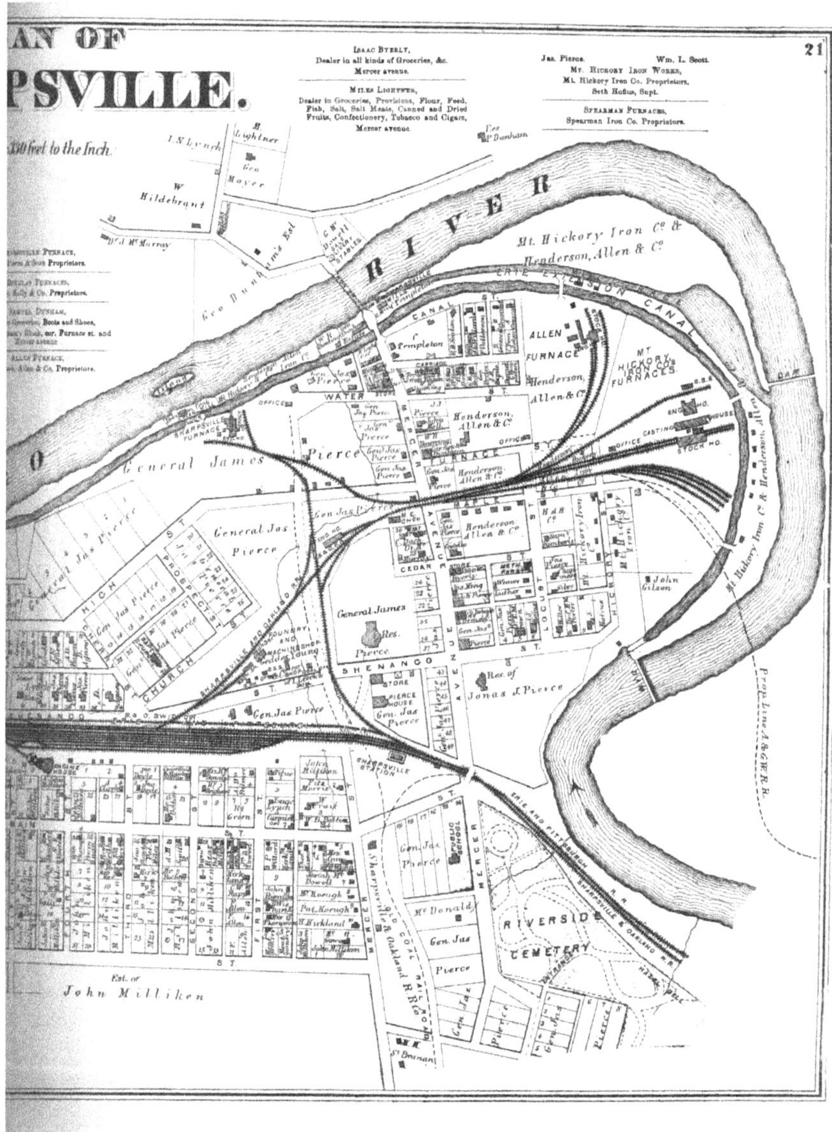

Railroads have moved in and taken the business of these iron furnaces along the canal in Sharpsville. The guard lock at the dam is preserved. *From the* Mercer County 1873 Atlas.

by an even bigger 600-foot-long and 100-foot-high aqueduct above the stream. After operating for twenty-six years, the canal was sold in 1870 in a sheriff's sale to the Erie and Pittsburgh Railroad Company, a subsidiary of the Pennsylvania Railroad Company. Collapse of the Elk Creek Aqueduct closed the canal one year later.

The only surviving feature of the canal is a guard lock in a public park below the Shenango Reservoir dam on the north side of Sharpsville. The Shenango Trail follows much of the towpath from Big Bend through Hamburg to the Kidd's Mill covered bridge in Shenango. A segment of watered canal, accessible by the abandoned railroad bed, provides waterfowl habitat in the state game lands south of Pulaski. The wall of upper Girard Lock, in Rochester, supports the Madison Street Pump Station.

In conclusion, doctors, lawyers, architects, surveyors and mechanics turned their abilities to engineering the canals and early railroads needed to develop our country. They designed transportation facilities using technology available at that time from the British Industrial Revolution. As time went on and new technology became available, engineers applied skills and methods first learned during the canal era to design and construct the transportation system we have today.

RAILROADS

By John F. Oyler, PhD, PE

Civil engineering heritage in Western Pennsylvania between 1850 and 1950 was dominated by the development and proliferation of railroads in this area. The image of the engineer, transit on his shoulder, trudging up the hollow cut by some small stream in an effort to find an acceptable minimum grade and curvature for a proposed railroad could well be the prototype for this era. We know the names of some of the well-publicized early railroaders, but it is the journeyman engineer who merits the credit for the massive network of rail lines that served this area so well.

The first example of railroad engineering in this region was associated with 1830 plans to build a railroad linking Washington, Pennsylvania and Pittsburgh to the newly constructed National Road. The Washington and Pittsburgh Railroad, incorporated in February 1831, hired a local engineer, Charles De Hass, to perform a preliminary design of the railroad and determine its estimated cost, as well as the revenue it could be expected to generate.

At a time when there were only four railroads in the whole world, and the one in this country was only twelve miles long, this assignment required an impressive combination of knowledge, ingenuity and imagination. Mr. De Hass was obviously the right choice for it. We know nothing of his background or education, but the product of his efforts is proof of his capability. His approach was to survey a route down the Chartiers Valley to the Ohio River and then along the south shores of the Ohio and the Monongahela River to the Monongahela Bridge (now the site of the Smithfield Street Bridge). His judgment that this route should be limited to a grade of 1.5 percent (1.5 feet per 100 feet) and a minimum radius of 385 feet was an impressive prediction of what would be appropriate a century later. The route was just over thirty-two miles long; his estimate of the cost to build it was just over $148,000, roughly $4,625 per mile. His unit costs were based on experience with canal construction, the small amount of B&O Railroad construction and appropriate local experience.

Mr. De Hass then proceeded to analyze the potential traffic and fees that could be generated to pay for building, maintaining and operating this new transportation mode in the Chartiers Valley. He anticipated cargoes of general merchandise, salt, flour, grain, pork, whiskey, wool, coal, boards and shingles and the U.S. Mail. He forecast revenue of about $15,000 per year, a very attractive value for potential investors. All told, his effort was an outstanding example of civil engineering accomplishment at a time when engineers lacked the information and resources available two generations later. Unfortunately, the financial and business minds behind the Washington and Pittsburgh Railroad were not as successful at their task as Mr. De Hass was at his. Although the corporation began to acquire rights-of-way and perform initial grading in the early years, it took forty years before the railroad was completed to Carnegie, where it could then follow the tracks of the Pennsylvania Railroad into Pittsburgh, following the original route Mr. De Hass had surveyed decades earlier.

The Pennsylvania Railroad (PRR) came into existence in 1846 with the specific goal of building a line that would connect Pittsburgh to Harrisburg and from there to the entire Eastern Seaboard. To achieve this goal, it hired John Edgar Thomson as its chief engineer. He was a self-educated engineer who had just completed construction of the Georgia Railroad, the longest line in the world at that time, linking Augusta and Atlanta. A route following the Susquehanna River north to the Juniata and then west to Allegheny Ridge was chosen from the east. From Pittsburgh, the western part of the route went southeast to Greensburg, then to Blairsville and then up the Conemaugh River to the western slope of Allegheny Ridge near Johnstown.

A decade earlier, the Pennsylvania Main Line Canal had overcome the obstacle of Allegheny Ridge with the Portage Railway, a series of ten separate inclined plane railways, five on each side of the mountain. Thomson's solution was to ascend the ridge from the east by a long, horseshoe-shaped curve climbing up one side of a ravine, crossing it on

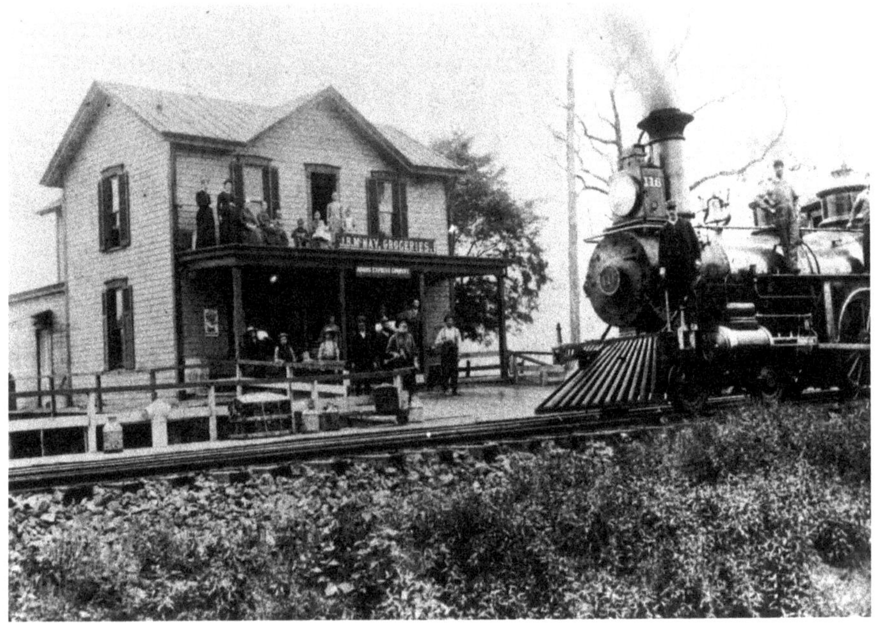

The Chartiers Valley Railroad at Boyce Station. *Historical Society of Upper St. Clair.*

a fill and continuing to climb up the other side. Just before reaching the summit of the ridge, the 3,612-foot-long Summit Tunnel was constructed through the mountain, emerging on the west side at the community of Gallitzin. Thomson's associate in engineering this passage through Allegheny Ridge was Herman Haupt, a West Point–trained civil engineer with considerable experience in canal, railroad and bridge design and construction. Haupt served with distinction during the Civil War, focusing on repair and maintenance of railroads. The "Horseshoe Curve" has been recognized by the American Society of Civil Engineers as a National Historic Civil Engineering Landmark. It ascends 122 feet in a length of 2,375 feet, a grade of about 1.8 percent. Its central angle is 220 degrees, with a diameter of about 1,300 feet. The curve was constructed without heavy equipment, requiring about three years to complete, in 1854. The Summit Tunnel at Gallitzin, also completed in 1854, was twice as long as the famous Central Pacific Summit (also known as No. 6) tunnel, an ASCE National Historic Landmark. Completed thirteen years earlier, the Gallitzin tunnel is itself an impressive achievement for its time. In 1854, it was the longest tunnel in the world. Both it and the Horseshoe Curve have been in continuous use since their construction.

With the route from Philadelphia to Pittsburgh in full operation, the Pennsylvania Railroad began to expand to the west. In 1869, it acquired the Pittsburgh, Fort Wayne and Chicago Railroad, giving it access to Chicago. It was the successor to three lines, each partially funded by the Pennsylvania Railroad, linking Allegheny City (now Pittsburgh's North Side neighborhood) and Chicago. In Pennsylvania, the route followed the northeast shore of the Ohio River. A light-duty bridge across the Allegheny River was built in 1857 to provide access to the main passenger station in Pittsburgh. It was replaced by a five span wrought-iron lattice truss in 1868 and then by the massive double-deck truss bridge constructed by the American Bridge Company in 1904 that is still in use today. In 1917, it was jacked up about thirteen feet and new pier caps added to enhance navigation on the Allegheny River. The upper deck carried the main line to Fort Wayne and Chicago, and the lower deck was used by trains serving the Strip District. Conrail ended use of the lower deck in the 1980s.

Similarly, in 1890, the Pennsylvania Railroad acquired the Pittsburgh, Cincinnati, Chicago and St. Louis Railroad, a combination of several

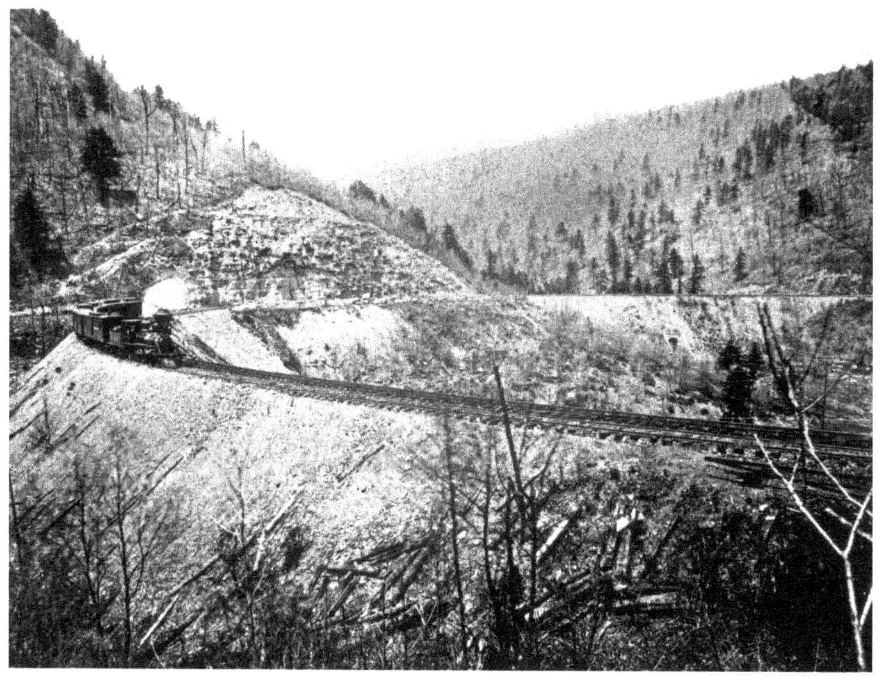

Horseshoe Curve, 1897. *Brady Stewart Collection.*

smaller midwestern lines, to have access to St. Louis. It was operated as the "Panhandle" Division. From Union Station, it went through a tunnel under downtown Pittsburgh, crossed the Monongahela River on the Panhandle Bridge and followed the southwest shore of the river to Pittsburgh's West End neighborhood and then to Crafton and Carnegie before going due west to Steubenville, Ohio. The third Panhandle Bridge, a steel truss structure built in 1903, has been repurposed and is in use today providing light-rail passenger service to Pittsburgh's southern city neighborhoods and suburbs.

Because Pittsburgh originally was the hub for three different lines, its main passenger station was called Union Station. The main building is a conventional twelve-story masonry structure constructed in 1903 and currently repurposed as an upscale apartment complex, "The Pennsylvanian." Peter Joseph Weber is credited with the design of the building under the supervision of architect Daniel Burnham. The architect's greatest achievement was the magnificent rotunda interfacing the station with the city street network.

In 1837, a charter was granted to the Pittsburgh and Connellsville Railroad to construct a line along the Monongahela and Youghiogheny Rivers to Connellsville. The actual route of the railroad was along the east shore of the Youghiogheny. Six years later, the charter was amended to permit extension beyond Connellsville "to any point in Pennsylvania." In 1853, Maryland granted permission for extending the line as far as Cumberland, Maryland, where it could connect with the Baltimore and Ohio Railroad (B&O). Once the line was complete as far as Connellsville, it was leased by the B&O, providing it with access into downtown Pittsburgh via P&LE tracks, also leased, in about 1870. The B&O built a large terminal and rail yard on the east side of Smithfield Street, between Second Avenue and the Monongahela River. The yard extended for a mile along the river. The terminal was razed in 1955 to permit construction of the Parkway East and replaced by a modest building on Grant Street. Commuter trains operated in this location until 1989. B&O became part of CSX in 1987; the property was eventually vacated and repurposed.

The original B&O mainline west bypassed Pennsylvania completely, running from Cumberland, Maryland, to Grafton, West Virginia, where one branch went northwest to Wheeling and on to Columbus, Ohio, and the other branch went due west to Parkersburg, West Virginia, and then on to Cincinnati, Ohio. Part of the original charter for the Pennsylvania Railroad included legislation limiting competition from the B&O.

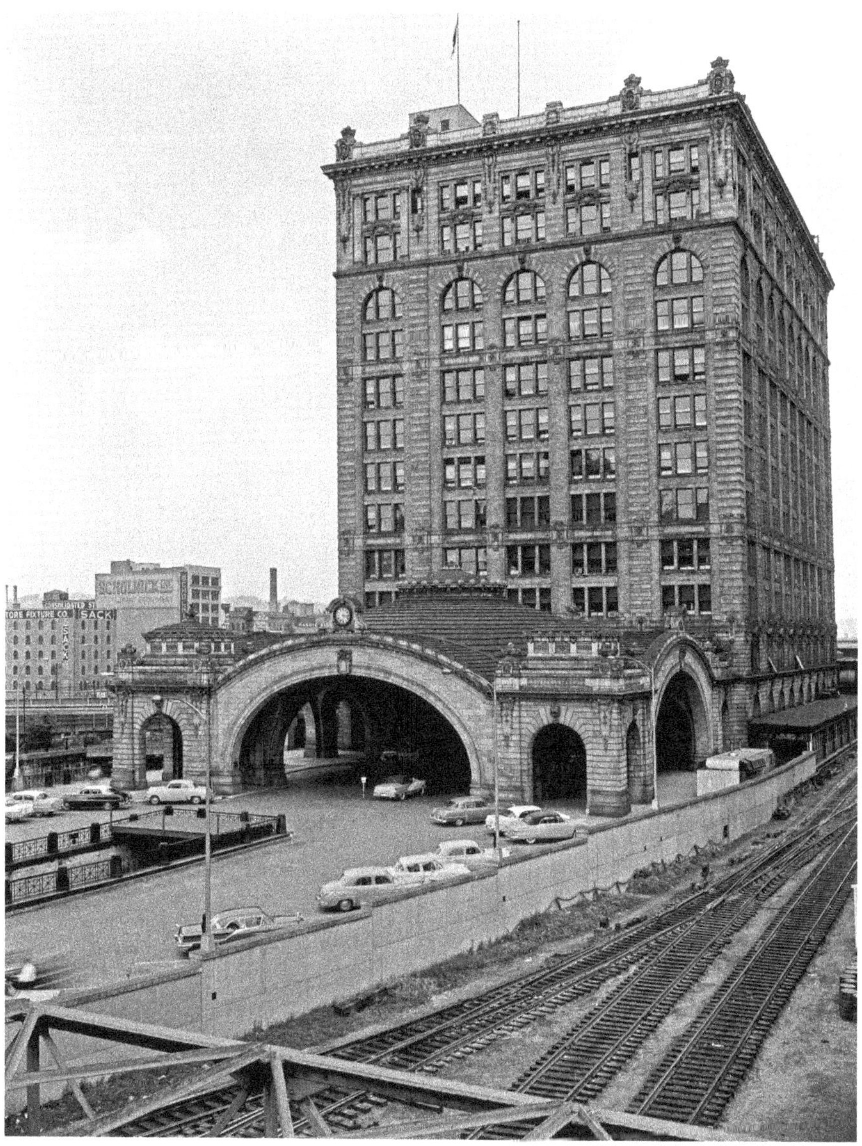

The Union Station was constructed between 1898 and 1903. In 1912, its name was changed to Penn Station to match the other Pennsylvania Railroad stations in the state. *Brady Stewart Collection.*

The Pittsburgh and Castle Shannon Railroad (P&CSRR) was an excellent example of the impact that small, narrow-gauge railroads had on the development of this area. It was the successor to the Coal Hill Railroad, built by the Pittsburgh Coal Company in 1861 to service a mine in the Saw Mill Run Valley. The line climbed the south slope of Mount Washington via a horseshoe curve, ran through the "mined out" Beltzhoover mine to an opening on the Pittsburgh side of the mountain and then descended to the Monongahela River on an inclined plane railway.

In 1871, a group of investors, headed by Milton Hayes, formed the Pittsburgh & Castle Shannon Railroad to promote development of communities along Saw Mill Run, including Castle Shannon. It purchased the Coal Hill Railroad and extended it up Saw Mill Run, still as a narrow-gauge (forty inches) line. In addition to coal cars, it began running passenger cars through the old mine tunnel. The cars have been described as similar to those on amusement park trains, to get through the tunnel that had an overhead clearance of sixty-five inches. The investors quickly realized the potential for passenger business to supplement their coal hauling function and enlarged the tunnel to make it possible for conventional locomotives and passenger cars to negotiate it. At that point, the passengers transferred to the incline to be transported down to Carson Street. By 1877, the railroad was running nine passenger trains per day, each way.

In 1891, a new incline was designed and built by the P&CSRR chief engineer, Samuel Diescher. Named the Castle Shannon Incline, its cars were large enough to haul wagons (and eventually automobiles), as well as passengers. The old incline it replaced continued to be used for transporting coal to the Carson Street transfer facilities. It was coupled with a new incline on the south face of Mount Washington, providing passengers with an easy passage over the mountain. The Castle Shannon Incline operated until 1964.

In 1900, after a long conflict with the Pittsburgh Southern Railroad for a route south to Washington, Pennsylvania, the P&CSRR was sold to the Pittsburgh Coal Company. In 1905, Pittsburgh Railways leased the track and added its standard-gauge (five feet, two and a half inches) rails to permit the use of streetcars. For a few years, streetcars and passenger trains used the track during the day, and coal trains operated on it at night. The coal hauling business ended in 1912, and three years later, passenger service using steam locomotives also ceased. Since then, the route has been dedicated to interurban trolleys and, eventually, to the current light-rail system.

The predecessor to the Little Saw Mill Run Railroad (LSMRR) was the "Horse Railway," a two-mile-long tramway that used horses to haul coal from a coal mine in the Little Saw Mill Run valley to the Ohio River at Temperanceville (now Pittsburgh's West End). The Horse Railway was the brainchild of Abraham Kirk Lewis, who is also credited with building the first tunnel (one mile long) through Mount Washington and the region's first inclined plane on the north face of the mountain.

In 1853, funded by the Harmony Society, the Little Saw Mill Run Railroad was constructed to replace the Horse Railway. The standard-gauge line ran three miles from a coaling dock in Temperanceville to a mine in Banksville. The line included five bridges and a 1,400-foot-long trestle and operated three 0-6-0 locomotives built at the Pittsburgh Locomotive Works plant in the Chateau/Woods Run area of Pittsburgh's North Side.

An engine house was located at the Banksville end of the railroad. In the early 1870s, the line moved about 150,000 tons of coal each year, some of which was converted to coke in twelve beehive ovens in Temperanceville. Passenger service was provided by a single un-propelled car that coasted downhill from Banksville to Temperanceville, with a brakeman assigned to stop it with handbrakes to take on and discharge passengers. The car was returned to Banksville coupled to a coal train. The railroad survived until 1897, when it was merged into the West Side Belt Railroad.

The Pittsburgh Southern Railway came into being as a result of the Pittsburgh and Castle Shannon Railroad's inability to complete an extension from Castle Shannon to Finleyville and then on to Washington, Pennsylvania. In 1877, a new company, the Pittsburgh, Castle Shannon and Washington Railroad (PCS&WRR), was chartered to provide the necessary extension. Milton Hayes, president of the P&CSRR, was also president of the new venture. At thirty-six miles long, it transported coal, agricultural products, timber and other freight on a narrow-gauge (forty inches) line from Castle Shannon to Washington.

At some point, the cooperative agreement between the P&CSRR and the PCS&WRR began to break down. Hayes contacted the Harmony Society (Jacob Henrici) and negotiated an agreement to use the Little Saw Mill Run Railroad's right-of-way into Temperanceville. His intention was to add a third rail to the LSM line to permit operation of rolling stock for a narrow-gauge line and to build a new route through Mount Lebanon from Banksville to the Arlington Station on the P&CSRR. It would then lease a mile of the P&CSRR to reach the terminus of the PCS&W at Castle Shannon.

This agreement was announced on April 2, 1878, along with the announcement that the railroad's name had been changed to the Pittsburgh Southern Railroad (PSRR). This was the final straw for the P&CS; it forced

Hayes to resign from the organization and dispatched a crew to Castle Shannon to tear up the third rail the PS had installed on its line to the Arlington Station.

According to the local papers, this initiated the "Castle Shannon Railway War" between the two track gangs, climaxing with P&CS master mechanic Matt Rapp giving Hayes a black eye. Nonetheless, the PSRR side prevailed, and the track continued to be used by its trains. Although the Pittsburgh Southern hoped to extend its lines south through West Virginia to the coal fields in Virginia, that ambition was never realized. After struggling financially for a few years, the line was sold to the B&O in 1883.

The Rochester and Pittsburgh Railroad was constructed in 1881 to connect the Pennsylvania coal fields with marine terminals in Buffalo and Rochester, New York. It entered Pennsylvania at Bradford, continued south through Ridgway to DuBois via the Kinzua Viaduct and then west to Butler before entering Pittsburgh through Allegheny City (today's North Side). It went bankrupt in 1881, an experience from which emerged the Buffalo, Rochester and Pittsburgh Railroad. It prospered until 1932, when it was acquired by the B&O, giving it access into western New York.

The Pittsburgh and Western Railroad was constructed as a narrow-gauge (thirty-six inches) line to serve the area north and northwest of Pittsburgh. It was acquired by the B&O in 1911, providing it with a northwest route to Ohio and beyond. It began in Rankin and followed the Monongahela north shore downstream to Junction Hollow and then through the Schenley Tunnel and across the Thirty-Third Street Railroad Bridge to Etna, Glenshaw, Elwood City and New Castle before exiting Pennsylvania.

The Pittsburgh and Lake Erie Railroad (P&LE) was the brainchild of Pittsburgh businessman William McCreery in response to a business failure he blamed on the PRR's discriminatory rates practice. Organized in 1870, it began to lay tracks in Beaver Falls, Pennsylvania, in 1877 for a line linking Pittsburgh and Youngstown, Ohio. Coincidentally, Beaver Falls was the location of a major business owned by the Harmony Society, one of whose members, Jacob Henrici, was a P&LE director. Harmony Society was a pietistic Christian sect centered near Ambridge, Pennsylvania, in a community named Economy. Its emphasis on frugality and hard work produced significant wealth that the society's elders, including Henrici, invested profitably in local businesses, like the P&LE. Its practice of celibacy, however, eventually doomed the society to extinction. During his lifetime, Henrici was a major factor in the railroad's development.

Another significant factor in the early life of the P&LE was William Vanderbilt's investment in it through New York Central System's subsidiary, the Lake Shore and Michigan Southern Railway (LS&MSR). The P&LE functioned effectively throughout its lifetime as an independent subsidiary of the NYC. From 1887 on, the president of the LS&MSR also served as P&LE president. In 1881, as part of his South Pennsylvania Railroad scheme to undermine the PRR's monopoly on traffic between Harrisburg and Pittsburgh, Vanderbilt acquired P&LE stock from the Harmony Society and Pittsburgh steel magnate Henry Oliver and financed the construction of the Pittsburgh, McKeesport and Youghiogheny Railroad between Pittsburgh and Connellsville, where it was intended to meet the South Penn. This eventually became the Youghiogheny Branch of the P&LE.

In 1901, the P&LE's Monongahela Branch was built down the east side of the Monongahela River to Brownsville, where it eventually met the Monongahela Railway, a joint venture of the PRR and the P&LE, serving the coal mines in Washington, Greene and Westmoreland Counties. The P&LE was nicknamed "The Little Giant" because of the massive amount of coal, coke, iron ore, limestone and steel it moved on a fairly short main line—ten times the ton-miles per mile of track of an average railroad. The P&LE boasted two landmarks that are still prominent today: the magnificent Ohio River bridge between Monaca and Beaver and the impressive passenger terminal on Pittsburgh's South Side. The terminal was constructed in 1898 and has been repurposed as the centerpiece of the popular Station Square complex at the south end of the Smithfield Street Bridge. The bridge was built in 1910 as a cantilever through-truss structure with a main span of 769 feet shortly after the highly publicized collapse of the similar Quebec cantilever bridge.

The Pittsburgh, Chartiers & Youghiogheny Railroad (PC&Y) was incorporated in 1881 to acquire and consolidate the assets of two proposed railroads—the Chartiers and Mansfield Valley Rail Way Company and the McLaughlin's and Saw Mill Run Rail Way Company—and to construct about twenty miles of track on its rights-of-way. In 1893, it was acquired jointly by the Pittsburgh and Lake Erie (P&LE) and Pittsburgh, Cincinnati, Chicago and St. Louis Railroads, each respectively subsidiaries of competitive rivals, the New York Central and Pennsylvania Railroads. The PC&Y originated at McKees Rocks and followed the Chartiers Creek Valley to Carnegie, where it joined the PRR and followed that line to Woodville. At Woodville, it split off two branches—one going southwest through Presto to the Beechmont coal mine and the other going southeast to Beadling and mines in the

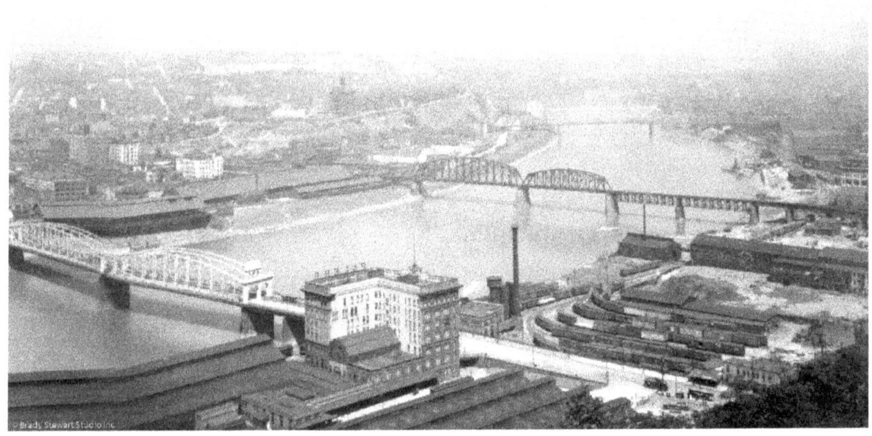

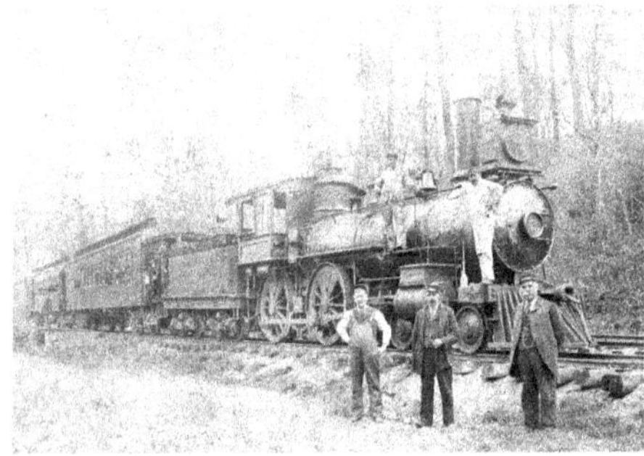

Above: View of the PL&E railroad building and yard, Smithfield Street Bridge, Monongahela Railroad Bridge and Mon Warehouses from Mount Washington, 1905. *Brady Stewart Collection.*

Left: The first train that came to Hickman, Pennsylvania, 1885. *From Pittsburgh, Chartiers & Youghiogheny Railway Company, courtesy Gene Czambel.*

Painter's Run Valley. At its peak, the PC&Y was a busy line, moving nearly 2 million tons of freight per year and handling a small amount of passenger traffic as well.

In the early 1880s, a syndicate led by William Vanderbilt, president of the New York Central Railroad, began construction of a new line from Harrisburg to Pittsburgh, aimed at competing with the PRR's highly successful main line. Included in the syndicate were steel barons Andrew Carnegie and Henry Oliver and Reading Railroad president Frank Gowen. They acquired more than two hundred miles of right-of-way along the route surveyed forty years earlier by Colonel Charles Schlatter and began construction in 1883. The construction included a wide, long bridge across the Susquehanna River and nine tunnels through the ridges of the Allegheny Mountains. It proved to be an expensive endeavor, both in lives lost (twenty-seven) and financially (a 100 percent budget overrun at the 60 percent completion stage).

At this point, J.P. Morgan, who had major financial interests in the New York Central, stepped in as a mediator between PRR president George Roberts and the Vanderbilt syndicate. Being the most influential businessman in the country in those days, Morgan's invitation for Roberts, Vanderbilt, Carnegie and the rest of the syndicate to spend a day discussing the situation on Morgan's yacht in Long Island Sound amounted to an order from on high. Two things happened concurrently: the participants were unable to reach a satisfactory solution and the wind came up, making the sound very rough. Morgan agreed to return his seasick guests to dry land as soon as they came to an agreement. The prompt response was that the syndicate would cease construction of the South Pennsylvania Railroad and sell the right-of-way to the PRR for a token price, and in return, the PRR would relinquish its interest in the New York, West Shore and Chicago Railroad, a venture attempting to build a line through New York State to compete with the NYC. Fifty years later, the Pennsylvania Turnpike Commission acquired the right-of-way and used it to construct the first limited-access, all-weather "superhighway" in North America. Despite its never reaching completion, the South Pennsylvania Railroad was a significant civil engineering accomplishment in the late nineteenth century.

George Jay Gould inherited a fortune from his father, Jay Gould, and the ambition to surpass his father's remarkable success in railroad building. His grand scheme was to create a transcontinental system of railroads linking the East and West Coasts. He had inherited control of the Western Pacific Railway, the Denver and Rio Grande Railroad and the Missouri Pacific Railroad, connecting California with the Mississippi River at St. Louis. The next step was acquisition of the Wabash Railroad, which brought the system as far east as Toledo, Ohio. He then gained control of the Wheeling and Lake Erie Railroad connecting Toledo with Wheeling, West Virginia, and bought the never-constructed Pittsburgh and Mansfield Railroad and its charter to build into downtown Pittsburgh.

Control of the Western Maryland Railroad and its access into Baltimore left the section through Pittsburgh and southwestern Pennsylvania the only missing link. The Pittsburgh, Carnegie and Western Railroad was chartered to construct this link. It was eventually combined with the Wheeling and Lake Erie and two other small lines to form the Wabash Pittsburgh Terminal Railway (WPT).

The WPT crossed the Ohio River at Mingo Junction, Ohio, and then proceeded east across the West Virginia Panhandle, eventually reaching Bridgeville and then Rook Yard before turning south through Bruceton and Monessen to link up with the Western Maryland at Connellsville. To enter downtown Pittsburgh, a spur ran through a new tunnel under Mount Washington before crossing the Monongahela River on a magnificent cantilever bridge and ending at an equally magnificent terminal on Liberty Avenue. The engineer for this impressive project was Joseph Ramsey, a Pittsburgher who had graduated from the Western University of Pennsylvania (later renamed the University of Pittsburgh).

By the time the WPT was constructed, all of the river-level routes had been preempted by other railroads, necessitating the numerous high trestles that are still in use by its successor, a later version of the W&LE. The WPT went into operation in 1904 with an excursion train to the Louisiana Purchase Exposition, also known as the St. Louis World's Fair. Unfortunately, the excessive construction costs had generated debts that couldn't be remediated during the Panic of 1907, and the system went into bankruptcy the following year. A series of railroads, including the W&LE, has managed to continue railroading profitably on the WPT main line. The Pittsburgh Terminal was destroyed by fires in 1946. The Wabash Bridge was demolished in 1948, leaving only its piers as hints of its splendor. The Mount Washington Tunnel survives as an underutilized HOV route.

In 1865, the Bear Creek Railroad was chartered to move coal from Pardoe to Shenango, where it could be transferred to the Erie Extension Canal and other railroads. By the time it began operation in 1869, it had been renamed the Shenango and Allegheny Railroad. By 1883, it had been extended south to Butler and north to Greenville. It reached the port of Conneaut, Ohio, in 1892, just in time to coincide with the arrival of the first ore boat from the Iron Range on Lake Superior. Renamed the Pittsburgh, Shenango and Lake Erie Railroad, in 1896 it became part of a joint venture involving the Union Railroad and the Carnegie Steel Company to build a connecting line from Butler to Carnegie's Edgar Thomson Works in Braddock. The new line was

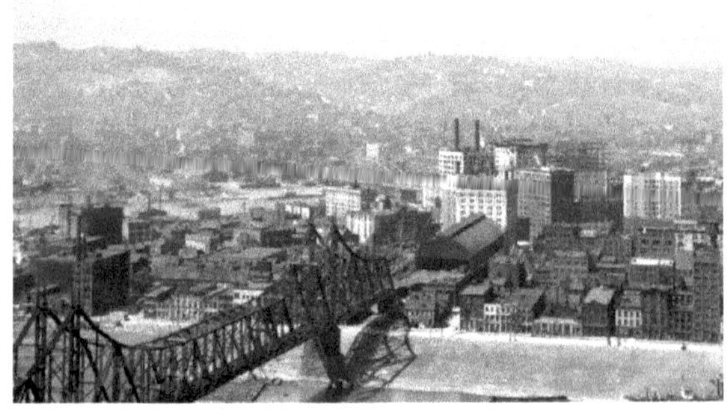

View of the Point buildings, Wabash Railroad Bridge, Wabash Railroad Terminal and adjacent Wabash RR office building from Mount Washington, 1905. *Brady Stewart Collection.*

called the Butler and Pittsburgh Railroad. At this point, Carnegie acquired majority equity and organized the two lines into the Pittsburgh, Bessemer and Lake Erie Railroad (B&LE). It soon became quite profitable, moving iron ore south from Conneaut to Pittsburgh and coal north to Conneaut to be loaded into lake vessels for shipment throughout the Great Lakes. The B&LE had major spurs. One line ran into Erie to interface with the Erie Railroad. Another ran to the Conneaut Lake Park, which became a popular destination for excursions from Pittsburgh and Cleveland. The single-track bridge across the Allegheny River at Cheswick was completed in 1897 and is still in service.

The Waynesburg and Washington Railroad (W&W) was chartered in 1875, built in 1877, acquired by the Pennsylvania Railroad in 1885 and operated into the 1970s. It was constructed as a narrow-gauge (thirty-six inches) line for about $5,000 per mile. In the 1800s, there was no advantage for an independent railroad dedicated to linking two cities to build the more expensive standard-gauge line; narrow-gauge railroads were quite common. The W&W initially had tiny rails (thirty pounds per yard) and ties that were only six feet long.

The route was filled with zigzags and sharp curves; sarcastic riders claimed that its original surveyor must have been a snake. A witty nineteenth-century poet described the W&W as follows:

It wriggles in and it wriggles out
And leaves the traveler still in doubt
Whether the snake who made the track
Was going south or coming back.

Its low point was at Waynesburg (900 feet above sea level), with a summit of about 1,400 feet, four miles south of Washington, requiring a grade of 2 percent in several areas. The curves were so sharp that locomotives with eight drive wheels could not be used. The main yard for the W&W was at Waynesburg. It included a roundhouse, a turntable, a freight house and the stockyard. On Saturdays, the local farmers shipped cattle to Pittsburgh. Fridays were "drovers' days," when the cattle were driven through the Waynesburg streets to the stockyard, where they were housed overnight before being loaded onto the train. Despite terminating passenger service fifteen years earlier, in 1944, the PRR converted the W&W to standard gauge. A few years later, the only traffic on the line was a gasoline-powered truck equipped with flanged steel wheels delivering small freight shipments. This

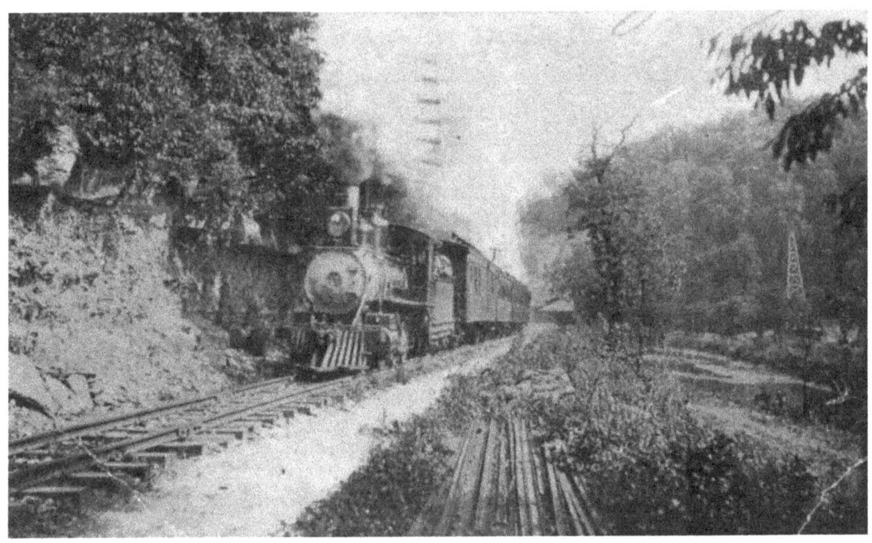

The Waynesburg and Washington leaving Waynesburg. *Greene County Historical Society.*

service ended in 1974. When Conrail acquired the assets of the bankrupt Penn Central Railroad, it elected to abandon the W&W.

The Montour Railroad was chartered in 1877 as a wholly owned subsidiary of the Imperial Coal Company, located at Imperial, Pennsylvania, to provide an outlet for marketing its product. Initially, it transferred coal to barges on the Ohio River, near Coraopolis; however, it soon became more profitable to transfer railcars full of coal to the P&LE at Montour Junction. Construction of 102 beehive coke ovens near Montour Junction provided the coal company an alternative market for its coal. By 1899, passenger and mail service was being provided on the twelve-mile-long line, and railroad shops had been constructed at Montour Junction. At that point, the Pittsburgh Coal Company was organized to purchase 140 independent coal companies in southwestern Pennsylvania, including the Imperial Coal Company and its railroad subsidiary. The advantage of expansion of the railroad to serve mines in southern Allegheny and northern Washington Counties was obvious.

By 1915, the Montour Railroad had been extended through McDonald, Venice, Hendersonville and Hills Station to West Mifflin, where it interchanged with the Union Railroad, providing it access to the Monongahela River as well as to the Ohio. The rail line included four tunnels and numerous steel bridges. When World War I broke out, the railroad was taken over by the

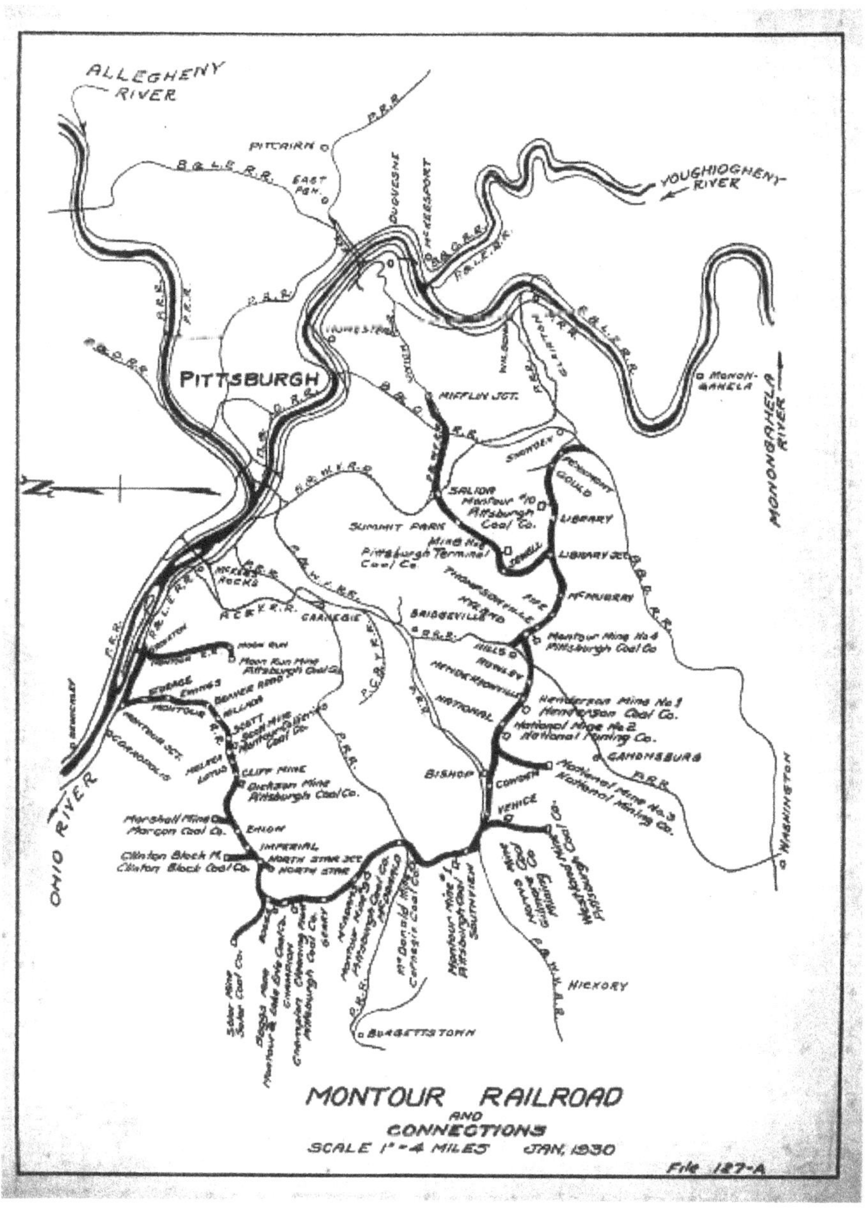

Montour Railroad and connections map, January 1930. *Montour Railroad Historical Society.*

federal government for a period of six months before being returned to private control. At its peak, the Montour Railroad served twenty-seven coal mines transporting 7 million tons of coal annually. When the Champion Coal Preparation Plant went into operation, it became the focus of the coal handling business, processing thirteen thousand tons of coal per day.

In 1946, Pittsburgh Coal Company sold the railroad to a combination of the PRR and P&LE, an arrangement that lasted until 1975, when the P&LE acquired full ownership. By then, the decline in production of most of the mines in the area and other economic factors had reduced traffic on the railroad significantly; in 1984, it ceased operation and was formally abandoned. Much of its right-of-way has been acquired by the Montour Trail Council and has been a popular recreational trail.

The legacy of the civil engineers who designed and constructed the massive infrastructure for the railroads that enabled the industrial and commercial development of Western Pennsylvania in the late 1800s and early 1900s is a combination of several robust lines still providing important service to society; a handful of buildings, bridges and tunnels, many of which have been repurposed for other uses; and the growing number of recreational "Rails-to-Trails" projects throughout the area. We are grateful to them for their achievements.

ROADS AND HIGHWAYS

The Ultimate Independence

By Jason Machuga, PE, and Carrie Machuga

The roads and highways in Western Pennsylvania have changed over time to reflect the needs of the populace and times in which they were developed. They show an evolution from the early adoption of deer paths into native paths, the military importance of early routes to link east to west and the economic importance of connecting the region to commercial centers throughout the United States. These roadways opened up Western Pennsylvania, allowing travel in new ways and to new locations, providing independence that had not been previously possible. Countless and nameless engineers, in particular civil engineers, played important roles in the development of this vital infrastructure.

Native American Paths in Western Pennsylvania

Native American paths served as the first transportation system in Pennsylvania. They were the first trails blazed through the wilderness that was then the Pennsylvania frontier. Different trails were used for trade, war, hunting and travel; each had a strategic location and design depending on their use. For example, war paths were unique from trade routes in that they were usually located at higher elevations to provide better observation of the enemy. But regardless of their purpose, these paths were the result of rudimentary engineering based on observation and experience. They marked routes with acceptable soil conditions, which were rarely undermined or washed out and were always protected from weather. Several of these paths have served as connections between important parts of Pennsylvania throughout history.

In the early period of settlement in Pennsylvania, travelers from the east would use several paths to reach the Allegheny River Valley. From Carlisle in central Pennsylvania, travelers could use the Frankstown Path (also called the Allegheny or Ohio Path) northwestward to Indiana, Pennsylvania, where it joined the Kittanning Path, which ended at the Allegheny River near Kittanning. A shorter alternate route to the Allegheny Valley would take travelers along the Kiskiminetas Path from just west of Indiana to the Pittsburgh area. This path was the preferred route used by traders during colonial times to traverse the Pennsylvania wilderness.

Prior to the French and Indian War (1756–63), roads were developed only as far west as the Susquehanna River at Carlisle, where the native trails and packhorse trails became the only route over the Alleghenies. George Washington used several of these trails on his first mission to the Allegheny and Ohio Valleys to deliver a message of "cease and desist" to the French and their Native American allies who occupied the area. That message would precipitate the conflict between the British and the French and native allies.

EARLY MILITARY AND PACKHORSE ROADS

General Edward Braddock embarked on an unprecedented campaign from Fort Cumberland in Maryland with the intent to attack the French at Fort Duquesne, where the forks of the Allegheny and Monongahela Rivers join the Ohio River in present-day Pittsburgh. The 125-mile journey took Braddock and his troops over the steep and rocky terrain of the Allegheny Mountains. Braddock led 2,200 men who included not just soldiers but also "hatchet men," blacksmiths, miners, teamsters, wheelwrights and military engineers, all of whom were necessary to build a twelve-foot-wide wagon road through the mountains. Just surmounting the first ridge from Fort Cumberland proved a challenge, with the loss of several horses and wagons

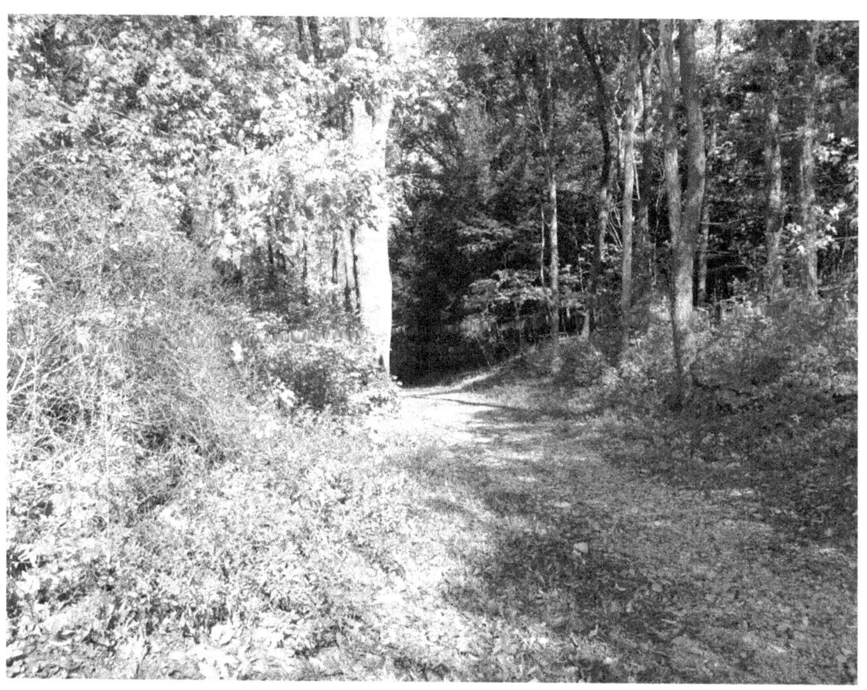

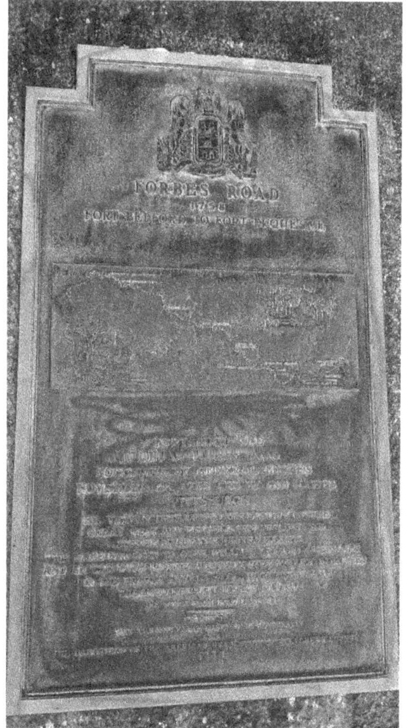

Above: Braddock's Road, located at Braddock's Grave, near Fort Necessity National Battlefield. *ASCE Pittsburgh Section.*

Left: Monument commemorating Forbes' Road from Fort Bedford to Fort Duquesne in Point State Park, Pittsburgh. *ASCE Pittsburgh Section.*

in those first few days. Braddock's Road followed Nemacolin's Path from Cumberland to Chestnut Ridge (just southeast of Uniontown), where it turned northward and toward Fort Duquesne, situated at the forks of the Ohio River, and the Point. In all, the road traversed eight major mountains. Braddock's troops dragged supplies and heavy artillery along the way just to suffer a horrific defeat in a French and Native American ambush a few miles from Fort Duquesne. Nearly two-thirds of the army was killed or wounded in the battle. General Braddock was fatally wounded and died during the retreat, retracing the road they had fought to build. Braddock was buried in the road, where the ruts from the wagons would make the grave less obvious to any enemy looking for the body.

General John Forbes led another mission to take the French Fort Duquesne in 1758. He built his road on a wagon trail that had been opened four years earlier between Shippensburg and Bedford. Forbes's army extended the road over the Raystown Path to just west of Ligonier. The army traveled through the woods from there to Fort Duquesne, in the hopes of surprising the French, only to arrive to find the fort burned and abandoned. In place of Fort Duquesne, the British built Fort Pitt, in honor of the British secretary of state William Pitt, who had been instrumental in turning the tide of the French and Indian War in favor of the British. Over the next five years, Forbes' Road, the reopened Braddock's Road and Burd's Road, a new road from Gist's plantation (about five miles southwest of Connellsville) to Brownsville, were maintained by the British army to transport supplies to support the final defeat of the French in the Pennsylvania frontier.

WESTERN PENNSYLVANIA'S FIRST BUILT ROADS

During the latter half of the eighteenth century, many roads were developed in the southeastern section of Pennsylvania (near Philadelphia), while the western region lagged far behind in road development. Forbes', Braddock's and Burd's Roads were maintained during the French and Indian War but were left to deteriorate until after the American Revolution.

The first formalized connection between Philadelphia and Pittsburgh was the Pennsylvania Road, completed in the 1790s. Its alignment included portions of some existing paths and roads, such as the Allegheny Path, the Raystown Path, Burd's Road and Forbes' Road. The Pennsylvania Road was a state road spearheaded by Hugh Henry Brackenridge, who first lobbied in the state legislature for improvement to the east–west transportation system in the early 1780s. Throughout the remainder of the eighteenth century, several acts and appropriations from the legislature authorized surveys and construction on the road's westward advance. The final alignment of the road was roughly the same as today's Lincoln Highway, following the main line of Forbes' Road over the Allegheny Mountains to Ligonier and diverging a few miles south to Greensburg and then on to Pittsburgh.

The William Penn Highway was surveyed first from Frankstown to the Conemaugh River in Blairsville in 1787. It was initially designed as a connection between the Susquehanna and Ohio River systems, by way of the Frankstown Road. The highway was extended along the Conemaugh River to Loyalhanna Creek and made passable for wagons in 1789. In the early years, the road was used primarily for transporting iron from the Juniata area to Pittsburgh. In 1807, the road was extended all the way into Pittsburgh. It was originally called the Huntington Pike, but over several years, the name evolved to the William Penn Highway.

The National Road, also known as the Cumberland Road, was the first road built entirely with federal funds. The road was initiated in an 1802 act that allowed the residents of Ohio to form a state government and join the United States. The act included a provision that said, "One-twentieth of the net proceeds of the lands lying within said State sold by Congress shall be applied to the laying and making of public roads." Previously, roads had been entirely the responsibility of the states, and this federal action in the realm of transportation caused considerable controversy that haunted the National Road throughout its history.

In 1805, President Thomas Jefferson authorized the study of potential routes to Ohio from the Eastern Seaboard. The committee studying possible routes recommended that the road begin in Cumberland, Maryland, and traverse Pennsylvania and present-day West Virginia to the Ohio River in Wheeling. In 1806, Jefferson signed a law "to regulate the laying out and making a road from Cumberland, in the State of Maryland, to the State of Ohio." The National Road between Cumberland and Wheeling officially opened in 1818 with a hard stone surface. As traffic exceeded expectations, the roadway was soon reconstructed with macadam, an early hard surface used for roadways. The completed alignment traveled over Nemacolin's Path, over the mountains, along the Youghiogheny River and Braddock's Road to Brownsville and Washington, Pennsylvania, and finally to Wheeling. Today, much of the National Road alignment is followed by US Route 40.

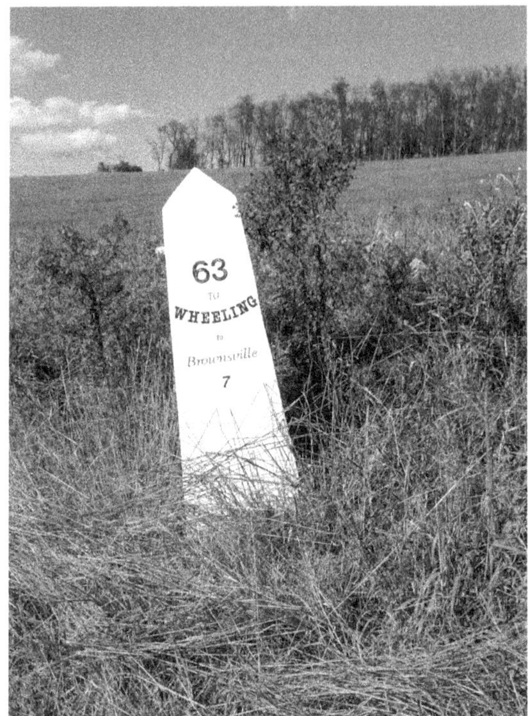

Left: Replica National Road marker. *ASCE Pittsburgh Section.*

Below: Searight's Tollhouse along the National Road, north of Uniontown. *ASCE Pittsburgh Section.*

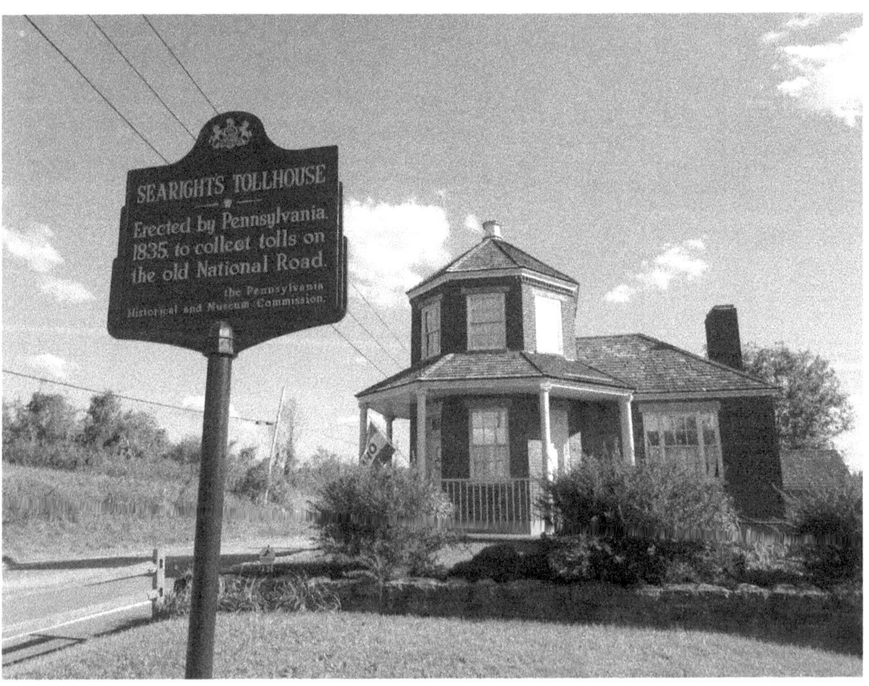

The National Road opened the western frontier to those searching for new, rich land to start their lives. Towns along the road began to grow, offering services to those traveling or for those travelers to stop and settle. As such, Cumberland, Uniontown, Brownsville, Washington and Wheeling became industrial centers. Congress originally planned to extend the road all the way to the Mississippi River. Extension required agreements, like the one made with Ohio, to be completed with each state that the road would pass through, and Congressional appropriations were needed for each stage. Maryland, Pennsylvania, Ohio and Virginia (now West Virginia) had accepted their portions of the National Road between 1831 and 1834 and immediately passed legislation to toll the road to maintain it. After $6,759,257 of federal funds had been spent on the road, the federal government turned the entire road back to the states in 1850.

By the 1850s, traffic had begun to decline on the National Road as railroads offered faster, more comfortable travel than the stagecoaches that used the road. In southwestern Pennsylvania, residents fought the expansion of the railroads in the area, knowing that they would begin the end of the National Road. When the Pennsylvania and B&O Railroads reached the area, the prosperity along the road began to decline as many of the businesses that had sprung up to support the National Road closed.

Another unique type of roadway that was found near Pittsburgh was part of the "Plank Road Craze," which began in Pennsylvania shortly after the first American plank road was built in upstate New York in 1846. Using wood to pave roads rather than stone was significantly cheaper: $1,500 per mile for a plank road compared to the $10,000 per mile cost of the National Road. The Alleghany and Butler Plank Road Company was one of the oldest and most successful of the private companies formed to build and toll these plank roads. Its Butler Plank Road was one of the most profitable plank road operations in the state. The road was twenty-seven miles long and connected Etna and Butler, Pennsylvania.

The Butler Plank Road, initially paved with flagstone, was popular with stagecoaches traveling between Butler and Pittsburgh. As the iron rims of the wagons using the road cut into the soft flagstone, it was replaced with wooden planks in the 1870s. This was considered an "engineering marvel of the times." According to the Shaler Historical Society, the wooden planks are still under the modern road that has replaced it. The planks were eight feet long and about three inches thick, split directly from logs and hand-hewn on top. It was typical of other plank roads, with the wooden pavement only wide enough for one-way traffic. The planks were occasionally offset at "turn-offs," where wagons could drop off the planks onto the adjacent dirt surface to allow others to pass. Tolls were collected at four toll gates along the Butler Plank Road.

Not surprisingly, plank roads survived just several decades at the most, due partly to competition from railroads at the time but also to the maintenance they needed. Wood planks had to be replaced on average every decade. There were at the time no wood preservatives that could protect the planks from rotting from the weather and sitting in the damp earth, and planks also often broke under the weight of the heavy wagon loads. Most of the plank road companies failed or closed before the end of the 1800s, unable to manage the repair and maintenance costs with their shrinking toll revenues.

THE FIRST AUTOMOBILE HIGHWAYS

As canals and railroads devalued the importance of earlier good roads, the birth of the automobile quickly reestablished the need for functional highways. One of the earliest and perhaps most important automobile highways was the Lincoln Highway. The Lincoln Highway was the brainchild of Carl Fisher, known previously for development of the Indianapolis Motor Speedway. The Lincoln Highway Association was founded in 1913 by Fisher and several other industrialists. Their goal was to create a hard-surfaced route extending from coast to coast that would keep motorists from getting stuck in the mud. Using private donations, the association promoted good roads along the designated route. Connecting New York City's Times Square with the Pacific Ocean in San Francisco, the Lincoln Highway route went directly through Pittsburgh. In Pennsylvania, the Lincoln Highway followed the path of the old Pennsylvania Road. Since its initial construction, the Lincoln Highway has taken several different routes through Pittsburgh and its environs.

The success of the Lincoln Highway led to other named routes across the country. In the late 1920s and early 1930s, construction was underway on the William Penn Highway, crossing the state via Pittsburgh, Harrisburg and Allentown. After nearly a century of decline, the National Road would find new life with the advent of the automobile and "motor-touring" in the 1910s and 1920s. The presence of the automobile on the National Road rejuvenated the towns along the road once again. The National Road again

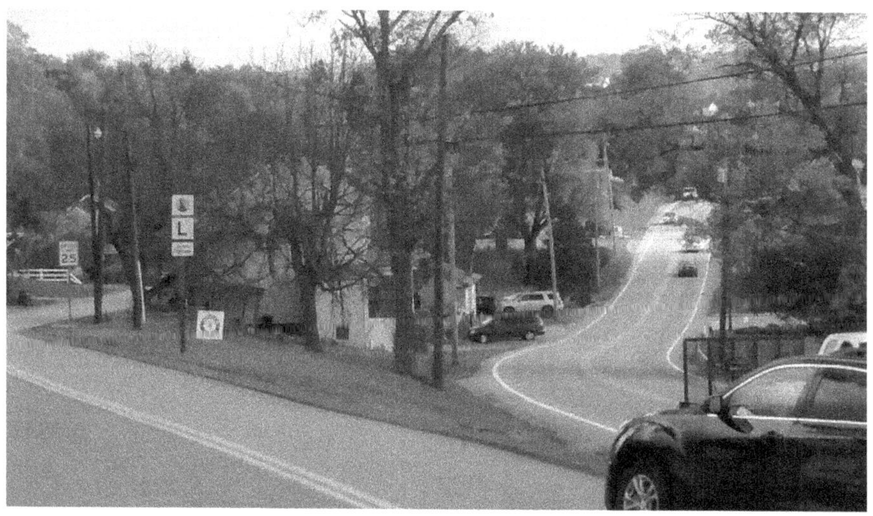

Lincoln Highway marker and two former alignments of the Lincoln Highway in North Huntingdon Township, Pennsylvania. *ASCE Pittsburgh Section.*

served as a major east–west route until the Pennsylvania Turnpike and the interstate system drew traffic away from the National Road.

The Federal Highway Act of 1921 created "an adequate and connected system of highways, interstate in character," as well as the numbering system for highways. In Pennsylvania, the National Road was revived as US Route 40, the William Penn Highway as US Route 22 and the Lincoln Highway as US Route 30. These three routes provided vital east–west routes for motorists and trucks in Western Pennsylvania. While vital, these routes were tough on the vehicles of the day, as they crossed the tops of mountains, and vehicles would often need to stop to cool down. Perhaps the most famous rest stop was the S.S. Grandview Ship Hotel along the Lincoln Highway in Bedford County. Built in the shape of a ship, the hotel boasted a view of three states and seven counties. The Ship Hotel stood until 2001, when it was lost to a fire.

Although these routes crossing the Appalachian Mountains were a vast improvement for travel across Pennsylvania, as vehicular technology improved and ownership increased, the demand for a modern highway connecting the east and the west grew. To meet this demand, attention was turned to history and the failed South Penn Railroad of the 1880s. The South Penn Railroad and William H. Vanderbilt of the New York Central Railroad intended to provide a direct railroad route with a gentle grade

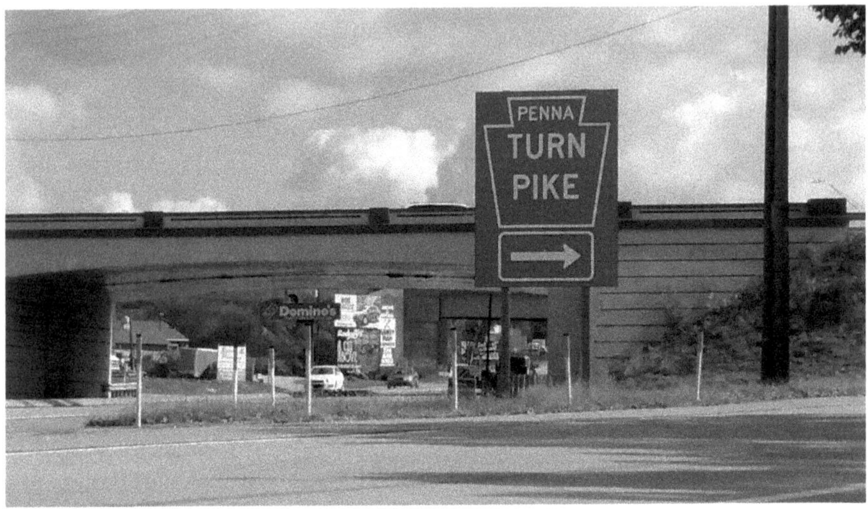

Original western terminus of the Pennsylvania Turnpike, Irwin, Pennsylvania. *ASCE Pittsburgh Section.*

connecting east with west as direct competition with the Pennsylvania Railroad. Construction abruptly ended due to a deal brokered to preserve the territorial rights of both the Pennsylvania Railroad and the New York Central Railroad, and the unused railroad grade and the partially built tunnels sat undisturbed for half a century.

Formed in 1935, the Pennsylvania Turnpike Commission began turnpike construction on October 26, 1938, and opened the route along the South Penn Railroad grade on October 1, 1940. The 160-mile highway connected US 30, the Lincoln Highway, at Irwin, Pennsylvania, outside Pittsburgh to US 11 at Carlisle, Pennsylvania, outside Harrisburg. The design was unique, modern and innovative. The grade-separated, limited-access toll highway provided quick and efficient access through the mountains connecting Pennsylvania's east and west like never before. It would be dubbed "America's first superhighway." The highway, its service plazas and its seven tunnels quickly captured the imagination of the nation and was commemorated in story, song, souvenirs and postcards. The Pennsylvania Turnpike was later extended from the Delaware River at the New Jersey border to the Ohio border. The Pennsylvania Turnpike blazed the way for toll roads in other states and eventually became a component of a series of toll roads that connected New York City and Chicago. The interstate system followed in 1956, with many of the Pennsylvania Turnpike's design features included.

GRAND BOULEVARDS

While the technology of highways and automobiles quickly improved in crossing the Alleghenies in the early twentieth century, the advent of the automobile also presented challenges to the existing city streets, which were designed for pedestrians, horse carts and streetcars. The City of Pittsburgh and the County of Allegheny needed to think big to accommodate the modal shift from human- to automotive-scale transportation.

As industrial development ensued, city engineer Edward Manning Bigelow made sure that Pittsburgh partook in the City Beautiful movement, an urban planning and architectural philosophy popular during the Victorian era that sought to make urban design beautiful as well as functional. After persuading Mary Schenley to donate the land for a large park in the city's east end, Bigelow knew that a boulevard connecting the new park to downtown was essential. This led to the development of Grant Boulevard, a low-grade boulevard connecting the park with downtown along the city's Bedford hillside early in the twentieth century. Today, Grant Boulevard is known as Bigelow Boulevard, named after the engineer who developed it. While Grant Boulevard was born from the City Beautiful movement, the need for future boulevards would be driven by age of the automobile. Beginning in 1920, a more direct route, Monongahela Boulevard, would be constructed connecting Schenley Park and east end neighborhoods with downtown.

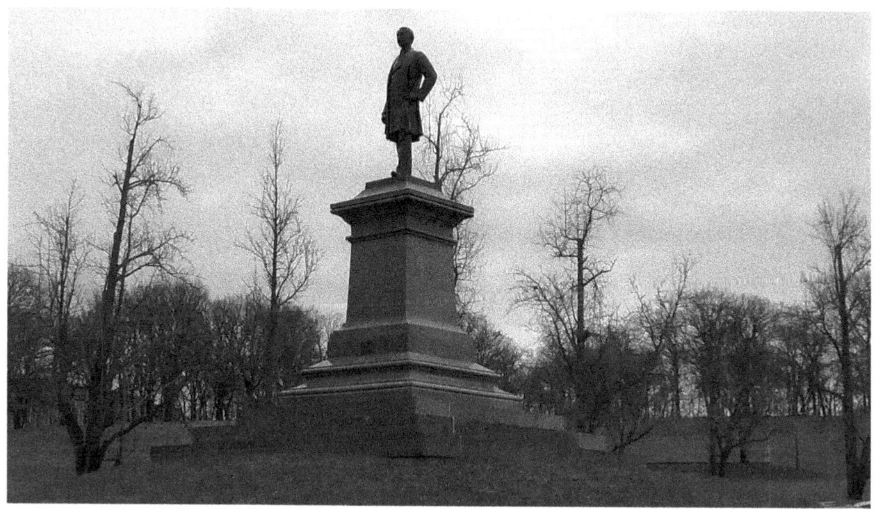

Statue of Edward Manning Bigelow in Schenley Park, Pittsburgh, Pennsylvania. *ASCE Pittsburgh Section.*

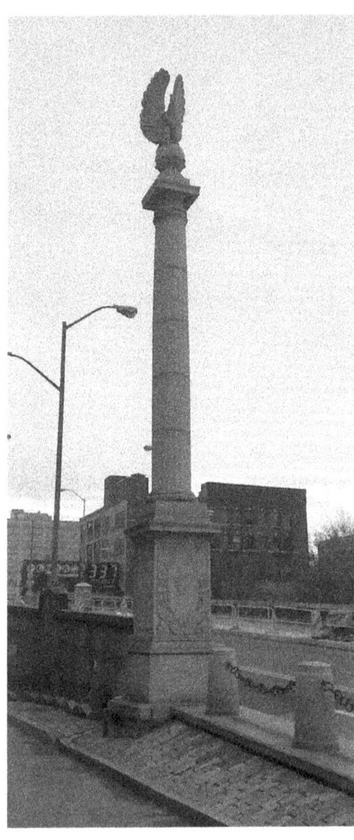

Decorative monument along the Boulevard of the Allies, downtown Pittsburgh, Pennsylvania. *ASCE Pittsburgh Section.*

Monongahela Boulevard was later renamed the "Boulevard of the Allies" in dedication to the Allies of World War I.

In 1910, Pittsburgh's Committee on City Planning commissioned a report by renowned landscape architect and city planner Frederick Law Olmsted Jr. to develop a plan to "meet the City's present and future needs." The report detailed technical approaches on appropriate roadway widths and specific thoroughfares that should be developed to meet the challenges of the city. Much of the report focused on the need to develop gentle-grade roadway solutions to improve mobility in an era of horse-cart transportation. One of the report's recommendations was to eliminate Grant's Hill, or the "Hump," in downtown Pittsburgh. Olmsted's "Hump Cut" was carried out in 1912 to minimize the grades of crucial downtown streets by lowering some streets by as much as sixteen feet. Remaining buildings in this section of downtown showcase the architectural anomaly of having to lower their entrances to the new street level. A fine example is the rear entrance to the Allegheny County Courthouse on Ross Street. Olmsted scoured the world for examples of how to develop thoroughfares to tackle Pittsburgh's complex terrain and drafted a report recommending improvements to the waterfront and utilizing hillsides for important roadways. In addition to widening many of the city's main streets, the report recommended many improvements and several new arteries that would come to fruition.

In an effort to connect the South Hills to downtown, Olmsted's proposed South Hills Artery would utilize a high level bridge and tunnel, which today is known as the Liberty Bridge and Tunnel. The report even provided details arguing the advantage of a low-grade bridge and tunnel in reaching the South Hills at a significantly higher elevation, thus reducing travel on steep roadways. The report details scores of other improvements to the city's

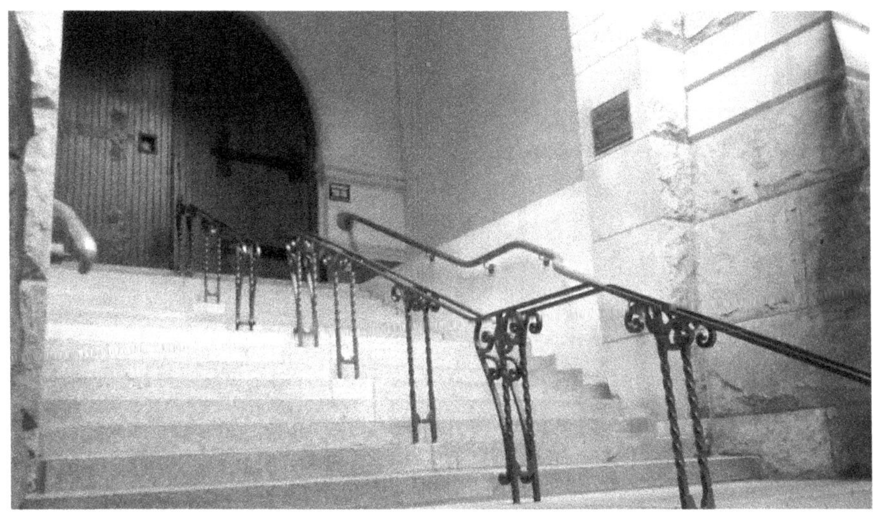

Above: Ross Street rear entrance of the Allegheny County Courthouse showing the architectural adjustments required as a result of the "Hump Cut." *ASCE Pittsburgh Section.*

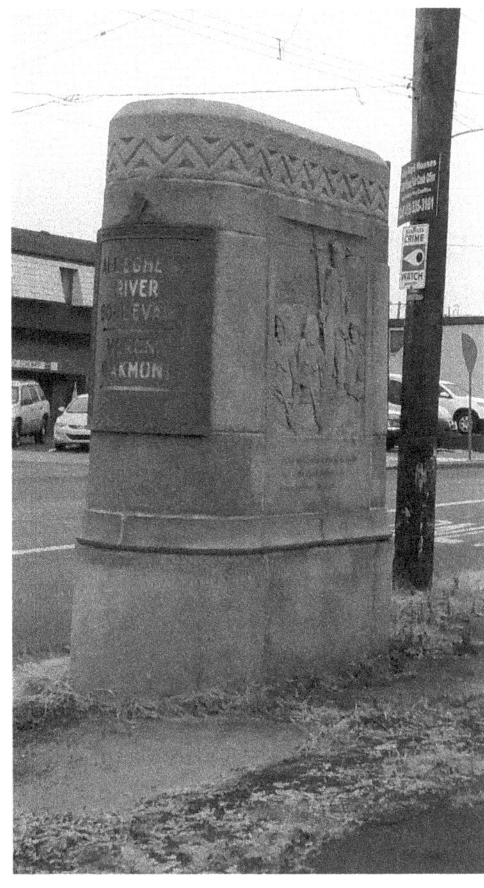

Right: Stone pylons along the Allegheny River Boulevard in Verona, Pennsylvania. *ASCE Pittsburgh Section.*

streets. Some were developed and some forgotten, but much of the city's backbone known today can be attributed to Olmsted's plan, connecting and improving on the city's organic growth. Not to be left out of the City Beautiful movement, the county constructed its own grand boulevards—Allegheny River, Ohio River and Saw Mill Run Boulevards—connecting Pittsburgh with its surrounding environs. On some of these boulevards, the county placed stone pylons dedicating the routes with ornate stone carvings. Several can still be seen along the Ohio River and Allegheny River Boulevards.

PARKWAYS AND INTERSTATE HIGHWAYS IN WESTERN PENNSYLVANIA

While the boulevards within Pittsburgh were a venerable early solution to getting high-speed vehicles in and around the city, they lacked connectivity and often ended abruptly, sending vehicles into the street grids. Efforts to improve access into the eastern suburbs began in the 1920s with plans to upgrade Second Avenue and, later, to extend the Boulevard of the Allies. In 1937, a delegation of state officials drove the route from Churchill to Campbells Run Road, west of Pittsburgh. After they experienced difficulties traveling through Pittsburgh, they agreed to develop the Penn-Lincoln Parkway to supersede the arterial Penn and Lincoln Highways. Robert Moses, who planned New York City's parkway network, was consulted on the project. His influence can be seen in the parkway's design, notably the mindful route choice through topography that would guarantee a park-like environment, as well as the complex interchange layouts along the Penn-Lincoln Parkway.

Ground was broken for the parkway in 1946, a full decade before the interstate system was created. The east–west route includes two dual-bore tunnels (Squirrel Hill and Fort Pitt), with two traffic lanes in each, and a dual-level major river crossing, the Fort Pitt Bridge. The last link to be completed was the Fort Pitt Tunnel, which opened in 1960, connecting Monroeville to the Greater Pittsburgh Airport. The Penn-Lincoln Parkway has a complex history of naming and route numbering. From the Point to Monroeville, the route is colloquially referred to as the "Parkway East." Likewise, the route from the Point to the airport is known as the "Parkway West." As interstate designations appeared on the route, the parkway's original namesakes, William Penn and Abraham Lincoln, have been obscured with time.

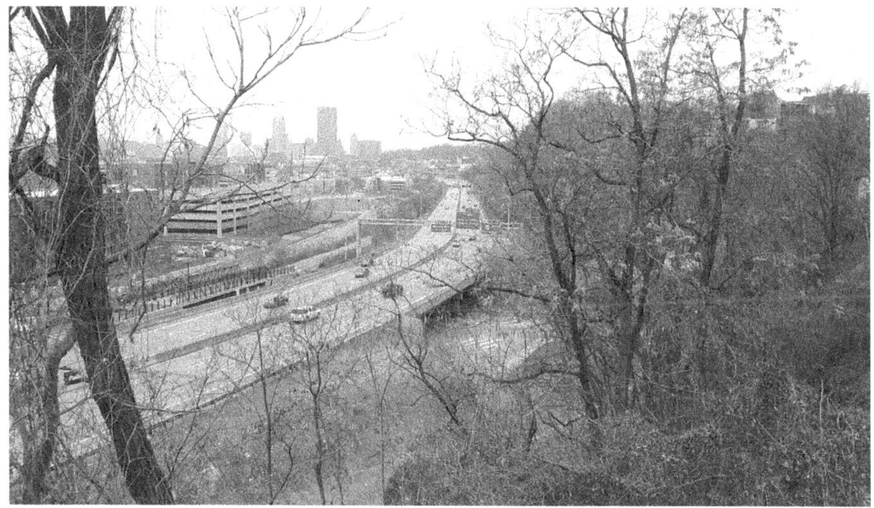

Penn-Lincoln Parkway East as seen from the Shrine of the Blessed Mother in South Oakland, Pittsburgh, Pennsylvania. *ASCE Pittsburgh Section.*

The Penn-Lincoln Parkway has carried many interstate designations, including I-70. The Point was also the original end of I-76, which, at the time, left the Pennsylvania Turnpike at Monroeville and was routed along the Parkway East into the city. The Parkway East became I-376 when I-76 was reassigned to follow the turnpike into Ohio. I-79 was planned to be routed along the Parkway West and along a yet-to-be-built Parkway North, while I-279 was intended to bypass the city to the west. After construction of the western bypass was completed in 1976 and it was the clear the Parkway North construction would be stalled, the route numbers were reassigned. I-79 bypassed the city to the west, and I-279 provided a loop through Pittsburgh with the completion of the Parkway North. The Parkway North and its reversible HOV (High Occupancy Vehicle) lanes opened in 1989, completing the loop and the route number swap. In 2009, to extend the interstate system past Pittsburgh International Airport, the numbering was again changed. I-376 would be extended along the Parkway West from the Point, past the airport, to end at I-80 outside Sharon, Pennsylvania. At this time, I-279 was also truncated at the Point.

While roads and highways will continue to play a critical role in Pittsburgh's transportation network, it remains to be seen how advances in technology, such as vehicle automation, will shape the roads and highways of the future.

BRIDGES

By Todd M. Wilson, PE

The Region's First Bridges

Western Pennsylvania is a dissected plateau with many valleys and streams forming the headwaters of America's most significant westward-flowing river, the Ohio. Natural and mineral resources along its waterways, combined with its challenging topography, set the stage for development that required many bridges over rivers, streams and valleys.

In the mid-1700s, British colonists formed land companies to develop the frontier west of the Appalachians. This area intersected with French trading routes along the Ohio and Allegheny Rivers that connected French colonies in Louisiana and Quebec. Central to the ensuing conflict of the French and Indian War was the strategic need to control the "Forks of the Ohio," as George Washington called the land that eventually became Pittsburgh.

Western Pennsylvania's illustrious bridge-building history has its origins in that war. The British hurried to fortify the "Forks" in 1754 but surrendered Fort Prince George to the French, who built Fort Duquesne later that year. Plans showed a bridge over the ditch into the fort. The British military constructed Braddock's Road (1755) and Forbes' Road (1758) to retake the land, which became major routes later upgraded with bridges. After the French retreat, the British constructed Fort Pitt in 1759–61, building several bridges over the moats. Ever since then, bridges have played an essential part in transporting people and goods in Western Pennsylvania.

EARLY ROAD BRIDGES

Western Pennsylvania's first bridges were constructed along primitive military roads, American Indian paths and new routes connecting emerging frontier towns. They were made of locally available materials such as stone or wood, which limited span lengths. By assembling wooden members together in triangular shapes called trusses, builders could create longer spans. Trusses were expensive to build and difficult to assemble, so bridge operators started covering them for protection, creating wooden covered bridges. Pittsburgh's first major wooden covered bridges were built in the late 1810s, about a decade after America's first prominent covered bridge was built in Philadelphia. Before bridges, private ferries were used for river crossings. Costly bridges were constructed later, when investors projected that sufficient traffic would make them economically viable.

American engineers started introducing iron for its strength and durability in the 1800s. While Chinese engineers had started building bridges with iron chains centuries earlier, the first documented European iron chain bridge was not built until 1734. The first all-iron arch bridge was completed in England in 1779. The second was planned for Philadelphia, but it was never built. Founding father Thomas Paine planned to have it fabricated and shipped from England in the late 1700s but lacked sufficient investment to do so. At that time, however, Fayette County's James Finley was serving as a state senator in Philadelphia. Was he exposed to the knowledge of European iron bridge building? Did that exposure develop his interest in designing bridges? After returning to Western Pennsylvania, he was awarded a contract in 1801 to construct a seventy-foot bridge over Jacobs Creek on Braddock's Road south of Mount Pleasant. There, Finley designed what is considered to be America's first iron bridge and the world's first modern suspension bridge. He patented his design in 1808. The bridge used externally anchored iron chains hung from towers, forming catenary curves. Stiffened by wooden trusses, the level road deck was supported by suspenders hung from the catenaries. Finley marketed and built similar chain bridges, including an eighty-foot bridge over Dunlap's Creek in Brownsville in 1809. Finley designed what were intended to be Pittsburgh's first bridges over the Monongahela and Allegheny Rivers in 1810, but the bridge company was unable to secure sufficient investment and financing. When Pittsburgh was incorporated as a city in 1816, the eventual "City of Bridges" had none.

America's first federally funded road, the National (Cumberland) Road, was built from Baltimore to Wheeling in 1811–18 to reach Ohio, which had just achieved statehood in 1803. The road was routed across Finley's Dunlap's Creek Bridge in Brownsville. To cross the nearby Monongahela River, fill was extended across the river in 1817 to form a sort of causeway—the Monongahela's first crossing. Along the road, stone bridges were used for smaller rivers and streams. The largest was the Great Crossings Bridge over the Youghiogheny River. Flooded by the Youghiogheny Reservoir in 1944, it reappears when water levels are low. The Little Crossings Bridge over the Casselman River still stands twenty miles to the west near Grantsville, Maryland. Its eighty-foot arch was recognized as America's largest when built.

Charters for Pittsburgh's first river bridges were reauthorized in 1816, the year Pittsburgh was incorporated as a city. Rather than using Finley's designs, the reorganized bridge companies hired Philadelphia engineer Lewis Wernwag to design covered bridges instead. Wernwag had achieved fame in 1812 by building a record-setting covered bridge in Philadelphia. His 1,500-foot, eight-span Monongahela Bridge opened in 1818, connecting Pittsburgh with the Washington Turnpike (Boggs Avenue) on the river's south side. The similar 1,037-foot, six-span Allegheny Bridge opened the

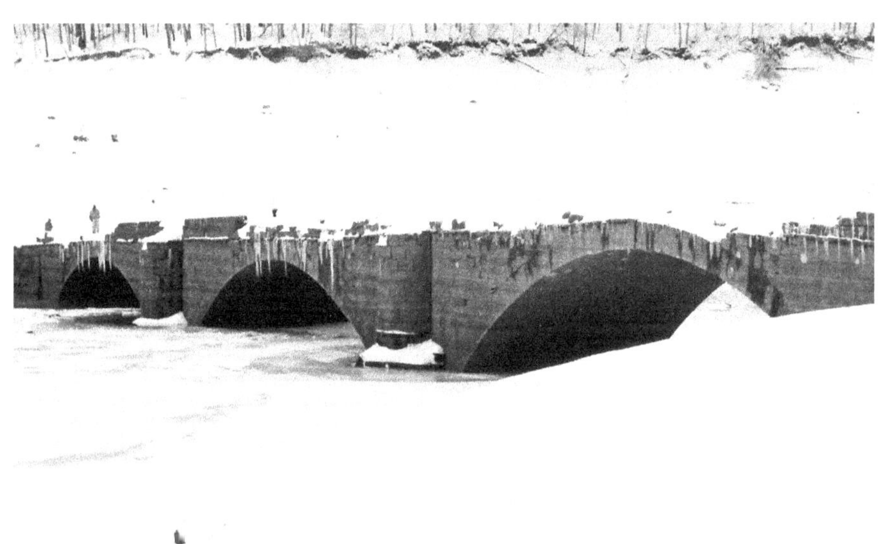

The 1818 Great Crossings Bridge, shown when it reappeared during low Youghiogheny Reservoir water levels in 1999. *Todd Wilson.*

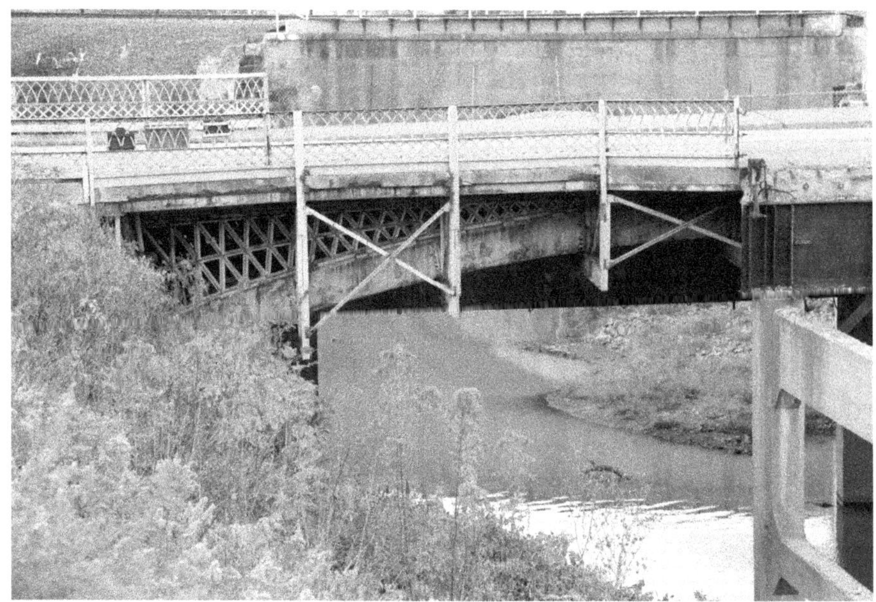

Brownsville's 1839 Dunlap's Creek Bridge, America's first iron arch bridge. *Todd Wilson.*

following year, connecting Sixth Street in Pittsburgh with Federal Street in Allegheny City (now Pittsburgh's North Side).

After Andrew Jackson's election in 1828, the federal government wanted to transfer National Road ownership to the states. Pennsylvania would assume ownership only if the federal government repaired the road first, including replacing the Dunlap's Creek Bridge in Brownsville. Finley's bridge had collapsed in 1820, and subsequent replacements were hastily built and short-lived. The federal government assigned the task to Captain Richard Delafield of the Army Corps of Engineers. Unlike America's untrained craftsmen-turned-engineers of the time, Delafield had acquired knowledge of English and French engineering practices at the U.S. Military Academy. Wanting to build America's first cast-iron bridge, he designed an eighty-foot arch consisting of five cast-iron tubes, each formed by nine iron *voussoirs* (wedge-shaped elements) bolted together. Built in 1836–39 and widened in 1920, America's first iron arch bridge still carries traffic in its original location.

AQUEDUCTS AND THE RISE OF JOHN ROEBLING

Pennsylvania's Main Line canal, constructed in 1826–34 from Philadelphia to Allegheny City (now Pittsburgh's North Side), gave the Pittsburgh area a means to compete economically with the National Road (1818) and the Erie Canal (1825). Aqueducts along the route were either wooden or stone. Since the canal was routed along the Allegheny River's north bank, Pittsburgh leaders demanded a connection to bring it into their city. The state constructed the seven-span Allegheny Aqueduct, a wooden covered bridge, at Eleventh Street into Pittsburgh in 1829. It became unsafe and had to be closed in 1843. Unable to afford its repair, the state granted the City of Pittsburgh authority to replace it in exchange for future tolls. John Roebling secured the low bid, promising to replace it as quickly and as cheaply as possible with a new bridge. This launched his noteworthy career, cumulating with New York's 1883 Brooklyn Bridge.

Originally from Saxony in eastern Germany, Roebling attended the Berlin Polytechnic Institute, where he studied the work of engineers, including James Finley. Roebling developed a love for suspension bridges. He left Europe and helped to found the agrarian community of Saxonburg, Butler County. Returning to engineering, he was working as a surveyor for the Main Line's Portage Railroad when he witnessed two people crushed when a hemp rope pulling an incline car snapped. Having studied the concept of wire rope in Europe, he patented a manufacturing method in 1842 and successfully lobbied the Portage Railroad to use it to replace hemp ropes on inclines. Roebling's ultimate goal was to use his wire rope for suspension bridges.

At the time, builders pre-manufactured wire rope, limiting its size and leading to damage during installation. Roebling's new technique of continuously spiral wrapping the cable in place ensured uniform tension on each rope strand. The Allegheny Aqueduct replacement was his first chance to use his rope for a suspension bridge, which was completed in May 1845 on time and on budget.

One month prior to the aqueduct's opening, Pittsburgh suffered a devastating fire that destroyed a third of the city, including the Monongahela Bridge at Smithfield Street. Roebling successfully submitted the low bid for its replacement, a suspension bridge, to be built atop the surviving piers in 1845–46. Meanwhile, Roebling's competitor, Charles Ellet, won the commission for what became the Wheeling Suspension Bridge to carry the National Road over the Ohio River. Completed in 1849, it was the first to cross the Ohio River and the first to surpass the one-thousand-

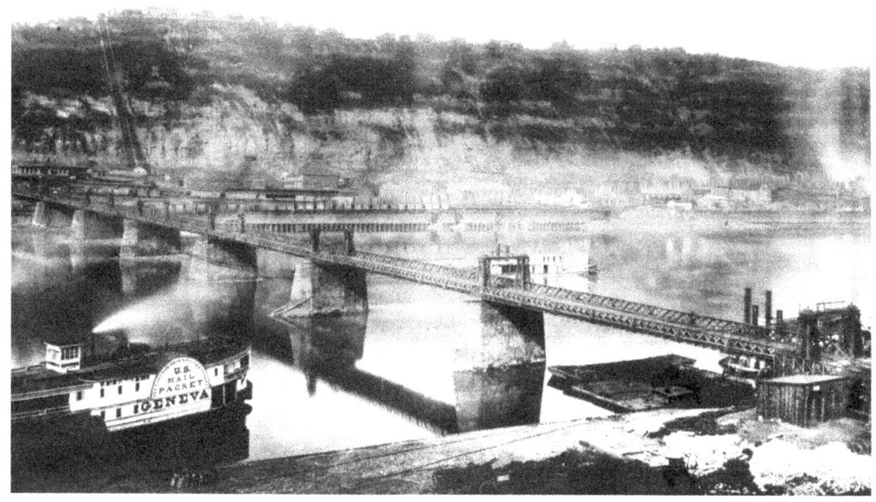

John Roebling's Monongahela River Bridge at Smithfield Street (1846–83). *Carnegie Library of Pittsburgh.*

foot-span barrier. It collapsed in a windstorm in 1854. Roebling was hired to rebuild it, adding diagonal stays from the towers to the deck for stiffening. Roebling's last work in Pittsburgh was his 1859 replacement for the original Allegheny River Bridge at Sixth Street. The toll company hired Roebling to design a suspension bridge so beautiful it would attract traffic away from the competing 1839 Ninth Street covered bridge while also improving nighttime safety for pedestrians.

RAILROAD BRIDGES AND THEIR ENGINEERING LEGACY

Through the 1700s and into the 1800s, bridge designers were military-trained engineers, apprenticed craftsmen or self-taught bridge builders. The title "engineer" was loosely defined. Engineering science was just developing. Early engineering was empirical, not theoretical. When a bridge collapsed, the craftsman turned engineer just built it stronger next time.

Losses per failure were generally limited to a horse-drawn vehicle and its occupants and cargo. This was not acceptable for railroads. Failures risked many deaths, significant equipment losses and costly service interruptions. Meanwhile, heavy locomotives needed unprecedented engineering solutions to cross wide rivers and deep valleys, requiring bridge design innovations. Trained engineers started to differentiate themselves from craftsmen, which cumulated in professional licensure. Engineers also started making great strides in structural analysis. American engineer Squire Whipple self-published *A Work on Bridge Building* in 1847, which was the first prominent publication to accurately analyze truss bridge members. Other bridge analysis methods soon followed.

Meanwhile, railroads needed not just stronger bridges but more durable ones. More advanced truss designs incorporating iron began to be patented in the 1840s. William Howe patented the Howe truss in 1840, which used vertical iron tension members and wooden compression members. This design was often built for early railroads, including the original Fort Wayne Railroad Bridge over the Allegheny River in Pittsburgh. Opening in 1857, it was Pittsburgh's first railroad bridge crossing a river. Thomas and Caleb Pratt patented the Pratt truss in 1844, which initially used diagonal iron tension members and vertical wooden compression members but soon became an all-metal design. It became the most common truss configuration.

Whipple devised a way to double the Pratt trusses per span in 1847 in an early all-iron configuration that used cast-iron compression members and wrought-iron tension members. In 1862–65, engineer Jacob Linville's Panhandle Railroad bridges over the Monongahela and Ohio Rivers in Pittsburgh and Steubenville ushered in the era of long-span metal truss bridge design. Using modified Whipple trusses, the bridges had record-breaking 260-foot and 320-foot main spans, respectively, leading to Whipple trusses being adopted for most first-generation large railroad bridges. When the Panhandle Railroad Bridge at Steubenville was replaced in 1889, two of the spans were moved to Allegheny City. They carried California Avenue over Woods Run until 1926. The Monongahela River Bridge was replaced in 1903 with the current Panhandle Bridge.

Other truss configurations were patented in subsequent years to improve strength or reduce material use. The 1848 Warren truss reduced materials by using equilateral triangles instead of right triangles. The 1870 Parker truss introduced a curved top chord to a Pratt truss. The 1871 Baltimore truss, developed by the B&O and Pennsylvania Railroads, used subdivided Pratt trusses for longer spans. The Pennsylvania Railroad began to subdivide

Parker trusses in 1875 for even longer spans. The resulting Pennsylvania truss replaced the Whipple as the definitive long-span truss.

One record-breaking Western Pennsylvania bridge built during this time was the 1882 Kinzua Viaduct along the New York, Lake Erie and Western Railway in McKean County. Erected in ninety-five days, the 2,052-foot-long, 301-foot-high iron viaduct was believed to be the world's tallest railroad bridge when it opened. It was designed by noted French-born engineer Octave Chanute, who later became known as one of the fathers of aviation. The viaduct was rebuilt of steel in 1900. Wooden Howe trusses were placed from one tower across an intermediate one to the next tower so the intermediate tower could be rebuilt, and the process shifted from one tower to the next until the bridge was entirely replaced. The bridge remained in service until 1959 and later became a state park, reopening in 1970. In 2003, a tornado toppled eleven of the bridge's twenty towers.

One of the most significant advances that brought about the next generation of long-span railroad bridges was the development and proliferation of steel. Andrew Carnegie constructed the Edgar Thompson Works as Pittsburgh's

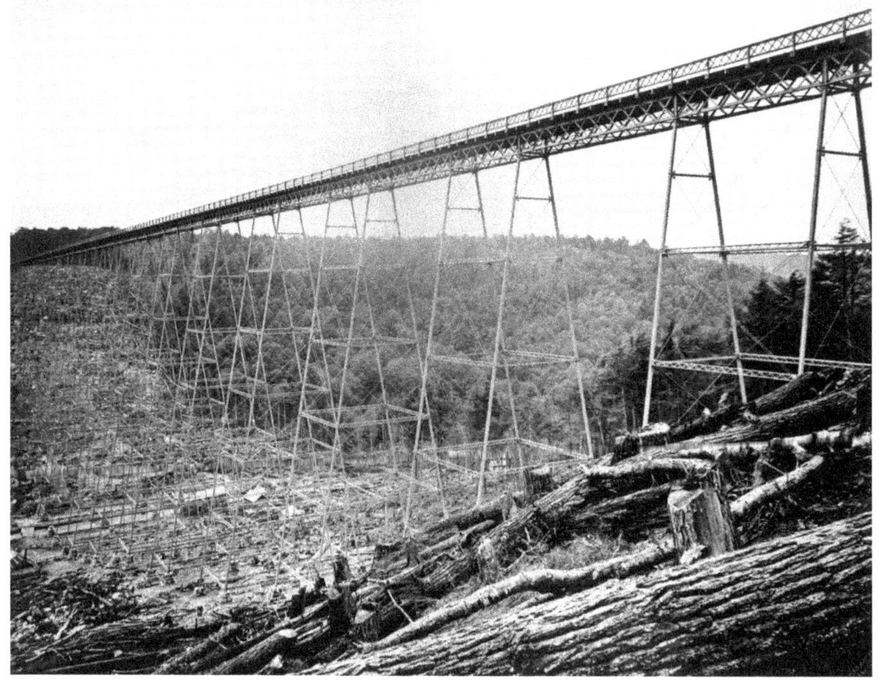

The original Kinzua Viaduct in McKean County (1882–1900). *Library of Congress, Prints & Photographs Division, HAER PA,42-MOJEW.V,1-.*

first steel mill using the Bessemer process. His Keystone Bridge Company constructed America's first major steel bridge, the steel arch Eads Bridge, over the Mississippi River at St. Louis in 1874. The first major steel truss opened in 1879, and by 1900, steel had entirely replaced iron in bridge construction. Almost all the major railroad bridges in Western Pennsylvania were replaced with steel structures around the turn of the century.

Early railroad bridges had spans simply supported from one pier to the next. Longer bridges were composed of multiple individual spans. Even with steel and improved trusses, engineers considered the economical limit of simple-span construction to be around 500 feet. This became problematic around the turn of the twentieth century after the 1890 Rivers and Harbors Act gave the U.S. War Department authority over new navigable waterway crossings, and the updated 1899 act gave the War Department the ability to order removal of older privately built structures if they impeded navigation. Longer-span designs were required, so cantilevered bridges started to be developed in the 1860s and rose to prominence around 1900. To explain cantilevering, imagine that you needed to span a 40-foot swimming pool, but you could only find a 30-foot board. However, the pool had diving platforms at each end, both cantilevered or extended over the pool by at least five feet. By connecting the board to the platform ends, the 40-foot pool can now be spanned with a shorter board. Likewise, a cantilever bridge has anchored spans extended out beyond their piers or abutments, and a suspended span is attached to those ends. Anchor spans are usually built deeper over their mid-span pier to resist bending. While several small-scale experimental examples were built for roads in the late 1800s, the Wabash Railroad built the area's first major cantilever bridge over the Monongahela River in Pittsburgh. Completed in 1904, its 812-foot span was the longest on record at the time. The bridge was removed in 1948, but its smaller twin over the Ohio River in Mingo Junction, West Virginia, still survives.

Another important Western Pennsylvania cantilever is the Pittsburgh and Lake Erie (P&LE) Railroad's Ohio River Bridge near Beaver. The P&LE needed to replace the original bridge, built in 1878, with a wider, stronger structure, but the War Department required a seven-hundred-foot-wide shipping channel. The railroad selected a cantilever design in 1907, one month before the infamous Quebec Bridge disaster that killed seventy-five workers. Famed engineer Theodore Cooper's attempted record-breaking cantilever had collapsed under construction. Engineers questioned whether long-span cantilevers could ever be built safely. P&LE's chief engineer, Albert Lucius, decided to keep the cantilever design for the bridge near Beaver, but only after reviewing and improving its design and construction methods. He rejected previous design assumptions unless he could verify them. Even so, the bridge contractor, McClintic-Marshall, was required to accept ultimate responsibility for design and construction, shifting responsibility away from the railroad. Lucius thoroughly checked and approved the drawings. The bridge was completed in 1910 and is still in use today.

The 1890 Ohio Connecting Railway Bridge in Pittsburgh spanned the Ohio River at Brunot Island, where the narrow river channels permitted simply supported main spans. The 4,500-foot single-track bridge was one of the longest and most innovative of the time. The Keystone Bridge Company built the main 523-foot Pennsylvania truss on a barge and floated it into place. The bridge also had a 413-foot span over the back channel. Soon overwhelmed by traffic, the bridge was replaced in 1913–16 with a double-track bridge. To maintain both rail and river traffic, the wider bridge was built around the previous single-track one. Unable to place falsework in the shipping channel, the American Bridge Company temporarily built each half of the back-channel span flanking the main channel as anchors so the main channel span could be built with cantilevered construction. Once the

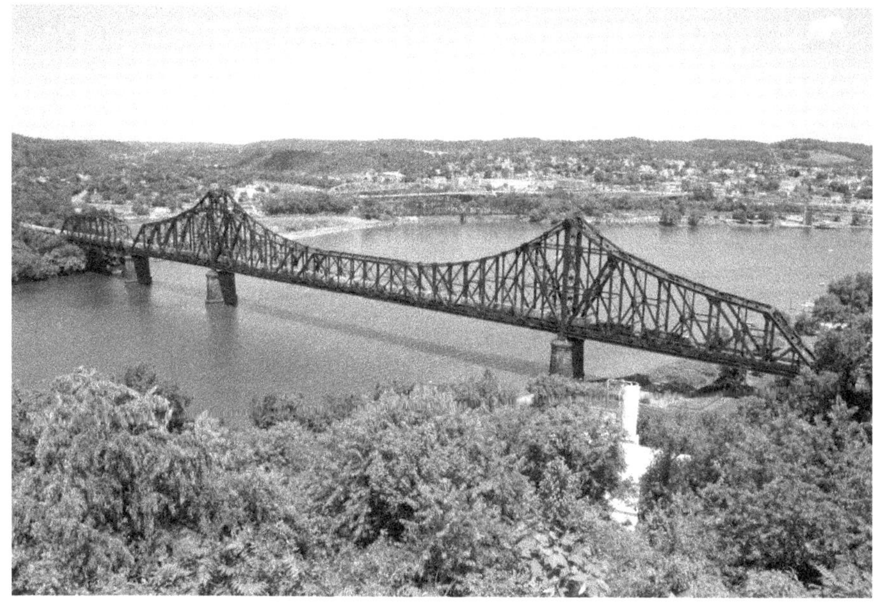

The Pittsburgh and Lake Erie Railroad Bridge over the Ohio River near Beaver, constructed in 1910. *Todd Wilson.*

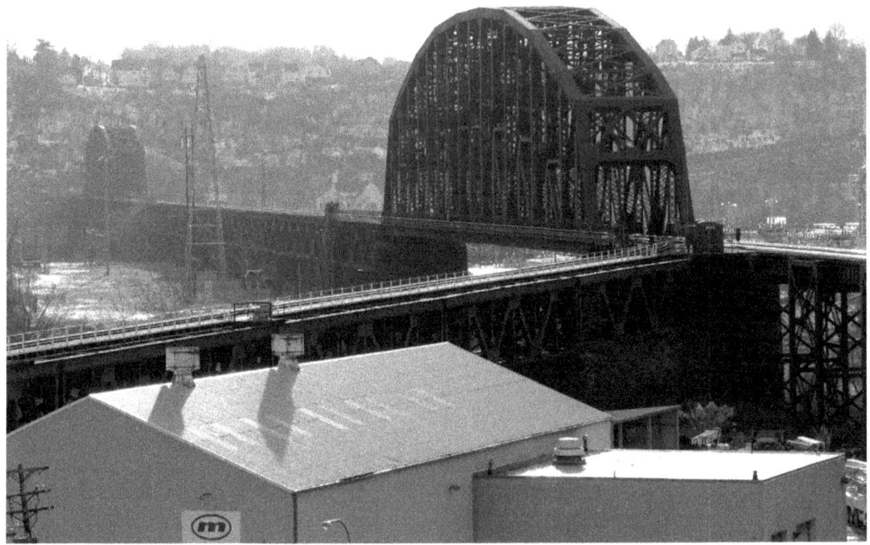

The Ohio Connecting Railway Bridge over Brunot Island, completed in 1916. *Todd Wilson.*

main channel span was complete, its anchors were re-erected as the back-channel span. Tensile and compressive forces are reversed in cantilever construction, so bridge members needed to withstand both. Therefore, rigid connections were used exclusively instead of pinned connections. The main span became the longest simply supported rigid truss span of its time.

These bridges represent a few of the many examples of innovative design and construction methods developed by railroad engineers and contractors in Western Pennsylvania. These advances were later applied to vehicular bridges.

EARLY BRIDGE BUILDING COMPANIES

It was initially a common practice for bridge owners—toll companies, railroads and government entities—to hire consulting engineers to design bridges and have separate companies build them. Beginning in the mid-1800s, private companies were formed offering combined services, located in many of America's emerging cities. Companies competed by offering exclusive designs or standard designs with patented connection details. Prominent Western Pennsylvania companies included Andrew Carnegie's Keystone Bridge Company (1865), the Penn Bridge Company (1868) and the Pittsburgh Bridge Company (1878). Their strongest competition came from eastern Ohio firms in Cleveland, Youngstown, Canton and Massillon. Companies like these offered their bridge designs in catalogues. They either constructed the bridges themselves or sold their bridge members to contractors for erection. For example, the Pittsburgh Bridge Company employed the Nelson & Buchanan Company as agents to sell and erect its designs.

Experimental and noteworthy bridges were built in Western Pennsylvania during this unique era of privately developed, competing bridge designs. Some bridges survived for a century or more before being upgraded with structures more capable of carrying the demands of modern traffic. Several were built by the Penn Bridge Company. The company's oldest surviving structure (one span remains, disassembled in storage) is Meadville's Mead Avenue Bridge, a Whipple truss built in 1871–72. It used the Keystone Company's patented tubular column compression members. The 1884 Fallston Bridge over the Beaver River in New Brighton is the company's

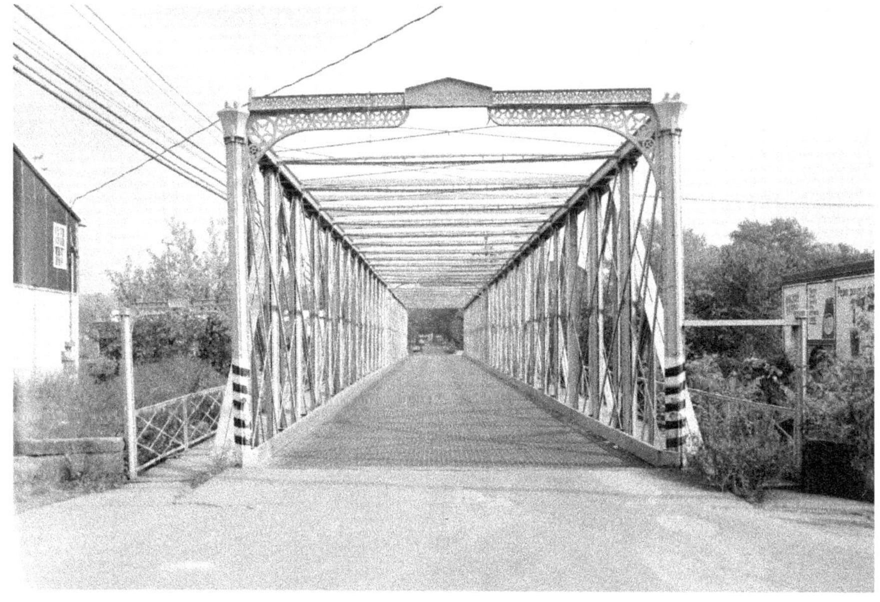

The 1872 Mead Avenue Bridge when it stood over French Creek in Meadville (removed and stored in 2015). *Library of Congress, Prints & Photographs Division, HAER PA,20-MEDVI,6-.*

last Whipple truss still standing in the region. Penn Bridge's 1878 Watts Mill Bridge over Little Beaver Creek in northwestern Beaver County has an experimental continuous truss design that allows its trusses to be smaller and thus more economical. Continuous truss bridges are statically indeterminate, in which reactions influence other connected spans. Continuous designs only became common after computers began to be used to assist with design calculations in the 1960s.

Lawrence County's 1888 Coverts Bridge over the Mahoning River, which lasted until 2003, was one of America's early experimental cantilever bridges. The unusual bridge was a product of Youngstown's Morse Bridge Company. Researchers from the Historic American Engineering Record (HAER) theorized that the pioneering design was done to reuse part of a smaller bridge from another location. Cantilever construction did not become popular worldwide until the successful completion of the 1889 Firth of Forth Bridge in Scotland.

Around the turn of the twentieth century, industry consolidation and the rise of municipal engineering departments led to the demise of the catalogue

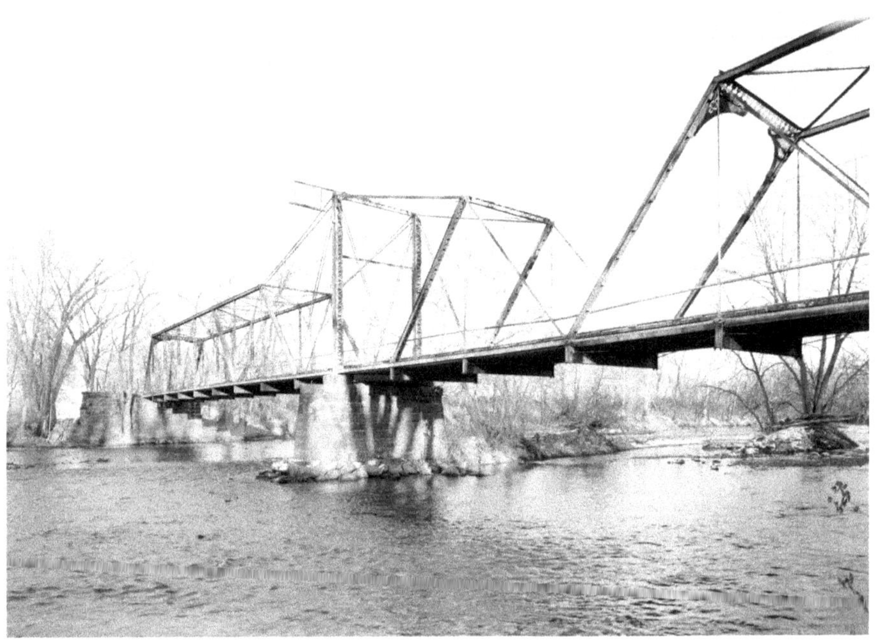

The 1888–2003 Coverts Bridge near New Castle, one of America's early cantilevers. *Library of Congress, Prints & Photographs Division, HAER PA,37-EDIN.V,1-.*

bridge companies, and structural engineering and contracting became separate. In 1900, twenty-eight companies were consolidated to form the American Bridge Company, including the Keystone Bridge Company and Pittsburgh Bridge Company. Together, they produced around half of America's output. Penn Bridge Company became strictly a contractor. Other Western Pennsylvania companies such as the Fort Pitt Bridge Works and McClintic-Marshall Construction Company formed in 1896 and 1900, respectively, to specialize in bridge construction. They built many bridges in the early 1900s. The American Bridge Company, based in Coraopolis, still builds some of the world's largest bridges.

PRIVATE AND STREETCAR BRIDGES

In the 1800s, larger bridges were built by private companies that charged tolls. Horse-drawn streetcars were introduced in Western Pennsylvania in the 1850s and electric streetcars in 1886. Private operators tried to secure streetcar routes to cross their bridges to stabilize and maximize revenue. Streetcar companies later began to own bridges. While the early bridges could generally support horsecars, few were tall or strong enough for heavier electric streetcars, so they were replaced around the turn of the twentieth century.

Pittsburgh's oldest streetcar-carrying river bridge—the 1883 Smithfield Street Bridge—is also one of the most significant. With the opening of the Monongahela Incline and the P&LE depot in present-day Station Square, the 1846 Roebling bridge at that location was unable to handle increasing traffic volumes in the 1870s. The bridge company decided to replace it in 1880, hiring Charles Davis, who designed a three-tower suspension bridge. Davis was a consulting engineer for the nearby 1877 Point Bridge over the Monongahela River. In February 1881, one of the P&LE founders took a controlling interest in the Smithfield Street Bridge Company's stock to potentially use the new bridge for a P&LE spur into Pittsburgh. The suspension design was neither expandable nor suitable for rail use. All work was stopped. Moravian self-taught engineer Gustav Lindenthal was hired to design a new bridge to fit the uncompleted suspension bridge's piers. He selected a lenticular truss because it was an attractive design for an urban bridge, it reduced materials compared to a typical truss by 9 percent and its suspended floor would be less affected by temperature variations. River shipping companies demanded that the new bridge be built twenty feet higher than the old suspension bridge, so it was constructed above the old bridge, which remained open during construction.

Lindenthal specified steel, despite iron having been ordered for Davis's suspension bridge. He selected open-hearth steel from the Kloman process, patented in 1881. The iron was used for the flooring system (replaced by aluminum in 1934) and approach girders. To make the bridge expandable, the two truss lines were placed on the downstream ends of the piers and the sidewalk cantilevered out over the river. The trusses were erected by the end of 1882, and the bridge was opened to traffic on March 19, 1883. It was notable for its beautiful Victorian cast-iron and wrought-iron portals. The P&LE extension never materialized, but the bridge was widened in 1890–91 with a third truss line on its upstream side for a single streetcar track. The 1904 Mount Washington Transit Tunnel increased streetcar traffic, so the bridge was widened in 1911 for two-track streetcar operation separate from roadway traffic. Civic architect Stanley Roush designed the current castle-like portals, which were installed in 1915. The original portals had deteriorated and were thought to be out of style. In 1985, streetcars were rerouted to the Panhandle Bridge as part of Pittsburgh's downtown subway project. The streetcar side of the Smithfield Street Bridge was converted for vehicular use, and the bridge was repainted in its original colors during its 1994–95 rehabilitation.

The Smithfield Street Bridge is the last major Pittsburgh-area survivor from the toll bridge era. Having an expandable design, using steel and being built higher over the river helped it to outlast many bridges that were built later. For example, the 1889 Dravosburg, 1890 Ninth Street, 1891 McKeesport-Duquesne, 1892 Sixth Street, 1894 Brown's (Homestead), 1895 Glenwood, 1897 Rankin, 1900 Sharpsburg and 1902 Highland Park bridges were all privately built streetcar-carrying bridges in Allegheny County that have since been replaced.

The Smithfield Street Bridge was Lindenthal's first major commission. He designed Pittsburgh's Seventh Street suspension bridge in 1884 and Thirtieth Street continuous truss bridge in 1887. Lindenthal became one of America's most important bridge engineers and ended his career as New York City's commissioner of bridges, most famous for New York's Hell Gate and Queensboro Bridges. Charles Davis served as Allegheny County engineer from 1881 until his death in 1907.

As with the Smithfield Street Bridge, private companies tried to keep their bridges open to traffic during their replacement to maintain revenue.

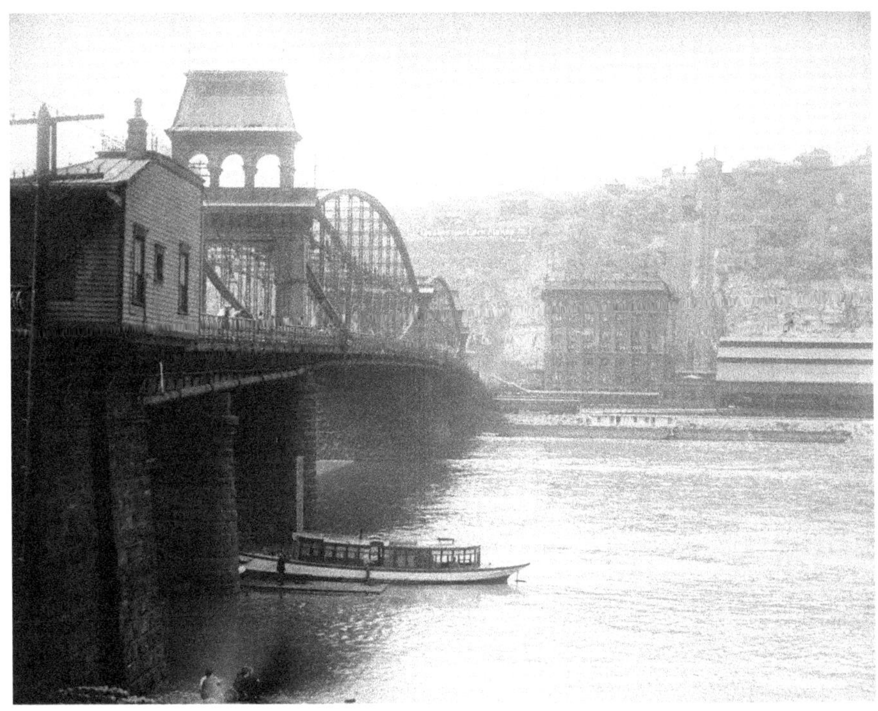

Gustav Lindenthal's 1883 Smithfield Street Bridge over the Monongahela River, as it appeared in about 1910. *Library of Congress, Prints & Photographs Division, LC-D4-70747.*

It was difficult and costly to build new bridges at different locations. Roebling's 1859 Sixth Street Bridge could not hold heavier electric streetcars introduced around 1890, so in 1892, engineer Theodore Cooper's Union Bridge Company was hired to replace the bridge. It took just ninety-five days to erect the new trusses around the suspension bridge. The 1839 Ninth Street wooden covered bridge was not tall enough for streetcars, so it was uncovered and a steel truss was built around it in 1890 by Ferris, Kaufman and Company. (George Ferris invented the Ferris wheel three years later.) The Sharpsburg Bridge was built over its 1856 wooden covered bridge predecessor in 1900. Once bridges became government owned, rapid bridge replacement rarely occurred. The government did not have to rely on a steady stream of toll revenue and could use eminent domain to force private property owners to sell their land.

CITY OF PITTSBURGH DEPARTMENT OF PUBLIC WORKS BRIDGES

The City of Pittsburgh Department of Public Works (City DPW) was created in an 1887 governmental reorganization. Pittsburgh was growing rapidly, both from immigration and from annexing adjacent municipalities. Residents from these new cross-river neighborhoods demanded toll-free crossings. The first City DPW–designed river bridge, the Brady Street Bridge, opened in 1896, connecting to Pittsburgh's new South Side neighborhood, formerly East Birmingham Borough (annexed in 1872). Pittsburgh purchased the Point, Smithfield and Tenth Street toll bridges in 1897 and replaced the Tenth Street Bridge in 1904. In 1907, Pittsburgh annexed Allegheny City (North Side) and built the Manchester Bridge at the Point in 1911–15. The City DPW designed bridges over Pittsburgh's valleys and parks as well, including the Panther Hollow and Schenley Drive Bridges in Schenley Park in 1896–97.

Most nineteenth-century bridges were economical structures. Railings were often their only ornamentation. Pittsburgh had grown into America's fifth-largest metropolitan area by 1910, but its adoption of the City Beautiful movement, which was influential at the time, was piecemeal. Pittsburgh's Civic Commission hired Frederick Law Olmsted Jr. to plan new automobile-focused thoroughfares in 1909–10. In 1911, the Civic Commission was reorganized into the City Planning Commission and the Municipal Art Commission. The Planning Commission was tasked with implementing Olmsted's thoroughfare system and the Art Commission with improving the appearance of new public structures, including bridges. The Art Commission was initially chaired by John Beatty of the Carnegie Institute and included committee members Henry Atkins MacNeal, president of the National Sculpture Society, and John Alexander, president of the National Academy of Design. The commission initially focused on embellishing bridges under construction at the time, including the Bloomfield and Manchester Bridges. Disappointed in the Manchester Bridge's design because the road went through the trusses, which obstructed the view of the city from the road, the Art Commission began considering structural design important to a bridge's artistic merit. The commission refused to approve additional through-truss bridges in Pittsburgh, although they continued to be commonly built outside of Pittsburgh for the next several decades.

Pittsburgh's inland ravine-spanning bridges were originally wooden or metal structures with functional designs. Schenley Park's mid-1890s

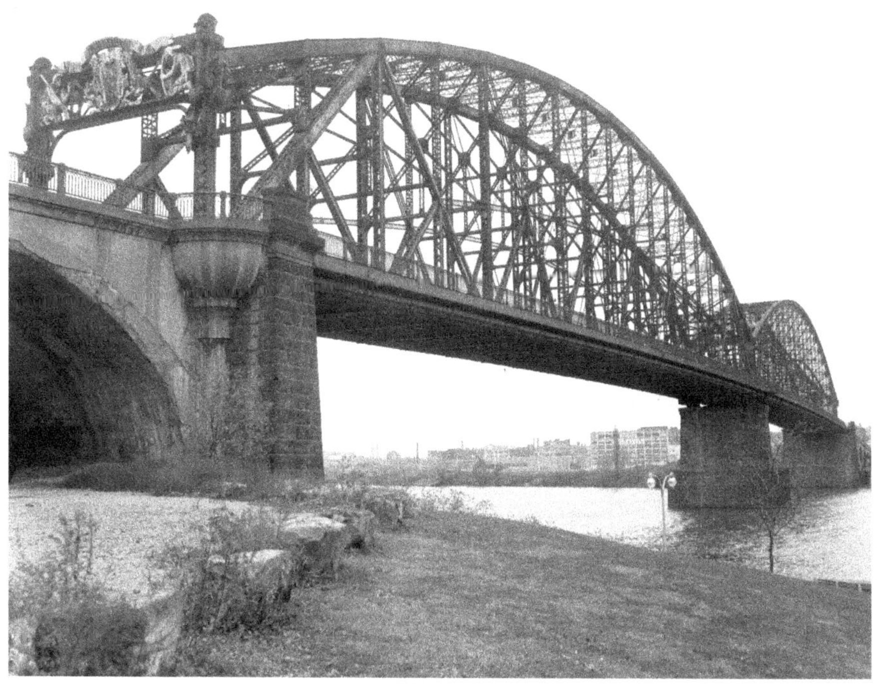

Pittsburgh's Manchester Bridge over the Allegheny River at the Point (1915–70). *Library of Congress, Prints & Photographs Division, HAER PA,2-PITBU,59-.*

steel arch bridges were Pittsburgh's first aesthetically focused designs. Philadelphia introduced large-scale concrete arch bridges to America with the landmark Walnut Lane Bridge in 1908 based on Luxembourg's 1903 Adolphe Bridge. The design was specifically chosen to beautify Fairmount Park. The large arch kept the valley free from intermediate supports, while the concrete, once considered unsightly, was molded with City Beautiful–style details such as Neoclassical balustrades, urns and sculptures. Reinforced concrete was a new material, assumed to be maintenance-free and thus thought to be worth the extra expense. Inspired by Philadelphia's bridge, Pittsburgh built the similar but slightly smaller Meadow Street Bridge in 1910 over Highland Park's Negley Run valley. With the Meadow Street Bridge's success, the City DPW used similar concrete arch designs for comparable ravine crossings for the next two decades, including on Larimer Avenue, Murray Avenue, Beechwood Boulevard, Baum Boulevard and McArdle Roadway.

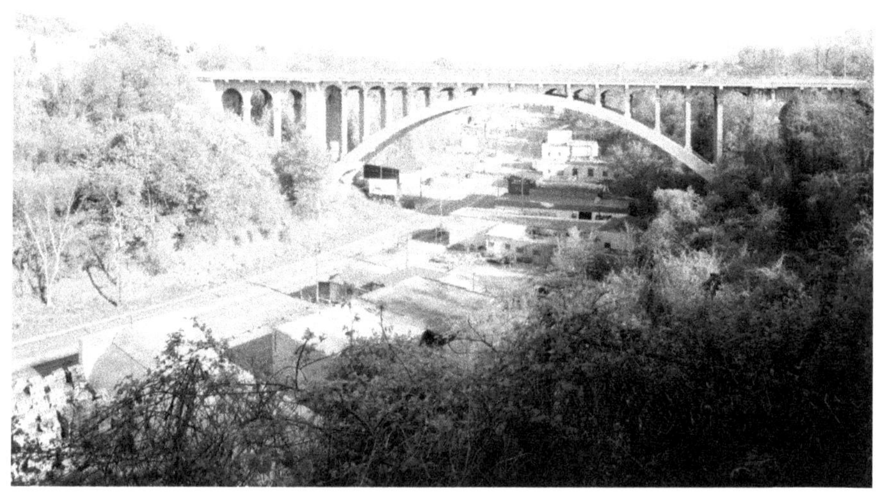

Pittsburgh's Larimer Avenue Bridge over Washington Boulevard, completed in 1912. *Library of Congress, Prints & Photographs Division, HAER PA,2-PITBU,73-.*

The 1911–12 Larimer Avenue Bridge is the most significant of these city arch bridges. Its three-hundred-foot span was considered the world's longest when it opened. It was built under City DPW director Joseph Armstrong, who later served as mayor in 1914–18 and then as county commissioner in 1924–32.

ALLEGHENY COUNTY DEPARTMENT OF PUBLIC WORKS BRIDGES

Charles Davis, consulting engineer for the first Monongahela Point Bridge, was hired as Allegheny County engineer in 1881. After reorganization, the Allegheny County Road Department was formed in 1895, the year Pennsylvania passed legislation allowing counties to take over local roads for improvement. The county initially built a number of small stone arch and steel girder bridges for these roads. With early 1900s public opinion increasingly favoring toll-free river crossings paid for through taxation, Allegheny County began purchasing toll bridges and building major new bridges. The first was the 1908–10 Jonathon Hulton Bridge over the Allegheny River in Oakmont, constructed by American Bridge. The five-span truss had a skewed 505-foot Pennsylvania truss main span. The county's second major bridge was at Sewickley over the Ohio River. The Fort Pitt Bridge Works constructed the cantilever with a 750-foot main span in 1909–11. It was the first vehicular truss bridge over the Ohio in Pennsylvania.

Industries were slower to develop along the Allegheny River than the Monongahela and Ohio Rivers because of the obstructive bridges near the Point between Pittsburgh and Allegheny City. By 1900, six bridges were located within a 1.5-mile stretch, each privately built before 1885. All were low to the water and had different pier arrangements. Congress and the Supreme Court intervened to pass and uphold legislation to force bridge demolition to open up the Allegheny River to shipping. In 1907, the Union Bridge crossing the Allegheny at the Point was demolished as a navigational obstruction. The remaining Allegheny River bridges were initially ruled not obstructive by the War Department, so at Pittsburgh's urging, Allegheny County purchased the Sixth through Thirtieth Street Bridges in 1911, freeing them of tolls. After the next election, the new

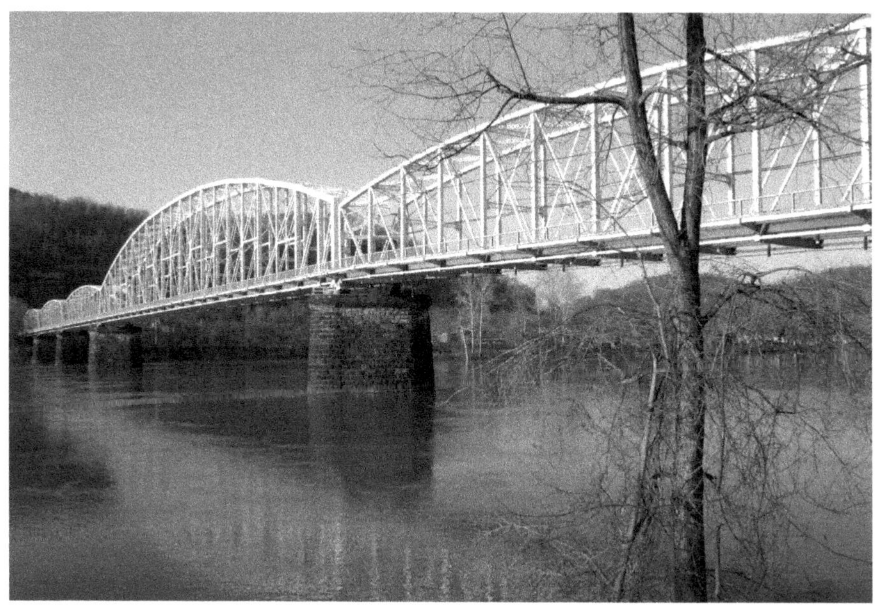

Jonathon Hulton Bridge over the Allegheny River in Oakmont (1910–2016). *Todd Wilson.*

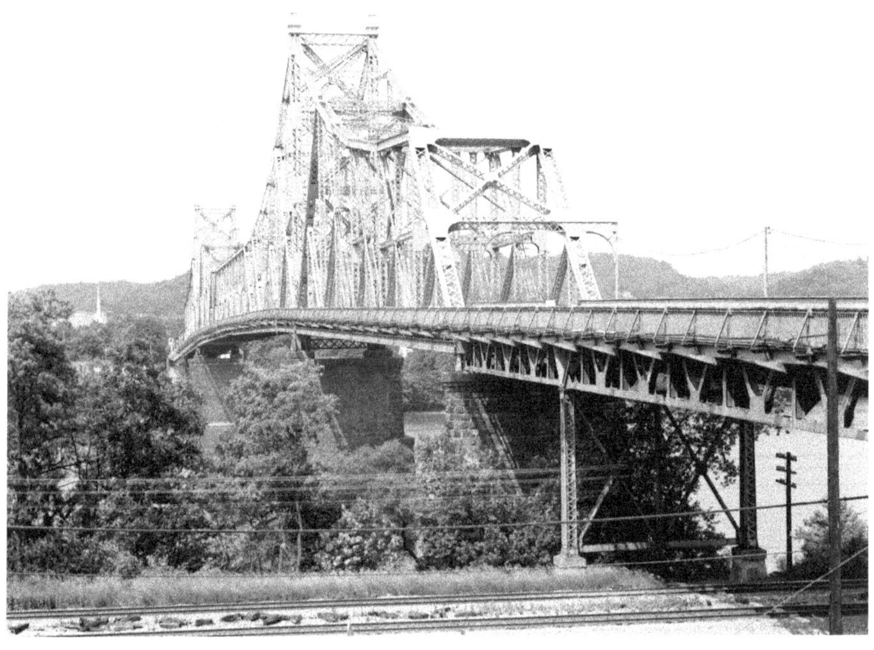

Sewickley Bridge over the Ohio River (1911–80). *Library of Congress, Prints & Photographs Division, HAER PA,2-SEW,1--23.*

War Department administration eventually labeled them as obstructive and in 1917 ordered their replacement. Having just purchased them five years before, Allegheny County now had to rebuild them. Pennsylvania subsequently passed an act giving counties the authority to build bridges over any stream, even within municipalities, and the power to collect taxes to construct and maintain them.

The first Allegheny River bridges to be replaced were the remaining covered bridges—the 1838 Sixteenth Street Bridge (rebuilt in 1851 and 1865 and destroyed by fire in 1919) and the 1870 Forty-Third Street Bridge. The city's Art Commission saw these replacements as opportunities for prominent architects to control the projects and design more beautiful bridges, taking final decision-making power away from engineers. The nationally known firm Warren & Wetmore was hired for the Sixteenth Street Bridge and locally prominent architect Benno Janssen for the Fortieth Street Bridge. The decision to put architects in control alarmed the engineering community. The Pittsburgh Section of ASCE protested nationally in the

Engineering News-Record in May 1923, and its successful campaign helped ensure that engineers would manage future bridge projects.

Regarding the architect-designed bridges, Warren & Wetmore, with engineer H.G. Balcom, selected a tied-arch design with three spans for the 1923 Sixteenth Street Bridge, the first local example of the type. Built by the Fort Pitt Bridge Works, it features stone portals topped with bronze armillary spheres based on the Observatory Fountain at the Luxembourg Gardens in Paris, France. Janssen, with engineer Charles S. Davis, designed a three-hinged deck arch at Fortieth Street. The bridge's location was shifted from that of the previous bridge at Forty-Third Street so it could end at higher ground to permit the deck arch design. The McClintic-Marshall built structure, named the Washington Crossing Bridge, opened in 1924. Its railings incorporate Allegheny County's seal and the seals of America's thirteen original colonies. Washington Monument–style obelisks adorn the ends of the bridge.

Designing bridges was one challenge; paying for them was another. Former Pittsburgh mayor Joseph Armstrong was elected county commissioner in the 1923 election. He created the Allegheny County Department of Public

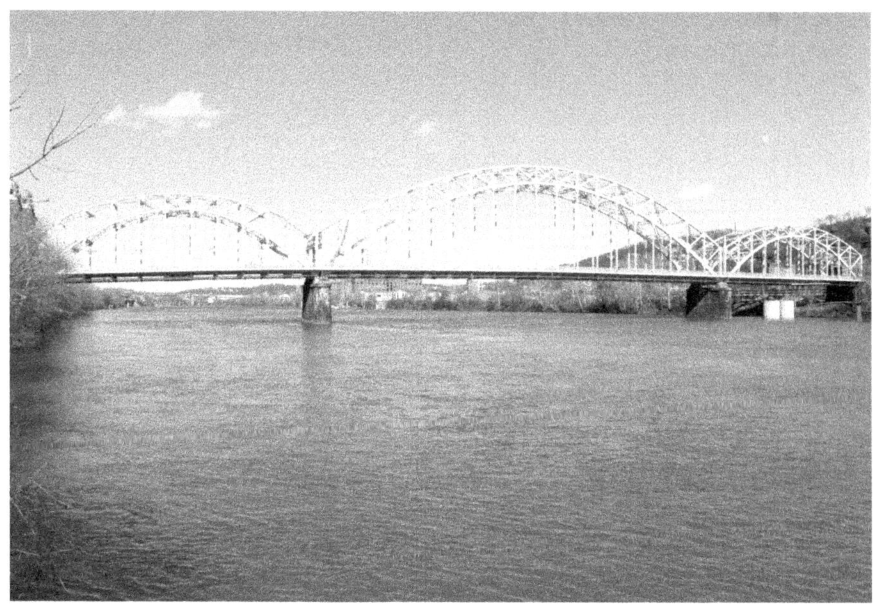

Pittsburgh's Sixteenth Street (David McCullough) Bridge over the Allegheny River, completed in 1923. *Todd Wilson.*

Works (County DPW) in 1924, led by engineer Norman Brown, as a full-service department able to design roads and bridges self-sufficiently. Vernon Covell led the Bureau of Bridges and Stanley Roush led the Bureau of Architecture, but Brown had the final authority. In March 1924, Armstrong announced the "Ultimate Highway System" for new automobile-focused highways and bridges throughout the county. After the measure to float bonds to pay for infrastructure passed, the county now had funding in place to design many of Pittsburgh's most famous and impressive bridges, linked by grand boulevards. A second bond was passed in 1928 after the 1927 elections to continue the work. Nearly 60 percent of the Allegheny County budget funded this program, and ninety-nine bridges were built.

In Pittsburgh, the next bridges to be replaced were at Sixth, Seventh and Ninth Streets, which had impeded navigation with varying span lengths and differing pier arrangements. Increased vertical clearance would require steeper roadway approach grades, problematic for horse and wagon use at the time. Engineers first recommended novel continuous-traffic lift bridges, in which bridge decks could be lifted fourteen feet for the times of the year when river levels were higher. Traffic could use the bridges in their lifted configuration. Those designs were rejected. Engineers then studied three-span arches similar to the Sixteenth Street Bridge, single-span trusses and continuous trusses, the last of which was selected. The plans were finished and advertised for bid when the County DPW submitted them to the Art Commission for approval. Shockingly, the commission rejected the designs, not wanting the view-blocking trusses. Through-truss bridges were never again approved for river bridges within the city limits.

The Art Commission believed that structural design was part of a bridge's artistic merit and that bridges should not obstruct views of the city skyline. Unconcerned by feasibility or cost, the commission preferred suspension bridges. The previous suspension bridges at Sixth and Seventh Streets, however, had problems with their external anchorages slipping. Constructing the external anchorages would greatly affect surrounding properties. County engineers instead designed America's first self-anchored suspension bridges based on a novel bridge in Cologne, Germany. Self-anchored suspension bridges have catenaries anchored directly into the bridge deck. The deck becomes a structural member that must be completed before the bridge can function. Building such a bridge was a challenge because the bridges needed to be built without blocking the river channel. The engineers selected eyebars rather than wire rope to better allow the bridges to be built as temporary truss bridges cantilevered over the river. The anchor spans were constructed

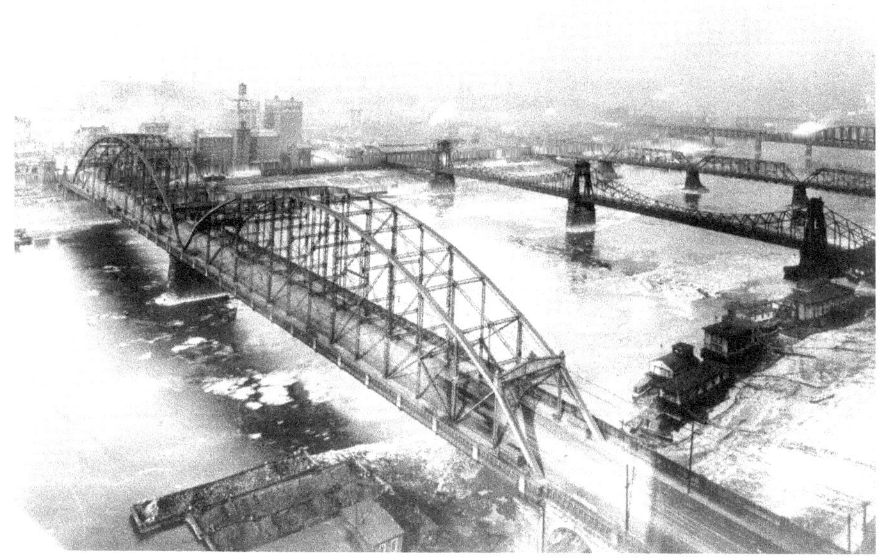

Theodore Cooper's 1892 Sixth Street Bridge (*left*), Gustav Lindenthal's 1884 Seventh Street Bridge (*center*) and Ferris, Kaufman and Company's 1890 Ninth Street Bridge (*right*). *Carnegie Library of Pittsburgh.*

first, then the cantilevered main spans. When the bridge was completed, the temporary trusses were removed. The Art Commission wanted the three bridges to be identical for aesthetic reasons, which also reduced costs. The previous Seventh and Ninth Street Bridges were demolished, and the previous Sixth Street Bridge was floated by barges to Coraopolis, where it carried traffic until being replaced in 1994–95.

Between 1924 and 1932, the County DPW designed many unique and innovative bridges. The Point Bridge over the Monongahela River was replaced in 1927 with an unusual cantilever design. The deck was suspended from overhead trusses and arced to provide some symmetry with the Manchester Bridge over the Allegheny at the Point while maintaining the view from the bridge deck. George S. Richardson became the engineer-in-charge, and he designed many Pittsburgh-area major crossings into the 1980s. The Liberty Bridge, a 2,663-foot-long deck cantilever, was the largest bridge in the county upon completion in 1928. Combined with the Liberty Tunnel,

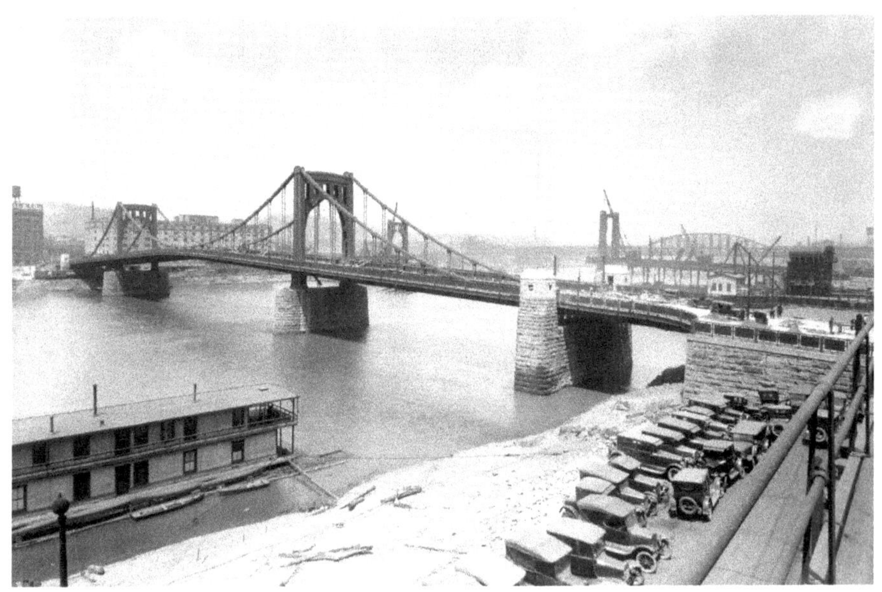

Seventh Street (Andy Warhol) Bridge nearing completion on June 8, 1926, with the Ninth Street (Rachel Carson) Bridge under construction in the background. *Carnegie Library of Pittsburgh.*

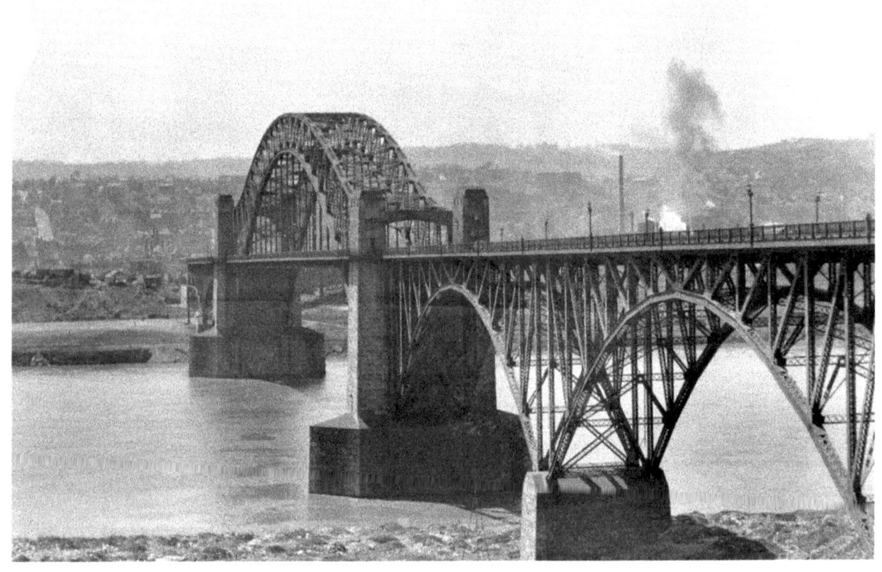

McKees Rocks Bridge over the Ohio River, completed in 1931. *Carnegie Library of Pittsburgh.*

it opened up the South Hills for automobile commuters. The 1931 McKees Rocks Bridge became Pittsburgh's first vehicular Ohio River crossing. Its design was based on Gustav Lindenthal's famous Hell Gate Bridge in New York City. Including solid fill sections, the 7,293-foot-long McKees Rocks Bridge is the longest in Western Pennsylvania. The 1932 West End Bridge over the Ohio River had a record-breaking 778-foot tied-arch span upon completion and used pre-stressed wire rope hangars for the deck. The 1933 South Tenth Street Bridge over the Monongahela River became Pittsburgh's largest suspension bridge.

Besides river bridges, the Allegheny County DPW designed grand urban boulevards that required bridges. The 1931 Ohio River Boulevard ran along the river's northern hillsides, crossing intersecting valleys on six open-spandrel concrete arch bridges. The largest was the record-breaking 400-foot Jacks Run Bridge. The following year, the county opened the George Westinghouse Memorial Bridge across the Turtle Creek valley, a five-span concrete arch bridge with a central 460-foot span, the largest in the world at the time. The bridge's dedication plaque reads, "In boldness of conception, in greatness and in usefulness to mankind, this bridge

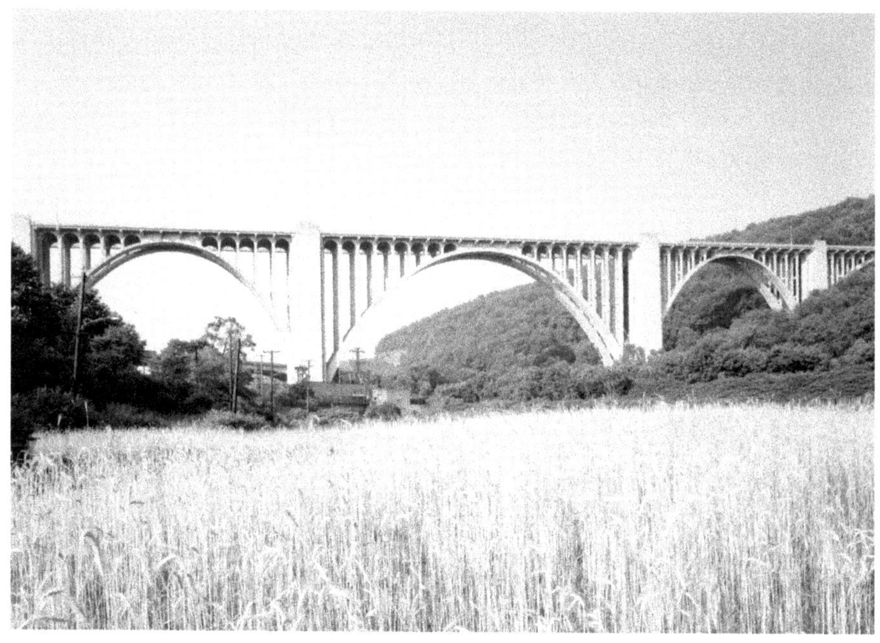

The 1932 George Westinghouse Memorial Bridge over the Turtle Creek Valley. *Library of Congress, Prints & Photographs Division, HAER PA,2-EAPIT,1--4.*

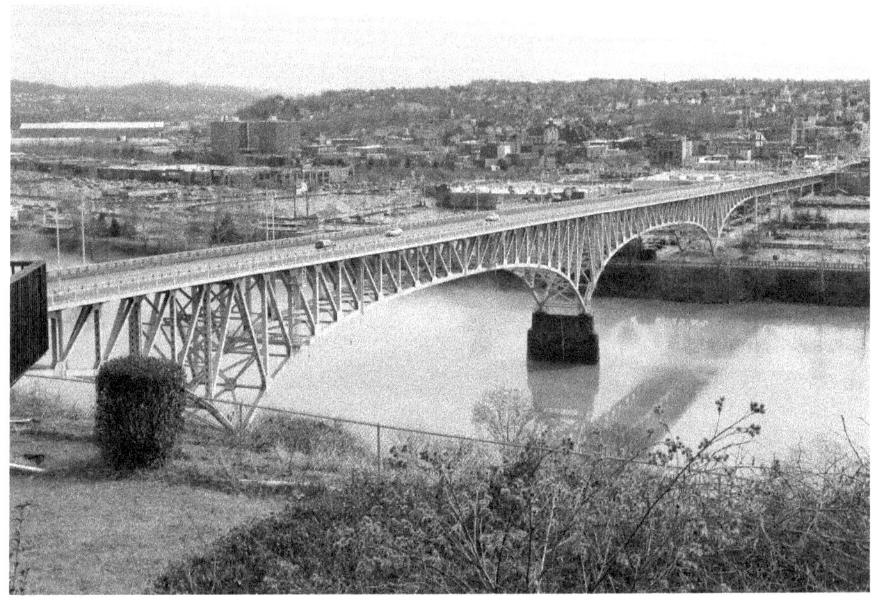

The Homestead High Level (Homestead Grays) Bridge over the Monongahela River, completed in 1937. *Todd Wilson.*

typifies the character and career of George Westinghouse 1846–1914 in whose honor it was dedicated on September 10, 1932." Four Stanley Roush–designed pylons with Art Deco–style granite reliefs by Frank Vittor were completed in 1936.

The 1931 elections halted Allegheny County's great bridge building program, but it was restarted after the 1935 elections as the Department of Works. With federal funding from the New Deal, bridges such as the 1937 Homestead High Level Bridge, 1938 Jerome Street Bridge and 1939 Highland Park Bridge were constructed over the Monongahela, Youghiogheny and Allegheny Rivers, respectively. The Homestead High Level Bridge is particularly significant because it was the first to use the Wichert truss, a patented hinged diamond assembly at pier points to allow otherwise continuous spans to flex independently. The bridge-building program was suspended in 1940 because steel was needed for the war effort. After the war, and with increasing use of outside consultants, the County DPW built other significant bridges. Cantilever bridges in Rankin and Dravosburg opened in 1951 and in Sharpsburg in 1962. The county's 1968 Glenwood Bridge was its first modern design, a continuous truss that pioneered welded instead of riveted members.

PENNSYLVANIA DEPARTMENT OF HIGHWAYS BRIDGES

Pennsylvania's State Highway Department was formed in 1903. Governor John Tener, who previously had formed the Mercantile Bridge Company to build the 1906 Charleroi-Monessen Bridge over the Monongahela River and is the namesake of its 2013 replacement, passed the Sproul Act in 1911. It led to the establishment of state highways, including the Lincoln Highway (State Route 1, now US 30) and the William Penn Highway (State Route 3, now US 22). "Good Roads" acts were passed every few years, increasing the development of state roads and the bridges along them. In 1931, the state took ownership of more than twenty thousand miles of county and municipal roads. In 1936, a devastating flood washed away hundreds of bridges. In the late 1930s, the Works Progress Administration (WPA) provided federal funding for infrastructure. Most of the state-standard bridges were built in the 1930s due to these circumstances.

The department started to design standard-plan bridges for these roads, similar to the catalogue bridges of the late 1800s. It created distinct designs—such as T-beams, concrete arches, steel stringers, through girders and steel trusses—and adapted them for bridges throughout Pennsylvania. The Allegheny River's 1917 Hollow Road Bridge in Potter County was one of the first to be built in the state. The 1932 Kittanning Citizens Bridge over the Allegheny River, a Parker truss, had the longest span of these bridges at four hundred feet. Other truss types included Pratt, Baltimore and Warren through trusses, Parker pony trusses and Pratt deck trusses. Hundreds were built across Pennsylvania, including Allegheny River bridges at Parker, East Brady and Tidioute; Kiskiminetas River bridges at Leechburg, Vandergift and Apollo; Beaver and Mahoning River bridges at Rochester, New Castle and Edinburg; and Conemaugh and Stonycreek River bridges at Blairsville, Seward and Johnstown.

After World War II and with the success of the 1940 Pennsylvania Turnpike, the department began designing high-speed automobile highways that needed bridges. The limited-access Penn-Lincoln Parkway was built from Wilkinsburg to Robinson Township in 1946–60 to bypass the congested combination of the Lincoln (US 30) and Penn (US 22) Highways, with an expressway segment to the new 1952 Greater Pittsburgh Airport. The parkway was the most expensive state-funded project at the time. Too large to be designed entirely within the State Highway Department, consulting engineering companies designed significant portions of the route. The

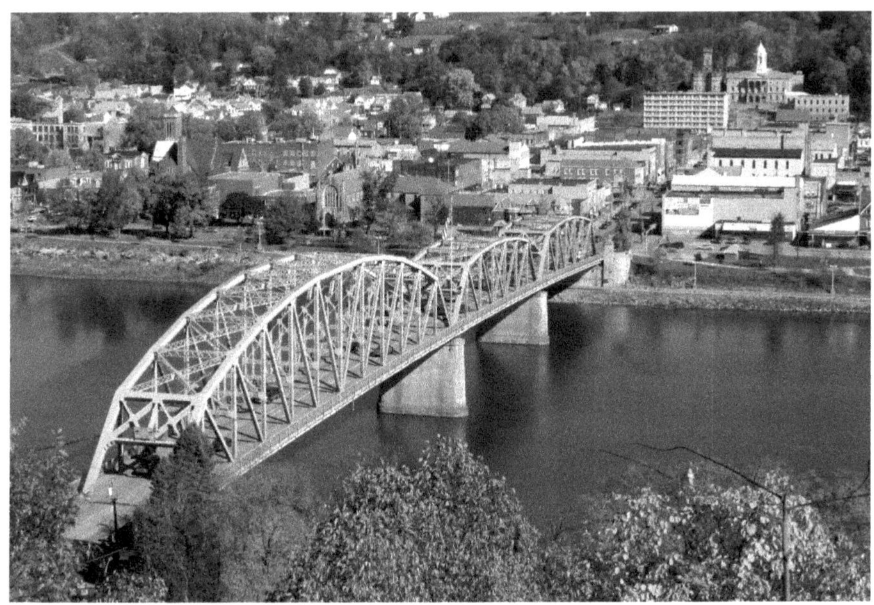

The 1932 Kittanning Citizens Bridge over the Allegheny River. *Todd Wilson.*

parkway was built with a variety of bridge types, including steel arches over Ardmore Boulevard and Campbells Run, open spandrel concrete arches over Nine Mile Run and on Brinton Road (over the parkway) and a continuous truss over Junction Hollow.

The parkway's most significant bridge was the revolutionary 1959 tied-arch Fort Pitt Bridge near the Point. By the 1930s, Pittsburgh leaders were seeking ways to revitalize the Point area. The Point Park Commission was established in 1945. Parkway plans necessitated a new Monongahela River crossing, so the commission decided on a comprehensive plan to incorporate the new bridge into a large-scale urban revitalization project called Renaissance I. Both of the existing Point bridges would be replaced with symmetrical ones farther upstream. The land at the Point would become a park with a fountain. When streetcars were eliminated from the plans, double-deck bridge designs were chosen to minimize intrusive looping ramps into the planned park. The Fort Pitt Bridge was one of the first to be designed using computer-assisted calculations. Its twin, the Fort Duquesne Bridge over the Allegheny River, was substantially completed in 1963, but it was the "Bridge to Nowhere" until 1969, when it finally opened to traffic after the first of two ramps was built. The other was completed nearly two decades later.

The state built several other expressways and limited-access highways in Western Pennsylvania in the late 1940s and early 1950s. This included the Route 51 expressway connecting Allegheny County's Saw Mill Run Boulevard with the National Road (US 40) in Uniontown and the Route 71 (now I-70) limited-access highway to connect the National Road (US 40) in Washington to the Turnpike (I-76) in New Stanton. Both required bridges crossing the Monongahela River, so the state created a design that could be used for both locations. The 1951 Elizabeth (Regis Malady) Bridge (Route 51) and 1952 Speers–Belle Vernon Bridge (I-70) were designed as arched continuous trusses with suspended decks.

The Federal Highway Act, established in 1956, created the Interstate Highway System. The higher-speed roads needed longer, wider and taller bridges than ever before. Western Pennsylvania's primary interstates—I-70, I-79, I-80 and I-90—were completed within the next twenty years. Taking advantage of the latest bridge technology, most of the new bridges were built as concrete or steel beam structures. Steel structural members were joined by either welded or bolted connections instead of being riveted. With computer-assisted calculations, the largest river crossings were built as either continuous trusses or tied arches. The 1968 Interstate 80 Allegheny River

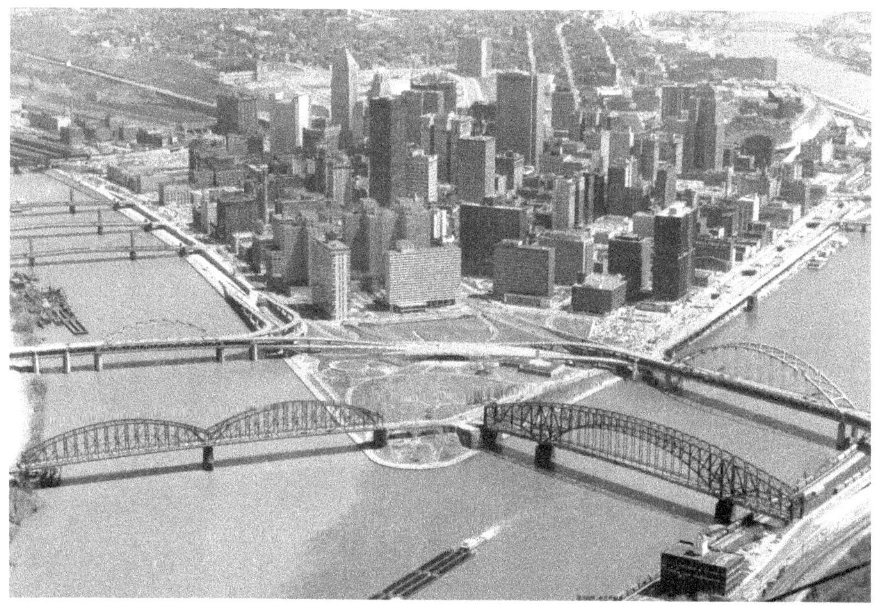

The Point in 1969 with the new Fort Pitt and Fort Duquesne Bridges replacing the former Point and Manchester Bridges. *Carnegie Library of Pittsburgh.*

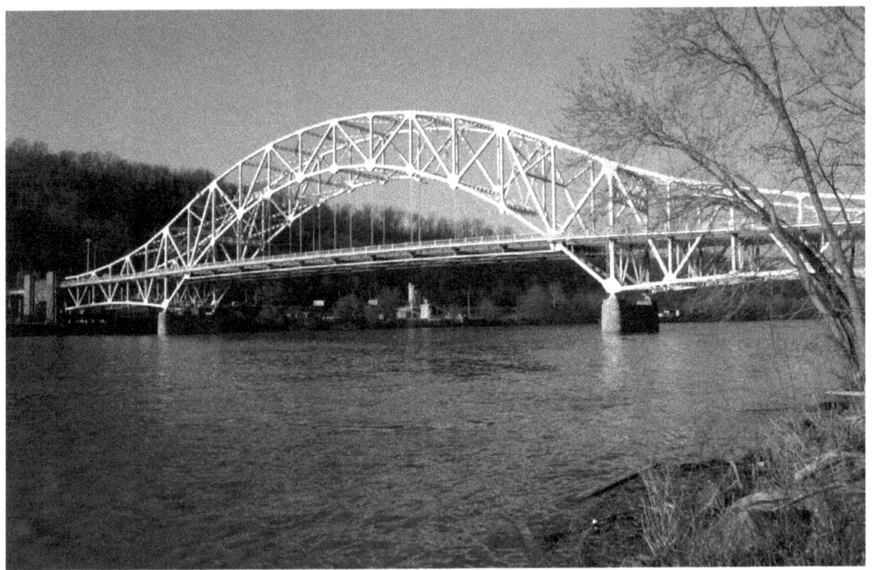

The 1951 Elizabeth (Regis Malady) Bridge over the Monongahela River. *Todd Wilson.*

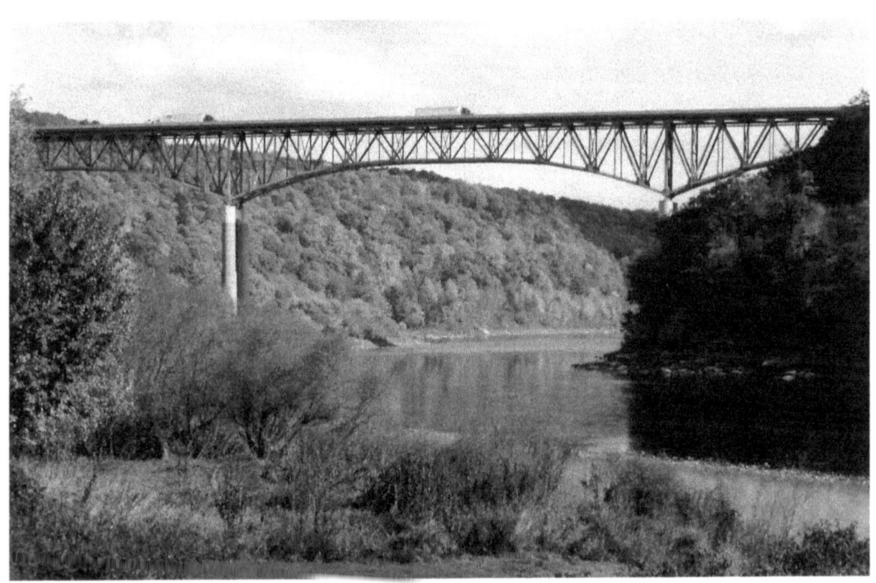

The 1968 Interstate 80 (Keystone Shortway) Bridge over the Allegheny River near Emlenton. *Todd Wilson.*

Bridge at Emlenton is a continuous deck truss example. The 270-foot-tall bridge was the highest bridge on the interstate system upon opening and is still the highest vehicular bridge in Pennsylvania. The 1976 Glenfield Bridge carrying I-79 over the Ohio River and Neville Island is a tied arch. It has a 750-foot main span and a total length of 4,544 feet, the longest (without interruption) in Western Pennsylvania. It was also infamous for having a main girder over the Ohio's back channel crack just five months after opening due to a defective weld.

In 1961, the state assumed ownership of many major county and municipal bridges. In 1970, various state departments with transportation-related functions were reorganized into the newly created Pennsylvania Department of Transportation, or PennDOT. Today, PennDOT, along with the Pennsylvania Turnpike Commission, takes the lead in planning, designing and maintaining new roads and bridges with their design consultants.

MODERN BRIDGES

After World War II, newer technology enabled engineers to design longer and stronger bridges than ever before, aiming for lower maintenance costs and one-hundred-year design lives. Sophisticated computer analyses; high-strength steel; precast, pre-stressed and post-tensioned concrete; and advanced construction techniques allowed for long, continuous and curved designs never before thought possible. Concrete and steel girder bridges, once limited to short spans, can now be used for almost all types of bridges in Western Pennsylvania. The Monongahela River's 1987 Clairton-Glassport Bridge was Western Pennsylvania's first to span 400 feet, and the 2015 Hulton Bridge was the area's first to span 500 feet. Both replaced county-built steel trusses, showing the technological change. The Pennsylvania Turnpike introduced segmental concrete box girder bridges to Western Pennsylvania that can span longer distances. Composed of box-shaped concrete segments, they are built from piers without falsework. The turnpike's Allegheny River Bridge near Oakmont, completed in 2010, has spans reaching 532 feet, and the similar Monongahela River Bridge near Brownsville, completed in 2012, has spans reaching 518 feet. Girder bridges are built crossing deep valleys, such as the 250-foot-tall Mon-Fayette Expressway's Joe Montana Bridges over Pigeon Creek. They use modern weathering steel, which does not need to be painted.

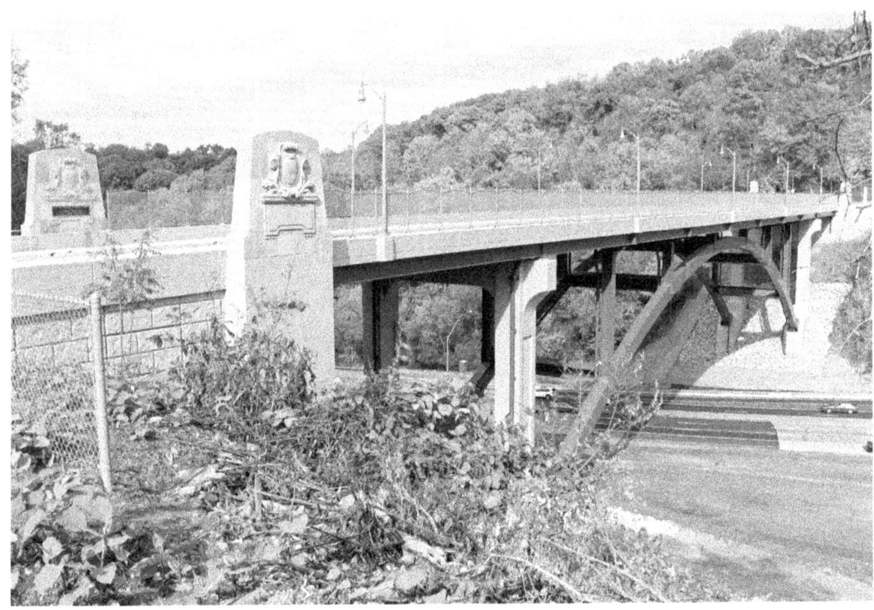

Pittsburgh's Beechwood Boulevard (Greenfield) Bridge II over I-376 Parkway East. *Todd Wilson.*

Engineers have also been improving other conventional bridge designs. Newer truss and arch bridges have been designed with internally redundant bridge members to protect against failure, such as the 2009 Point Marion Bridge over the Monongahela River, a 413-foot Parker truss. Another is the 2017 Beechwood Boulevard (Greenfield) Bridge in Pittsburgh, the winner of ASCE Pittsburgh Section's 2017 Award of Merit. Replacing a deteriorated concrete arch, the bridge was designed to replicate the shape and ornamentation of the original, serving both as a grand entrance into Schenley Park and a gateway arch above the Parkway East (I-376) into Pittsburgh. Innovative design and construction techniques were used, allowing the arch sections to be erected in just one weekend over the busy highway below. Such structures and techniques show the promise of civil engineering's future of bridge building—combining design and construction innovations and ingenuity to create the next generation of great public structures.

HOW MANY BRIDGES ARE THERE IN PITTSBURGH?

Pittsburgh is rightfully known as the "City of Bridges," but how many bridges are there? Many have wondered and a few have attempted to count, but the answer is far more complicated than a simple number can provide. Aside from civil engineering projects changing the number every so often, the total depends on the specific definition of "bridge." For the purposes of this book, we define a bridge to be an engineered structure designed specifically to function as a connected crossing to transport people over an obstruction. Elevated platforms, stairs and buildings are thus not considered, even if they happen to cross a road or extend over a hillside. Only permanent bridges are counted, which excludes structures connecting to floating docks. However, gray areas still remain. The National Bridge Inventory (NBI) lists only government-owned bridges spanning at least twenty feet, subject to federal inspection requirements. What about smaller and privately owned structures? What about bridges between buildings, into buildings or within buildings (such as ones that have ground-level paths with footbridges)? What about major ramps? While no exact answer may be possible, this chapter attempts to quantify both Pittsburgh's definitive bridges and debatable bridges into the following categories:

- river crossings: Pittsburgh's definitive river bridges
- major structures: other large non-river bridges
- intermediate structures: smaller than major structures, but spanning at least twenty feet
- ramps: NBI-listed structures connecting to distinct bridges
- minor structures: pedestrian and driveway bridges; road or rail bridges less than twenty feet
- buildings: crossings to buildings and between them; stacked multi-floor crossings are counted together
- insignificant crossings: least definitive, such as culverts and small footpath crossings

The first three categories are bridges by any engineering standards, totaling at least 370. The rest are debatable so we leave it up to the reader's interpretation to make the final determination. If all categories are counted, Pittsburgh's bridge total exceeds 700 structures. Refer to the

APPROXIMATE NUMBER OF PITTSBURGH'S BRIDGES BY TYPE

Type	*Approximate Count*
River Crossings	30
Major Structures	50
Intermediate Structures	290
Ramps	60
Minor Structures	110
Buildings	120
Insignificant Crossings	40
Total	**370 to 700**

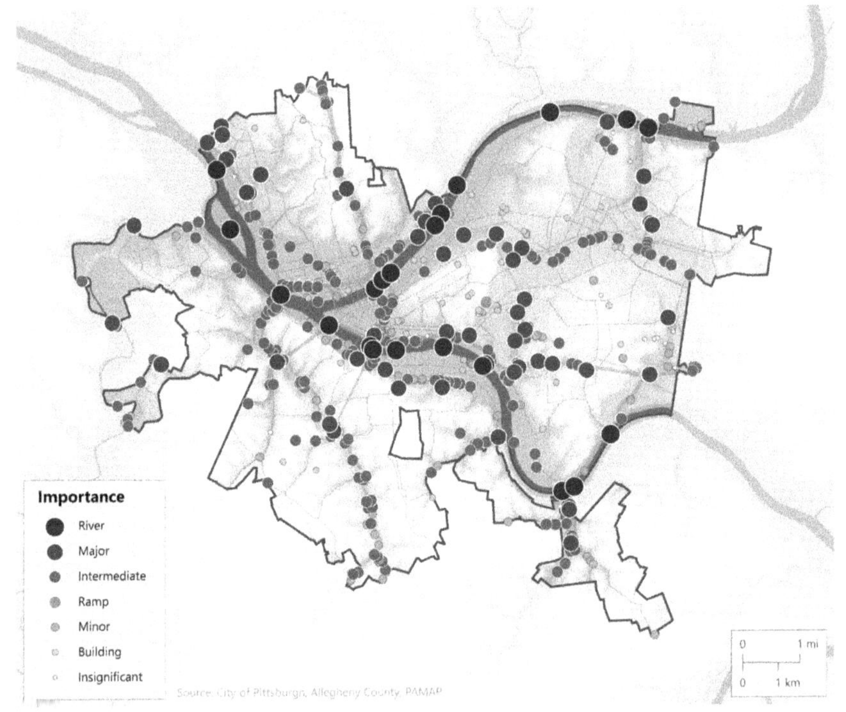

The *Complete Map of Pittsburgh's Bridges. Map created by Lauren Winkler, Michael Baker International from data compiled by Todd Wilson.*

table showing an approximate count of Pittsburgh's bridges per category. A map showing their location is also provided. Categorizing by structural type, about 75 percent are beam bridges, 12 percent are arch bridges, 8 percent are truss bridges, 4 percent are frame bridges and 1 percent are suspension bridges. Regionally, there are about ten thousand NBI-listed bridges in the twenty-eight counties that compose Western Pennsylvania. Of those, Allegheny County has approximately 15 percent. Any way you count it, there are a lot of bridges.

PUBLIC TRANSPORTATION

Mobility for All

By Jason Machuga, PE, and Carrie Machuga

Public Staircases

Walking: the most basic form of transportation. As such, walking in the public right-of-way is the most basic form of public transportation. In Pittsburgh, because of the city's complex topography, with its steep hills and deep valleys, the pedestrian has been afforded a unique solution: the public staircase. According to Bob Regan in his book *Pittsburgh Steps*, "These city steps were, in essence, the city's first mass transportation system." Like any successful public transportation system, public staircases have played an important role in the development of Pittsburgh by connecting people within and between neighborhoods, as well as to and from school, employment, shopping and other daily activities. Pittsburgh's some seven hundred public staircases have left their mark on the city and its neighborhoods and still perform their original purpose, even though much of the traffic has been displaced to other transportation modes.

Pittsburgh's public stairs have several interesting features. Some staircases are actually streets in themselves, maintained by the city. Many even have their own street sign, like Mann Street at the intersection of Woodruff Street. There is even a set of public staircases that meet, creating a car-less intersection just the size of a landing on a wooded hillside. There are many

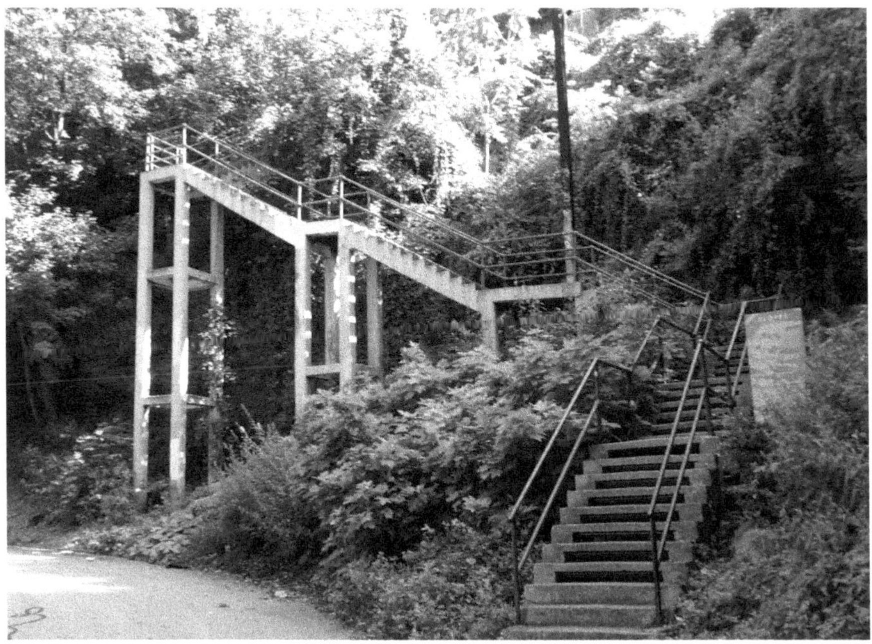

Above: The South Eighteenth Street Stairs, in the South Side Slopes neighborhood. *ASCE Pittsburgh Section.*

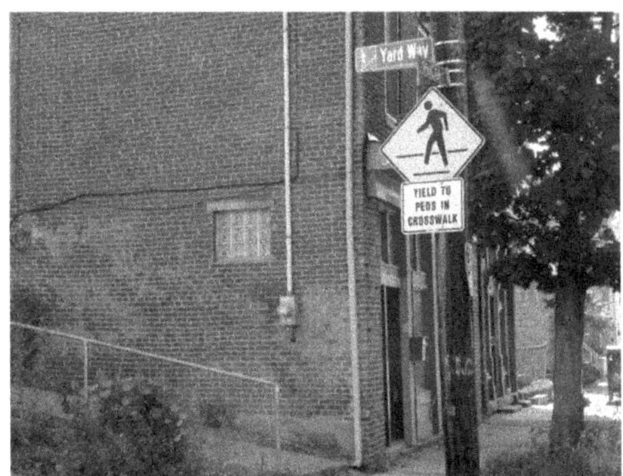

Right: Yard Way Stairs "street" sign, in the South Side Slopes neighborhood. *ASCE Pittsburgh Section.*

houses within the city that are only accessible by public staircases. Take a field trip (virtual or terrestrial) to Bering Street on Pittsburgh's South Side to see houses with their stoops connected directly to the public staircases.

Time, lack of funding and disinterest have taken their toll on many of these staircases, but recent public awareness efforts have, in some cases, protected them. The annual autumnal event "Step Trek" in Pittsburgh's South Side has generated much interest and has led to rehabilitation of several staircases. Additionally, permanent wayfinding signs were recently installed for the "Church Route," which created a route linking several staircases in the South Side neighborhood.

INCLINES

Pittsburgh's topography produced a second specific public transportation solution: inclined planes—or, colloquially, the "inclines." Two counterbalanced railcars ride on two adjacent parallel sets of track placed at a constant slope or incline in order to traverse large changes in elevation. At the peak, the city of Pittsburgh had numerous inclines. Only two remain: the Monongahela Incline and the Duquesne Incline. Both ascend the slopes of the Mount Washington and Duquesne Heights neighborhoods, respectively, and are nearly one mile apart. Both were designed to be near bridges that provided walking or streetcar connections to the city.

The Duquesne Incline was built by prominent local resident Kirk Bigham, who lived atop Coal Hill, as Mount Washington and Duquesne Heights were then known. While this region has geographic proximity to downtown Pittsburgh, it is separated by the Monongahela River and a four-hundred-foot vertical precipice. In a time before automobiles, Mr. Bigham had the foresight to see that in order to unlock the potential of this elevated land, a transportation solution must be developed to overcome the condensed contours. He hired Samuel Diescher, who designed and built the incline for a sum of $47,000. Diescher, who was born in Budapest and educated in Germany and Switzerland as a civil and mechanical engineer, designed many of the inclines in the United States. The Duquesne Incline opened to revenue service on May 20, 1877, providing a much-needed connection between Coal Hill, the Point Bridge and downtown.

After eighty-five years of service, the Duquesne Incline was shut down in 1962. Much like Mr. Bigham before them, the residents of Mount Washington and Duquesne Heights banded together to save the incline. It reopened in 1964 and is now operated by the Society for the Preservation of the Duquesne Heights Incline. This nonprofit organization not only continues to provide the crucial transportation link for Mount Washington residents but also provides an educational museum and a unique experience to the throngs of tourists who visit this iconic symbol of Pittsburgh. While the cars are not the originals, they are among the oldest operating transit vehicles in the country.

The nearby Monongahela Incline opened on May 28, 1870, and is the only other operating incline remaining in Pittsburgh. Unlike the Duquesne Incline, this incline is operated by the Port Authority of Allegheny County (PAAC). When riding on the incline, one can look to the east and see foundations from a parallel incline, the Monongahela Freight Incline, which

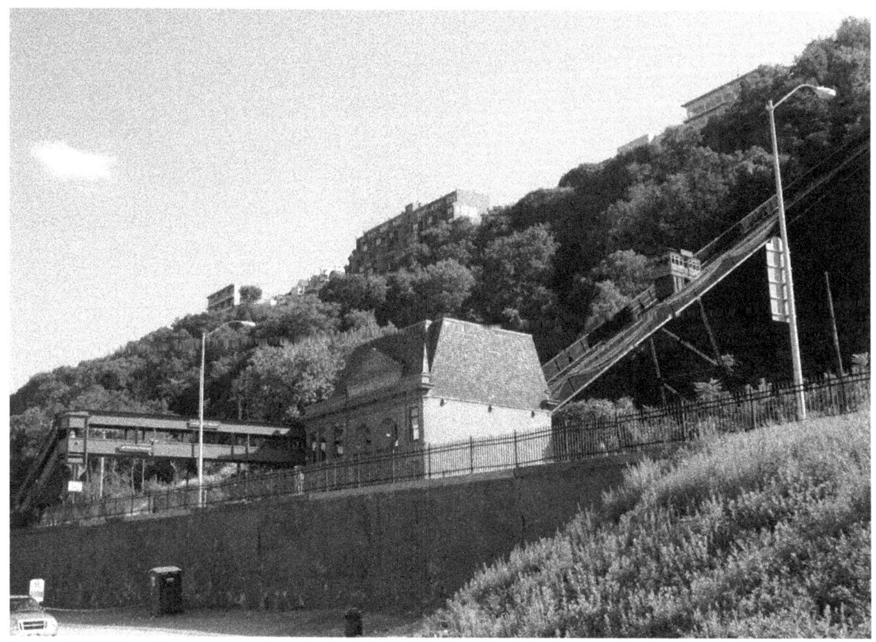

Duquesne Incline Lower Station, with vehicle departing station. *ASCE Pittsburgh Section.*

operated from 1884 to 1935. These sister inclines worked in concert to provide a quick lift for people and freight. There is a still-functioning freight incline in nearby Johnstown, Pennsylvania, at Yoder Hill. Passengers can drive their automobiles onto the incline to ride up the 70.9 percent grade.

Pittsburgh had another pair of sister inclines: the Castle Shannon Incline and the Castle Shannon South Incline. But unlike the Monongahela passenger and freight inclines, these inclines operated in series rather than parallel. The Castle Shannon Incline carried passengers along the front face of Mount Washington, and then passengers would disembark, cross the street and transfer to the Castle Shannon South incline, which would take passengers along the backside of Mount Washington, where many of them transferred to the trolleys to take them into the South Hills neighborhoods and boroughs, such as Castle Shannon.

The Knoxville Incline, Pittsburgh's famous incline with the bend, traversed the South Side Slopes to connect Pittsburgh's Allentown neighborhood with the South Side Flats. Operational from 1890 to 1960, a sharp curve allowed the incline to navigate the natural topography of the valley from which it rose. Although this incline suffered the same fate as most of Pittsburgh's

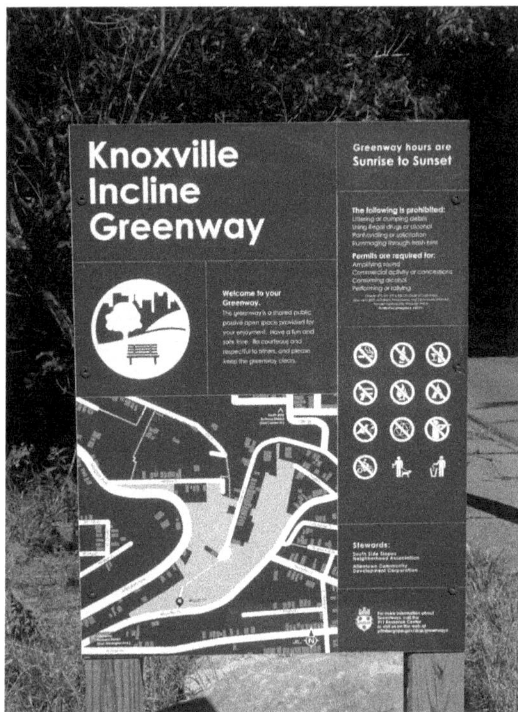

Left: Informational sign pertaining to the Knoxville Incline Greenway. *ASCE Pittsburgh Section.*

Below: Rehabilitated bridge that formerly crossed the Knoxville Incline and is now part of the Knoxville Incline Greenway. *ASCE Pittsburgh Section.*

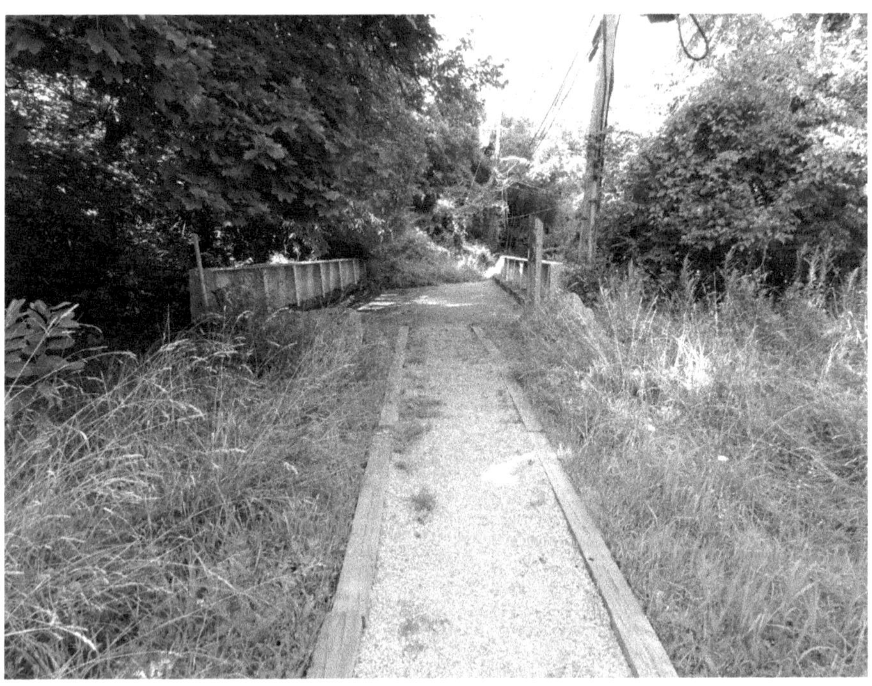

inclines, it has been given a new life in an unexpected way. Portions of the former right-of-way of the Knoxville Incline have been converted into a park. With the help of the community, the site has been cleaned, an original bridge painted and it is now ready to be enjoyed as a quiet respite in a bustling city with a deep connection to its history.

COMMUTER RAIL

Commuter rail also played an important role in serving Pittsburgh's commuters for decades. Service was provided by several railroads, including the Baltimore and Ohio Railroad (B&O), Pittsburgh and Lake Erie Railroad (P&LERR) and the vaunted Pennsylvania Railroad (later Conrail and Norfolk Southern). Between them, there were several major stations or terminals in or near downtown Pittsburgh. The development of the city followed the railroad lines. The Pennsylvania Railroad line snaked through the east end, connecting East Liberty, Wilkinsburg and Edgewood with downtown. These communities are excellent examples of railroad-induced development. Commuter rail began to taper off as passengers began diverting to automobiles. Ironically, one of Pittsburgh's last commuter trains, the "Parkway Limited," was developed to divert passengers from the Penn-Lincoln Parkway East during a major reconstruction project. The "Parkway Limited," a Pennsylvania Department of Transportation (PennDOT) and Conrail operation, traveled between Pittsburgh and Greensburg, with various station stops along the way. The service was cancelled in 1981 after nine months of operation due to low ridership.

HORSECARS, CABLE CARS AND STREETCARS

Adapting rail technology to the region's public right-of-way proved to be a challenge. Steam engines were not suitable in the street, but horsecar lines were an early solution. A hybrid of carriage and rail technology, horsecar lines provided smooth transportation when they were introduced in Pittsburgh in 1859. The first line was operated by the Citizens Passenger Railway connecting the Allegheny Cemetery in the Lawrenceville neighborhood with downtown.

The city's hills once again proved to be a challenge, leading to the introduction of cable car technology in Pittsburgh's East End neighborhoods in 1887. A steam engine was placed at the highest elevation along the line that drove a network of cables beneath the street. Each cable car would grip onto the cables and be pulled along the street, stopping by releasing the gripper from the cable and applying the brakes.

Cable cars were, however, quickly replaced by electric traction trolleys or streetcars. In 1890, Pittsburgh's first electric streetcar began operation, powered by overhead catenary. Electric streetcars and trolleys offered faster speeds and longer ranges than horse and cable cars. The network quickly expanded, with many private companies developing lines and competing for riders. This technology quickly grew outside the city of Pittsburgh. In the early twentieth century, it was possible to travel by interurban electric trolley from Pittsburgh as far south as Fairchance, Pennsylvania, and as far north as Buffalo, New York. An interurban trolley line also connected Pittsburgh and Washington, Pennsylvania. Parts of this line have been restored and are operated at the Western Pennsylvania Trolley Museum. After World War II, interurban electric trolleys could not compete with advances in highway and vehicle reliability and convenience and were mostly abandoned.

In 1902, the Pittsburgh Railways Company was formed as a merger of several independent streetcar companies. The hub and spoke system

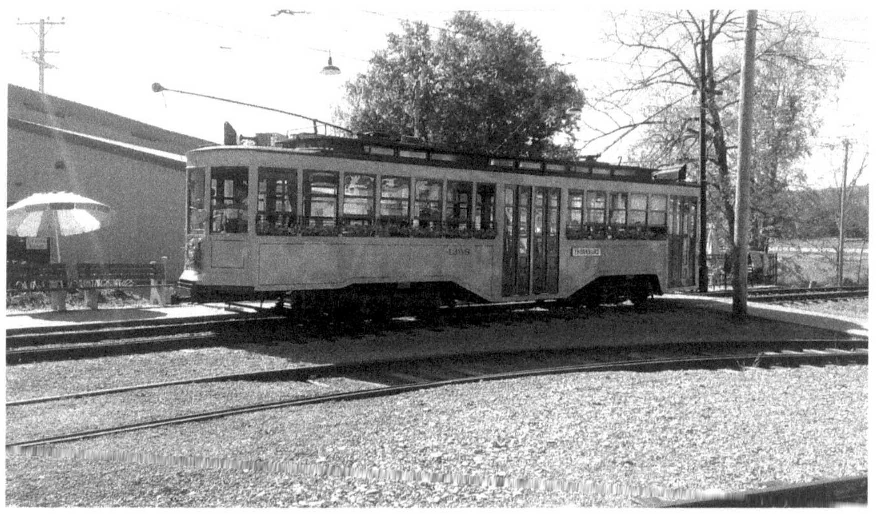

Car no. 4398 at the Western Pennsylvania Trolley Museum. *ASCE Pittsburgh Section.*

carried passengers in all directions from downtown Pittsburgh. In 1937, the Pittsburgh Railway Company operated the first President's Conference Committee (PCC) streamlined trolley used in revenue service in the United States. In 1950, the Pittsburgh Railway Company had more than one thousand cars; however, after World War II, ridership declined from 255 million passengers in 1947 to 66 million in 1962.

LIGHT RAIL TRANSIT

The PAAC commenced operations on March 1, 1964, and assumed operations of the bankrupt Pittsburgh Railways Company and many independent bus lines within Allegheny County. After the PAAC takeover of the streetcar/trolley network in Pittsburgh, the agency decided to abandon most of the routes. However, several routes into Pittsburgh's South Hills neighborhoods and suburbs continued.

The existing lines were upgraded and converted into Light Rail Transit (LRT) in the 1980s and 2000s. However, as the network was being planned, the street-level tracks over the Smithfield Street Bridge and through downtown Pittsburgh were not deemed suitable for the LRT system. As a result, the LRT network in downtown was routed across the Panhandle Bridge (originally a Pennsylvania Railroad bridge), over the Monongahela River and then into tunnels below Sixth Street and Liberty Avenue. The downtown subway was constructed and opened in 1985. The subway was connected with an existing tunnel, formerly part of the Pennsylvania Railroad at the Steel Plaza Station near Grant Street in downtown Pittsburgh. The line then continues south over the rehabilitated Panhandle Bridge before joining the original routing of the Mount Washington Transit Tunnel just past Station Square.

Because the subway was constructed during the transition period from streetcar and trolley to the LRT, there are several unique features of the original design. The streetcars and trolleys owned by the PAAC at the time were President's Conference Committee (PCC) cars, which, unlike LRT vehicles, could only travel in one direction. This meant that the system originally had trolley loops at both the Gateway Center and Penn Plaza termini, as well as a loop just outside the tunnel section to provide local downtown subway service. These loops have been removed now that all vehicles can run in both directions; however, a keen eye can still spot reminders of their presence, including the original Gateway Center Platform.

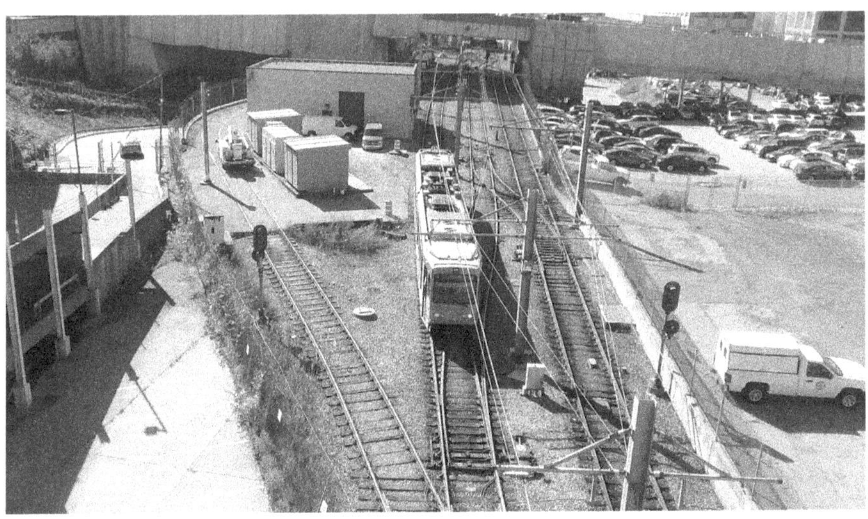

A light-rail vehicle traveling through the remains of a trolley loop before entering the downtown subway tunnel. *ASCE Pittsburgh Section.*

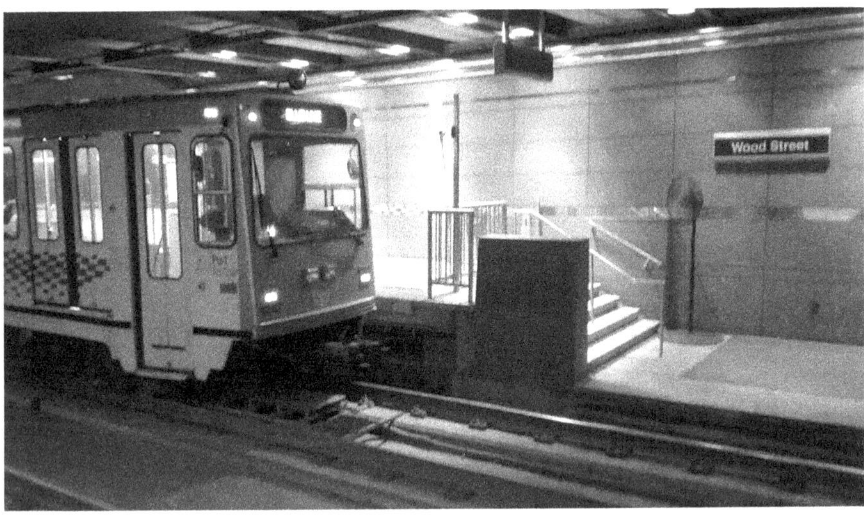

A light-rail vehicle stopped adjacent to the current high-level platforms; the abandoned low-level trolley platform can be seen to the right. *ASCE Pittsburgh Section.*

The Wood Street and Steel Plaza stations have lower-level platforms, which are now closed but previously provided access to the PCC cars while they ran underground.

Stage I of the LRT conversion focused on the underground subway and upgrading the Beechview and South Hills Village Lines. The Overbrook Line was closed in 1993, ending operation of the PCC cars into the downtown subway. The Overbrook Line was reconstructed and reopened in 2004 under the Stage II LRT project. In 2012, the North Shore Connector opened, reconstructing the Gateway Station and extending the line under the Allegheny River to provide two new stations near the city's baseball and football stadiums, as well as providing access to satellite parking and catalyzing new development opportunities near the stadiums and on the North Side.

BUSWAYS

In addition to the development of Pittsburgh's light-rail network, the PAAC was a pioneer in the development of Bus Rapid Transit (BRT) in the form of the busway. A busway is a limited-access roadway exclusively for buses. Much like conventional rapid transit, a busway has stations and a spine line that serves all of the stations. Many of the stations provide bypass lanes, and there are ramps along the busways where buses can enter and exit. The busways are well suited to provide express bus service and one-seat rides from locations throughout the region, providing a much-needed bypass of the traffic of the surface streets and highways.

Pittsburgh's first busway, the South Busway, opened in 1977 and was among the first in the nation. The South Busway connects the Mount Washington Transit Tunnel with Glenbury Street in Overbrook, runs parallel to Saw Mill Run Boulevard (PA Route 51) and provides relief to the congestion along that corridor. The corresponding Mount Washington Transit Tunnel provides a bypass of the Liberty Tunnel for local and long-distance bus routes.

The Martin Luther King Jr. East Busway, which opened in 1983, connects downtown Pittsburgh with Swissvale, serving the city's eastern neighborhoods and eastern and southeastern suburbs in Allegheny County. It was built within the original Pennsylvania Railroad Line right-of-way. Carrying a design speed of fifty-five miles per hour throughout most of the

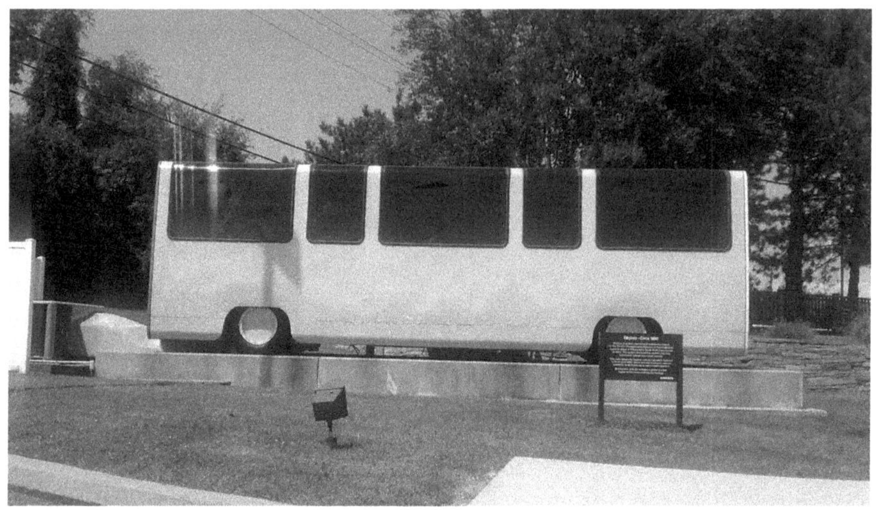

Photo of a SkyBus on display outside Bombardier, at 1501 Lebanon Church Road, Pittsburgh. *ASCE Pittsburgh Section.*

corridor, a trip from Wilkinsburg to downtown was reduced from forty-five minutes to fifteen. As a result, the Martin Luther King Jr. East Busway has seen average daily ridership as high as thirty thousand.

The West Busway, added in 2000, provides a bypass of the congested Parkway West and Fort Pitt Tunnel by connecting the Parkway in Carnegie with West Carson Street in the South Side. The original plan included extending the busway parallel to West Carson Street and constructing a new Monongahela River Bridge in conjunction with the Wabash Tunnel Project, but those elements were never built.

The Wabash Tunnel, originally built by the Wabash Pittsburgh Terminal Railway, was reopened as a High Occupancy Vehicle (HOV) tunnel connecting Saw Mill Run Boulevard with West Carson Street. After years of abandonment, the tunnel was purchased by the PAAC for the SkyBus Project, a sophisticated people-mover system developed by the Westinghouse Company to be built in the South Hills to replace the trolleys and streetcars. A demonstration line was constructed in South Park and ran for several years. Although the Skybus never gained traction, the technology developed locally at the Westinghouse Company, now Bombardier, has been used to provide public transportation solutions throughout the world. The Pittsburgh International Airport's automated people mover, built with the 1992 Airside & Landside Terminals, is a descendant of this technology. A SkyBus vehicle is still on display outside the Bombardier building.

Self-Driving Vehicles

The city of Pittsburgh is also a pioneer in robotics and self-driving vehicles. Eric Meyhofer, a founder of the Carnegie Mellon Robotics Institute, joined with Uber in 2015 to further develop the self-driving vehicle. Uber, which provides on-demand rides via its smartphone application, launched public rides in autonomous vehicles in Pittsburgh on September 14, 2016. The autonomous vehicles provide riders with point-to-point service with a driving monitor behind the wheel and a technician aboard.

Engineers from across many disciplines have played an important role in developing public transportation throughout the history of Pittsburgh. The significant innovations from inclined planes to people-movers and autonomous vehicle technology would not have taken place without a strong history of Pittsburgh supporting its engineers and Pittsburgh's engineers supporting the city.

AIRPORTS AND AVIATION

Connection to the World

By Patrick Mulvihill, DEd

The story of the pioneering days of aviation would be incomplete if the contributions of the early airfields, aircraft and personalities that emerged from Western Pennsylvania were excluded. Although the larger narrative of powered, heavier-than-air flight deserves to include notable names such as Wright, Curtiss, Lindbergh and Earhart woven into the narrative of this great story, you will also find the names of Pierpont-Langley, Mayer, Rodgers, Bettis and Bell.

The region of Western Pennsylvania, specifically Pittsburgh and its surrounding communities, played an important role in establishing the network of waypoints and airways for aircraft navigating the highway in the sky. It is important to understand that this collection is certainly by no means complete. These airfields and personalities were selected for inclusion because their stories, all of which are connected, provided the infrastructure from which an emerging transportation network would emerge.

The Emergence of Aviation in Western Pennsylvania

Hanging quietly in Wesley H. Posvar Hall on the campus of the University of Pittsburgh is Samuel Pierpont Langley's Aerodrome no. 6. During the 1890s, while serving as the director of the Allegheny Observatory and professor of physics at what would later become the University of Pittsburgh, Langley contributed a significant level of scholarly knowledge to the emerging field of powered, heavier-than-air flight. Although his efforts to create the first manned flying machine fell short, his legacy among aviation pioneers certainly placed Western Pennsylvania on the map in the early days of powered flight.

Less than ten years later, the Wright brothers became the first to successfully achieve manned powered flight in December 1903. Following in their footsteps, Glenn H. Curtiss flew his own "June Bug" aeroplane in 1908. Although many in Western Pennsylvania had not come to fully understand the idea of a flying machine, the arrival of Glenn Curtiss would soon bring about great change to the landscape of the region.

In 1909, real estate broker W.L. Smith conceived of an idea that would be supported by the creation of the Aero Club of Pittsburgh. The Aero Club, located on Brunot's Island on the Ohio River, would host a one-day exhibition featuring Glenn Curtiss and his team of demonstration pilots. The event, held in August 1910, would be the first time many Pittsburghers would see an aeroplane in flight. Although there are varying accounts within newspapers from the region, it is believed that Curtiss made three successful flights during his time in Pittsburgh. One flight followed a track around Brunot's Island, over the North Shore of the Ohio River, across the smokestacks located within the mills nearby, above Western Penitentiary toward McKees Rocks and then returned over the mills again as he returned to Brunot's Island to land.

These early airfields did not often require any infrastructure—just an open field. Therefore, they did not have much need for civil engineers. However, through the work of the early aviation pioneers, the aviation industry evolved to become critical to the fast, efficient transport of people and goods.

This necessity eventually challenged engineers to design supporting infrastructure and complex airports that allowed for the efficient movement of passengers, planes and cargo through the development of advanced road and rail infrastructure to connect passengers to their final destinations.

STEPPINGSTONES: EARLY AIRFIELDS AND AVIATION PIONEERS

It is believed that more than thirty thousand spectators made their way to Brunot's Island to meet and observe, with great curiosity, Glenn Curtiss and his flying machine. Although it may not have been known at the time, the race to achieve manned powered flight set in motion an entrepreneurial desire within the region to contribute, even if in a small way, to the future of aviation. What emerged from the spectators that day on Brunot's Island would be a tightly woven series of airfields, events and influential personalities that would shape not only the earliest footprints in our region but also the vision that shapes the Greater Pittsburgh International Airport today. The story begins in a small town south of Pittsburgh, Pennsylvania.

Mayer Air Field (1919–circa 1950)

With the Great War nearing an end, many of the advances in aviation were beginning to find their way back to the United States. It was not long before visions of a connected transportation system in the sky began to take shape. Mayer Field, located in Bridgeville, Pennsylvania, was one of the region's earliest airfields that developed from a desire to be a part of this burgeoning industry.

Established in 1919, Mayer Air Field was inspired by the vision of Casper P. Mayer. While serving as the mayor of Bridgeville, Mayer broadened his interests from an already successful paving and brick company to pursue the development of the Mayer Aircraft Corporation. Mayer intended for his fleet of aircraft to operate out of the new airfield, with service between Pittsburgh, New York and other Atlantic coast destinations.

In support of this vision, Mayer secured roughly sixty acres and quickly constructed two unpaved runways along with several small hangars. The timing of this new company and construction of Mayer Field could not have been better. With the U.S. Postal Service beginning airmail service roughly a year earlier in 1918, the airfield was selected as the original airmail delivery site for the Pittsburgh area.

Although the Curtiss JN-4 Jenny Biplane gained famed during the war and its role in launching airmail service, several other popular biplanes could be spotted at Mayer Field with regularity. The first, the Laird Swallow, designed and built by the Swallow Airplane Manufacturing

Company, was used by Mayer Aircraft Corporation for flight lessons. Mayer also quickly secured rights to market the Ryan B-1 Brougham high wing monoplane shortly after Charles Lindbergh flew solo across the Atlantic to Paris, France. The first of these aircraft to arrive was aptly named the "Pride of Pittsburgh."

Mayer Field existed until about the mid-1950s, when more modern development began to diminish its presence within Bridgeville. As of today, the previous site of Mayer Field can be located by traveling to the intersection of Route 50 and Mayer Road where the Great Southern Shopping Center currently resides.

Rodgers Air Field (1924–circa 1934)

In about 1922, the same Pittsburgh Aero Club that developed the land on Brunot's Island negotiated a deal that transferred ownership of roughly forty-two acres of land at the current site of the Fox Chapel Area High School. Once developed, the field came to be known as Rodgers Field, after Calbraith Rodgers, and was used from 1923 through about 1934. Rodgers was a larger-than-life aviator from southwestern Pennsylvania. Although he was known for being the great-grandson of Oliver Perry, whose heroics won the Battle of Lake Erie in the War of 1812, Calbraith Rodgers would eventually distinguish himself by making the first transcontinental flight in 1911.

Rodgers Field did host its own share of notable aviators, some more well known than others. It is believed that in early 1911, John Kowalsky of Verona, Pennsylvania, was one of the first locals to successfully build as well as fly his experimental aircraft on the same land that would eventually become Rodgers Field.

Amelia Earhart also touched down at this famed airport; during her touchdown and rollout, however, she encountered what many Pittsburghers experience throughout the winter months as they travel the roadways: a pothole. As the story goes, Amelia decided to take some time off after the completion of her book and had just taken off after refueling in Bellefonte, Pennsylvania. As she approached the Pittsburgh area, she experienced a few mechanical issues that required her to land. Although she made a smooth landing on the grassy runway at Rodgers Field, the aircraft struck a concealed ditch, which caused her gear to collapse and nose over. It is believed that members of the Pittsburgh Aero Club helped repair the plane, allowing Amelia to continue onward across the country after a short stay in Pittsburgh.

In fact, the Earharts are quite connected to the region. In addition to several stops at local airfields by Amelia, her father attended Thiel College in Greenville, Pennsylvania. The college has undertaken significant efforts to preserve this legacy, including a roadway named Amelia Earhart Drive on the campus.

Today, the site of Rodgers Field is still somewhat distinguishable in aerial photos. It is primarily located just north of the Fox Chapel High School in a triangular area between the Fox Chapel Field Club and Powers Run Road. In fact, as of this publication, there remains a residential street in the area named Rodgers Drive.

McKeesport Air Field/Bettis Field (1924–circa 1949)

Clifford Ball, owner of the Diamond Motor Sales Company in McKeesport, Pennsylvania, was often intrigued by the aeroplanes flying around the skies above his dealership. The aircraft were departing and returning to a field owned by Harry Neel, a local farmer. D. Barr Peat, a friend of Neel's, convinced Neel to allow them to begin using the land north of Dravosburg, Pennsylvania, in 1924 for aerial sightseeing services. Very quickly, Ball and Peat became business partners with a singular vision: building an airfield.

Ball and Peat began lobbying local congressman M. Clyde Kelly about further development of the aviation industry in Pittsburgh. Through a combination of their own efforts and help from the congressman, Ball and Peat raised enough funds to purchase the land from Harry Neel. With a $35,000 investment, they purchased close to forty acres around the original field with the hopes of developing a larger airfield. It was during this period of development in 1925 that several hangars and a machine shop emerged along with a new name, the McKeesport Air Field. The operation flourished, and in short time, the airfield was not only offering plane rides and flight instruction but also hosting airshows for curious spectators from around the region.

In 1918, Ball and Peat leveraged a significant industry shift that occurred as a result of the Kelly Act. No longer would the federal government be the sole proprietors of shipping mail and parcels by air. The Kelly Act required the government to contract with commercial carriers to provide this service. Pittsburgh postmaster George W. Gosser designated Pittsburgh McKeesport

Airfield as the best local field for receiving and shipping mail. As a result of this announcement, Ball and Peat began to prepare their bid for the airmail route and founded the Skyline Transport Company to carry both passengers and airmail to and from their airfield.

After a review of the bid and visit to the airfield, Ball and Peat were awarded the contract. The new Pittsburgh-Cleveland airmail route was inaugurated on April 21, 1927. Flying the route for the Skyline Transport Company that day were three aircraft appropriately named *Miss Youngstown*, *Miss Pittsburgh* and *Miss McKeesport*. Today, *Miss Pittsburgh* hangs proudly in the Pittsburgh International Airport and greets millions of passengers annually as they proceed in and out of the landside terminal security checkpoint.

The McKeesport Airfield was eventually renamed in 1926 to Bettis Field after Lieutenant Cyrus Bettis. Aside from being one of the earliest airfields in the region, Bettis Airfield is the original location of one of the first aeronautic schools to be approved by the Civil Aeronautics Authority (later renamed Federal Aviation Administration). Originally incorporated as the Curtiss-Wright Flight Services, Glenn Curtiss and Orville Wright offered both flight training and aircraft sales and service. In 1929, August Becker, then manager for the Curtiss-Wright Corporation, which leased the operation at Bettis Airfield, purchased the school and its facilities. At that time, the name of the operation was changed to the Pittsburgh Institute of Aeronautics.

Bettis Field also hosted a list of notable aircraft and aviators throughout its history. Probably the most famous of these was the *Spirit of St. Louis*, flown by Charles Lindbergh. Lindbergh arrived at Bettis Field around 2:00 p.m. on August 3, 1927, and was greeted by thousands of Pittsburghers. It was written that when Lindbergh returned to the airfield the next day to continue his tour of America, even more people gathered to wish him well as he departed westward.

In 1932, Allegheny County Airport, located about one mile from Bettis Airfield, officially opened for business. As it was the largest airport in the region at the time, many commercial and transport operations left Bettis Airfield for the county airport, leaving only a handful of small private planes on the field. The Pittsburgh Institute of Aeronautics did acquire and use the site in the early 1930s to train aircraft and engine mechanics for future careers in both civil and military aviation.

In early 1949, it is believed that Curtiss-Wright sold Bettis Airfield to Westinghouse Electric Company. Westinghouse eventually closed the airfield and redeveloped the land to support the Bettis Laboratory, which developed nuclear propulsion technology for submarines and aircraft carriers. The current site of Bettis Field is located north of the intersection of Pittsburgh McKeesport Boulevard and Bettis Road, one mile east of the Allegheny County Airport.

Longview Flying Club (1924)

While working as a mechanic and car salesman from Scottdale, Pennsylvania, Charles Carroll developed an interest in aviation. He established a flying club in a field near Latrobe, Pennsylvania, that would eventually evolve into Arnold Palmer Regional Airport. As with many of these early aviation pioneers, Carroll's team, which became known as the "Longview Boys," supported its flying club by performing stunts at local airshows. In just under two years, the Longview Flying Field had one of the highest numbers of aircraft on its field in Pennsylvania and was ranked fourth in number of flights and passengers as well.

This growth didn't go unnoticed. Shortly after the field was renamed the J.D. Hill Airport after James DeWitt in 1928, Saint Vincent College began what is believed to be the world's first aviation program. The relationship was developed out of the idea that the airplane, an emerging technology, would allow the college's missionaries to reach parts of the world once thought hard to reach. Although the relationship between Carroll's operation and Saint Vincent did not fully bloom, the college did purchase an aircraft to move the vision forward. Unfortunately, the timing of these events occurred too close to the beginning of the Great Depression to allow either opportunity to really develop.

Although the relationship did not come to fruition in the early 1930s, the late 1930s proved to be better timing for both Carroll and Saint Vincent. With World War II starting to heat up, along with a growing need for pilots to support the United States military, cadets were enrolled in a newly created ground school at Saint Vincent College and conducted flight training at the renamed Latrobe Airport next to campus.

While the relationship between Carroll and the college was developing, a local dentist, Dr. Lytle Adams, had perfected a nonstop airmail pickup system that would allow airmail delivery to rural and isolated communities. In May 1939, All-American Aviation integrated this system at Latrobe Airport, thus establishing what is believed to be the world's first scheduled airmail pickup. Eventually, in 1949, All-American Aviation began a series of transitions that would change the name from All-American to Allegheny Airlines and, finally, to US Airways.

Since 1940, Latrobe Airport has continued to experience significant growth and investment. The airport was renamed the Arnold Palmer Regional Airport after the local golf icon in September 1999.

WELCOMING MODERN AIRFIELDS

It is believed that members of the original Pittsburgh Aero Club, which first brought Glenn Curtiss to the region with his flying machines, also played a role in selecting and developing the land slated for both the Allegheny and Greater Pittsburgh Airports.

Allegheny County Airport (1931)

Less than one mile from Bettis Airfield and built on a former steel industry slag dump, Stanley Roush, the architect for City of Pittsburgh in the 1920s and 1930s and then the County of Allegheny, led the construction of the main terminal for the Allegheny County Airport in West Mifflin, Pennsylvania. In addition to the engineering that went into building the terminal, hangars, runways and more, the county built Saw Mill Run Boulevard and Lebanon Church Road to connect Pittsburgh to the airport after a bond issued in 1928.

When it was dedicated on September 11, 1931, the new airport encompassed roughly 432 acres and was considered to be the third-largest airport in the country. It was also believed to have, at the time, the largest amount of runway paving in the world with more than fifty combined miles of paved surface.

As one of the highest points within Allegheny County at an elevation of 1,252 feet above mean sea level, the airport's acreage and location are certainly visible to aircraft traveling through the region. In fact, in addition to his visit in 1927, Charles Lindbergh made two additional unexpected stops at Allegheny County Airport in 1930 and 1933 due to mechanical issues with his aircraft.

Clifford Ball, whose legacy of service to aviation in the region included the opening of Bettis Field, had some early influence within the county airport project. The original Clifford Ball Airline, which operated out of Bettis Airfield, eventually became Pennsylvania Airlines in the early 1930s. Around that same time, Central Airlines was formed by a group that had originally formed Pittsburgh Airlines in 1929. Of historical importance, Central Airlines is noted for hiring the first female commercial pilot, Helen Richey, in the United States. Richey was a Pittsburgh native, having been born and raised in the McKeesport area.

The competition between Pennsylvania Airlines and Central Airlines did significantly affect the commercial tenants of the new Allegheny County Airport. Because of a severe price war between the two airlines, the economic conditions that resulted forced the two airlines to merge in November 1936 to remain solvent. This resulted in the newly created Pennsylvania Central Airlines, based at the new county airport. Although the airline continued to expand its routes, by 1941 PCA had opted to relocate its headquarters to the newer Washington National Airport in Arlington, Virginia. Although Pennsylvania Central Airlines eventually changed its name to Capital Airlines, it did retain Allegheny County Airport as a stop on the Chicago–New York route so that it could continue to compete with railroad service between these two destinations.

Although the county airport continued to serve as the primary commercial airport for the region for some time, the beginning of World War II set into motion a series of events that would shift commercial airlines from the Allegheny County Airport to the significantly larger Greater Pittsburgh Airport in 1952.

Greater Pittsburgh Airport (1952)

Before World War II, Moon Township was primarily an agricultural area. One of the more significant landowners in the area, John Bell of Carnegie, Pennsylvania, had established a 1,900-acre commercial dairy farm on his land. Eventually, Bell sold his successful operation to Rieck's Dairy, which nearly doubled the size of the operation in later years.

By the 1940s, it had become apparent that the United States was becoming more involved in World War II. The Works Progress Administration (WPA), developed to help employ those affected by the Great Depression, identified the need to protect the industrial resources of the region. More specifically, it was seeking military presence to serve as a deterrent, training base and en route facility for military aircraft. Alongside planners from the region, the

WPA identified the vast undeveloped agricultural land in Moon Township as a primary site for development. Eventually, the WPA purchased the Bell Farm acreage and broke ground for the construction of runways.

In 1944, Allegheny County officials decided to expand the original military field to include commercial air service. The decision to replace Allegheny County Airport became a reality on July 18, 1946, when ground was broken for the expansion. That same year, ground was broken on the Penn Lincoln Parkway (in Churchill, Pennsylvania). The original parkway was completed in 1960 with the opening of the Fort Pitt Tunnel, providing a high-speed connection from Pittsburgh to its airport for the first time. With the new terminal building complete, the Greater Pittsburgh Airport opened on May 31, 1952, as one of the largest airports in the United States. During its first year of operation, more than 1.4 million passengers traveled through the airport.

Although the airport would undergo numerous expansions to support growth within the aviation industry, by the early 1980s, the main terminal was quickly becoming outdated and overcrowded. Just as the city of Pittsburgh transformed itself from an economy based on steel manufacturing to an emerging international economy rooted within technology and healthcare, the Greater Pittsburgh Airport would have to undertake a purposeful and strategic evolution.

Through the leadership of the Allegheny Country Airport Authority and visionaries from around the region, a new midfield terminal introduced a new vision for air travel within the region and beyond. The airport and supporting infrastructure formed one of the largest public works programs of the 1990s, engaging both architects and a wide range engineering disciplines.

On October 1, 1992, the newly developed Pittsburgh International Airport was opened with the intention of becoming a gateway to international commerce. The county's director of aviation was Scott O'Donnell, and the director of capital projects was John F. Graham Jr. For his work on the airport, Mr. Graham was awarded the Distinguished Civil Engineer Award from the Pittsburgh Section of ASCE in 1992 and named an honorary member of ASCE in 2006, the society's highest honor. Michael Baker Jr. Inc. was the airport's project engineer, later relocating its corporate headquarters to the site of the Greater Pittsburgh Airport's terminal.

The new vision, terminal and name were just one facet of the multidimensional plan created by leadership within the region. In support of this bold endeavor, the Pennsylvania Department of Transportation also led the development and construction of the Southern Expressway to support the new airport and the region's growing economy. In terms of engineering, the new airport's passenger building was intended to be revolutionary. Early airports had just a terminal building and an apron. With the advent of powerful jet engines and significantly greater numbers of airplanes, airport designers experimented with different ways of creating structures that would be the most efficient passenger buildings. Emerging mid-century airports, like Greater Pittsburgh, tended to be finger-pier concepts, in which linear concourses would extend from a terminal building.

While most convenient for originating and departing passengers, this design was less efficient for aircraft operations. In the 1960s, airport planners looked at ways of creating aircraft movement–focused designs, such as small satellite concourses away from the terminal or transporter concepts in which vehicles such as buses would transport passengers from the terminal to the plane. Later in the 1960s, designers experimented with linear terminals with decentralized operations, with the roadway infrastructure and parking on the long side of a terminal building and gates on the other. This design is most convenient for originating and departing passengers but requires many security checkpoints, long buildings and inconvenient connections. Therefore, major airports began to move to midfield designs, with long concourses in the middle of the airfield, separate from the passenger terminals. While less convenient for origin and destination passengers, this allowed for easy connections and simple airfield movements.

Until Pittsburgh International, all of these designs were arranged in linear configurations. Pittsburgh International pioneered the X-shaped midfield to optimize airfield movements and reduce passenger connections as much as possible. When this design opened, it met the needs of Pittsburgh as a connecting hub. Now that Pittsburgh just serves the needs of local passengers, it is an overbuilt complex with high maintenance costs.

Just as the region's infrastructure continues to evolve strategically to meet current and future demand, Pittsburgh International Airport in 2017 announced an ambitious plan to reposition the airport for the future. The forward-looking plan includes extensive renovation and merging of the terminals to leverage the paradigm shift away from being a major airline hub to position the airport focus on passengers within the region.

Supporting the development of Pittsburgh International is the Southern Beltway. As of this publication, construction has begun to connect the airport with Interstate 79 and will eventually connect to Interstate 376 in Monroeville. The high-growth areas in the metro region are generally along the airport corridor, both near the airport and in Washington and Butler Counties. The newly redesigned airport will require substantial civil engineering, both in the new building addition and in the supporting roadway infrastructure. This illuminates the challenge of balancing the needs of the airlines with the needs of support infrastructure. The midfield project was designed to be the world's most efficient connecting hub at the time when the older Greater Pittsburgh Airport served the connection market. Airports built too small have faced many challenges or needed to be replaced entirely, such as Pittsburgh's airports of the past. However, Pittsburgh's current airport was likely built too large for industry consolidation and high jet fuel prices.

It is also relevant to consider transportation to and from an airport. The wide median of the Southern Expressway was specifically designed to accommodate rail transit. Today, Pittsburgh is one of the few airports of its size that is not connected to a greater fixed guideway transit system. However, it was also one of the first to designate an area for ride sharing. It will be interesting to see how the autonomous vehicle revolution and potential new market entrants like the hyperloop will both connect to airports and affect the industry in the future.

THE FUTURE

As we continue to scan the horizon, always looking toward the future, the region's great optimism is balanced with pragmatic uncertainty. Airports such as the Pittsburgh International Airport and local regional airports that support commercial and private air travel will continue to respond and position themselves according to ever-changing market conditions.

The smaller airfields that support general aviation will likely continue to face further uncertainty. Market and industry conditions will force local municipalities and airport managers to make the difficult decisions related to the resources that are required to keep these airfields operational. As exemplified by the region's early pioneers, the general aviation community will need to move forward with purposeful steps, ensuring that its response stabilizes the operating environment for the foreseeable future.

DRINKING WATER

Civil Engineering Protecting Life

By Gregory Scott, PE, and Rachel Rampa

Drinking water is essential for human life. From mankind's earliest days, humans have settled where water was available, but human habitation brings with it the problem of disposing of human-generated waste and garbage. As the density of habitation grows, so do the occurrences of waterborne illness. Additionally, droughts can reduce or eliminate a water supply, making a location unsustainable. In mankind's earliest days, these issues did not present much of a problem since the population migrated with food sources and water supplies and would only occupy a location with available water for a short period of time. With the rise of agrarian societies, mankind became more settled and required water for livestock and irrigation of crops, in addition to human consumption. Towns and cities arose around abundant water supplies such as rivers and lakes, which also aided in waterborne transportation and waste disposal.

The sub-discipline of civil engineering that is involved in the treatment and distribution of drinking water supplies has been called "sanitation engineering" and, more recently, "environmental engineering" or "water resource engineering." All these terms touch on other aspects of engineering such as handling of solid waste, protecting and restoring wetlands and measuring and controlling rivers and streams. For the purpose of this chapter, the term "drinking water engineering" will be used to reference the work civil engineers perform that focuses strictly on drinking water supplies.

Drinking water engineers are tasked with designing and maintaining water systems that draw raw, untreated water from a source; remove potentially harmful and bad-tasting organic and inorganic contaminants; and transport the water to locations for storage and ultimately distribution to locations for purposes as widely variable as consumption, fire protection, industrial use and agriculture.

Humans were first known to build water systems as early as Crete's wooden water pipes in 2000 BC. The Roman empire was renowned for its massive aqueducts and water tunnels. In 1664, the king of France had twenty-five kilometers of cast-iron pipe installed to supply water to the Palace of Versailles. In Pennsylvania, the earliest water systems consisted of bored-out logs with leaded joints, which were soon replaced with cast-iron pipes. In 1829, the first sand filter was constructed in London at the Chelsea Waterworks, marking the beginning of water treatment.

As of 2018, there are more than ten thousand public and private drinking water systems in Pennsylvania, and more than 1 million people in the state still rely on private wells for their water supply. It is useful to focus on the history of one system as representative of the history of the development of Western Pennsylvania's drinking water systems. This chapter will focus on the history of the drinking water system for the city of Pittsburgh.

EARLY YEARS AND INCORPORATION

Pittsburgh was organized as a borough in 1794 and incorporated as a city in 1816. Before 1800, the local inhabitants relied primarily on river water for all household purposes, since there were only a few accessible springs, such as the spring that existed at the foot of Grant's Hill. People complained that much of the spring water tasted of sulfur, and wells were too hard to dig. Outsiders teased the townspeople with the claim that they stirred up the mud in the bottom of the water bucket before they took a drink. However, as the population continued to grow, private wells started to increase in number. Being private, their owners were reluctant to permit them to be used by the public.

The first documented effort to establish a public water system in Pittsburgh occurred in 1802, when the municipality had about 1,600 persons. A public system was needed not just for sanitary reasons but because of the constantly increasing danger of fire. At that time, the burgesses of the Borough of

Pittsburgh passed an ordinance authorizing construction of four forty-seven-foot-deep, stone-lined public wells with pumps on Market Street. This project was actually the beginning of the public water supply in Pittsburgh. The system cost $525, which was paid by placing a tax on residents.

As time passed, the system of public and private wells became inadequate to satisfy the needs of the growing population. By 1820, the water problem had become acute. Lines of people formed in the morning before public and private wells, and every morning and evening, women and children could be seen making their way to the rivers. Many households kept tanks in their backyards that were filled by "water carters," old men using barrels on carts. The going rate for this water was three cents per tubful or six cents per barrel. These water carters, whose livelihood was at stake, were the most vocal opposition to the public's demand to construct a citywide water system. In 1824, public outcry won out, and an ordinance was passed for the construction of waterworks.

THE FIRST PUMPING STATIONS: KEEPING PACE WITH A GROWING CITY

Because of the growing population and the increasing need for water, the city constructed a pumped water system utilizing Allegheny River water and put it into service in 1828. The river pumping station was located at the foot of Cecil Alley on the Allegheny River (Cecil Alley and Duquesne Way), and a 1-million-gallon reservoir was constructed at the corner of Fifth and Grant (the present site of the Allegheny County Courthouse). The average daily pumping rate of this original piped system during the first three years was 40,000 gallons of water per day.

The small system at Cecil Alley was replaced in 1844 with an expanded system consisting of a larger pumping station at Eleventh and Etna Streets, as well as a larger reservoir with a capacity of 7.5 million gallons on Quarry Hill. Part of the reason for the upgrade was to increase the capacity of the supply, as by this time, the city had expanded to the Hill District east of Grant Street. Additionally, there were complaints about the amount of river water contamination near the intake of the Cecil Alley Pumping Station, necessitating the upstream relocation of the intake. Furthermore, the first of three public works project aimed at cutting away at Grant's Hill had removed 10 feet and left the original reservoir high in the air (7 more feet were removed in 1849, and the hill was completely leveled by removing up to 16.3 more feet in 1912).

The new pumping station at Eleventh and Etna Street was equipped with two steam-driven pumps known as "Samson" and "Hercules" that had a combined capacity of 9 MGD (million gallons per day). These pumps functioned almost continuously until 1884, a period of forty years. The cost of city water at this time was relatively cheap, with householders paying $3 to $10 per year, hotels $20 to $40 and factories $15 to $150 for water.

In 1848, the continued expansion of the city to the eastern hill section forced the building of an additional reservoir (2.7 million gallons) on Bedford Avenue, as well as a small pumping station to pump to it. The town continued to grow, and in 1867, fourteen wards were annexed to the original city. This sudden addition of thirty-five thousand people brought about a general shortage of the water supply. Additional pumping units were installed, and a temporary pumping station was constructed at Forty-Fifth Street and the Allegheny River in 1870. This station, with a capacity of less than 1 MGD, pumped river water directly into the distribution system.

LATE 1800S: THE HIGHLAND PARK RESERVOIRS

By 1878, the population of Pittsburgh had increased to 106,000 people, and daily water pumping rate had risen to more than 15 MGD. In 1879, a 125-million-gallon reservoir, which is still in use and called Highland No. 1, was put into service at the top of Highland Avenue, and a river water pumping station called the Brilliant Pumping Station was erected on the river upstream of Negley Run to feed it. Another low-service reservoir was constructed at the same time on Brilliant Hill. However, although practically completed, it was never actually used as part of the drinking water system but was rather converted into a lake known today as Carnegie Lake within Highland Park. An additional reservoir, Herron Hill Reservoir, and a dedicated pumping station were added in 1880.

Small tanks and pump stations were built to serve the Garfield and Lincoln sections of the city in the early 1890s. From 1897 to 1903, a 126-million-gallon lower reservoir, which is also still in use and called Highland No. 2, was constructed in Highland Park to serve the low-lying sections of the city along the Allegheny and Monongahela Rivers. This reservoir performed the functions originally intended for the abandoned Brilliant Hill Reservoir. Two major additions were made to the water system with the consolidation of the city of Pittsburgh and the city of Allegheny (now called the North Side of Pittsburgh) in 1907, as well as the purchase of the privately owned Monongahela Water System (now called the South Side of Pittsburgh) in 1908. The three waterworks were merged into a single greater city-owned waterworks.

NEW CHALLENGES: WATERBORNE ILLNESS IN PITTSBURGH

Throughout the nineteenth century, river water was pumped to homes and businesses with no treatment other than the crude settling of suspended solids that occurred in the holding reservoirs. This was typical of public water supplies throughout the United States and Europe at that time. By the end of the nineteenth century, contamination of the Allegheny River had reached the point that there was an obvious need for some type of purification. Furthermore, it had become apparent that, as was the case in other cities, waterborne disease was also a problem in Pittsburgh. While the germ theory of disease was first proposed by Italian physician Girolamo Fracastoro in 1564, it was an accepted belief that diseases such as cholera, typhoid fever and the plague were spread by noxious air. This miasma theory was the accepted norm until the mid-nineteenth century, when it was finally documented that impure drinking water could negatively affect health. In 1849, the British physician John Snow published *On the Mode of Communication of Cholera*, which proposed that this particular disease was waterborne. He was able to clearly demonstrate his theory in 1854, when another cholera epidemic occurred in London's Soho district. His famous study, released in 1855, correctly concluded that the outbreak was caused by a water supply that had been founded with human waste from a nearby cesspit. For the first time, waterborne pollution was shown to be a cause of illness.

Like London, Pittsburgh in the 1800s experienced a number of outbreaks of cholera. While it is probable that at least some cholera originated with the drinking water, it was the link between untreated water and typhoid fever that was clearly evident in Pittsburgh. In the late 1800s and early 1900s, there were many cases of typhoid fever in Pittsburgh, a number resulting in many deaths. It was widely believed that these outbreaks were associated with untreated drinking water, and the highly visible contamination of the Allegheny River prompted residents and officials in the mid-1890s to press for the institution of a water purification system.

In 1896, the City of Pittsburgh authorized the appointment of a Filtration Commission to "thoroughly investigate the character of the present water supply of the city of Pittsburgh in its relation to public health" and recommend treatment options to the city council "for the best public interest in this matter." In 1899, the Filtration Commission issued its report documenting that a total of 2,245 deaths from typhoid fever occurred over the prior decade, with no fewer than 4 deaths per month. During the same period, Boston had 1,589 deaths and New York City had 3,522 deaths from typhoid fever. Both of these cites had far larger populations than Pittsburgh, however, so the deaths per year per 100,000 inhabitants produced the figures of 31.9 in Boston, 21.0 in New York City and 81.6 in Pittsburgh. The 1899 report spurred Pittsburgh leaders into action, but until water treatment was made available, disease continued to plague the population. For example, in 1907, with a combined total population of 535,330 people in Pittsburgh and Allegheny City, there were 5,652 cases of typhoid fever—648 of those cases proved fatal.

NEW SOLUTIONS: FILTRATION AND PURIFICATION

In 1905, after years of intense argument concerning the design of the plant, construction began on a slow-sand filtration plant at the site of the present treatment plant on the Allegheny River near Aspinwall. By October 1908, the water supply of peninsular Pittsburgh was being filtered. In 1909 and in 1914, the South Side and the North Side, respectively, began receiving filtered water.

The original plant included a river pumping station, the still existing Ross Station, a receiving basin, two sedimentation basins, forty-six covered slow-sand filters and an underground filtered water basin or clearwell. In 1912–13, ten more filters were added to the plant to meet the requirements of the North Side, and a contact baffle (or Reisler) pre-filtration system was installed to enhance removal of suspended solids. Chlorine began being widely used for disinfection of water supplies at that time and was included in the City of Pittsburgh's treatment scheme by 1911. The benefits of filtration and chlorination of the water supply were readily apparent. By 1911 and subsequent years, the annual number of cases of typhoid fever had dropped to fewer than five hundred and the number of typhoid fever deaths to fewer than one hundred.

THREE RIVERS, THREE SYSTEMS: CONSOLIDATION AND EXPANSION

With the consolidation of the Pittsburgh, Allegheny and Monongahela Water Companies in 1908, the city faced the problem of merging three water systems and extending its filtered water service to a city divided by rivers. To serve the North Side, Aspinwall Pump Station was built at the filtration plant from 1911 to 1914 and began delivering filtered water to the North Side. Lanpher Reservoir was constructed in Shaler Township simultaneously to store filtered water from the Aspinwall Pump Station. This reservoir has a capacity of 155 million gallons and sits at an elevation identical to that of Highland No. 2.

The low-lying portions of the South Side were fed directly from Highland Reservoir No. 2. The old Monongahela Water Company's South Twenty-Ninth Street Station was relieved of this function and took over the job of pumping water to the Allentown tanks. In 1912, Mission Street Pumping Station (in the South Side) was placed into service and replaced the antiquated South Twenty-Ninth Street Station, which was retired. The Garfield Pumping Station and tanks were eliminated in 1912 in favor of the Herron Hill Reservoir. Then, in the late 1920s, two additional reservoirs, McNaugher and Brashear, were constructed in the high district of the North Side to replace the older Montgomery, Lafayette and Green Tree tanks.

CHEMISTRY AND MODERNITY

From the initiation of filtration in 1907 until the 1950s, there was no further chemical treatment performed on the water—only the addition of chlorine for disinfection and soda ash, during periods of acid river water, to reduce the water prior to filtration. However, by the mid-1950s, the slow-sand filters had aged and become less effective. Treatment of the drinking water source by the addition of aluminum sulfate, commonly called alum, was then introduced to enhance removal of suspended solids, but that addition could still not keep up with the demand. The requirement to continue to provide satisfactory water pointed to a need for a modern and rapid sand filtration plant.

This upgrade to the system was undertaken in two stages. The first stage involved the construction of a clarifier pretreatment system to treat the water before it reached the slow-sand filters. This structure was constructed in 1962 just west of Ross Pumping Station and, for the first time, provided complete chemical treatment for removal of iron, manganese, tastes, odors and colors from the water. The second stage involved replacement of the outmoded slow-sand filters in 1969 with a dual-media, rapid-sand filtration system.

The modern-day Pittsburgh Water and Sewer Authority (PWSA), created in 1984, absorbed the City of Pittsburgh's water department in 1995 and became the sole proprietor of the sewer system in 1999. At its inception, the primary function of PWSA was to oversee a $200 million capital improvement program designed to refurbish the infrastructure of the entire water system. This budget included the water treatment plant and distribution system. The program was to ensure that the water system met the rapidly expanding water quality requirements of the federal and state Safe Drinking Water Acts.

One of the major requirements PWSA worked vigorously to comply with was to cover all existing open finished water reservoirs or replace them with closed tanks. Currently, all of PWSA's reservoirs are covered except for the Highland Reservoir No. 1, which remains an open reservoir. At the time when PWSA was covering the reservoirs, the Highland Park community was against covering Highland Reservoir No. 1. For more than 122 years, Highland Reservoir No. 1 had been the focal point of Highland Park—a place where the public enjoyed walking and recreation. The community worked for many years with PWSA and the City of Pittsburgh and arrived at an alternative solution that pleased everyone and fulfilled all of the requirements of the state and federal Safe Drinking Water Acts. Instead of covering the reservoir, PWSA built a membrane filtration plant where the water from the reservoir would be filtered through banks of microfilters before being sent to customers. The testing proved that the water leaving the membrane filtration plant would meet or exceed all water quality regulations. Thus, the Highland Reservoir No. 1 Membrane Filtration Plant went online the summer of 2002 and has the capacity to produce 20 MGD of water.

Today, PWSA provides quality water and services to about eighty-three thousand customers throughout the city of Pittsburgh daily. PWSA's vision is to provide water and wastewater services that meet or exceed all regulations and customer expectations at the lowest possible cost. Currently, a goal that PWSA is striving toward is to market water to other communities outside the city of Pittsburgh service area. This is an activity intended to move PWSA into its third century of service.

In the future and with the help of civil engineers, it is anticipated that the system can apply some of its excess capacity to become a regional water supplier for the Greater Pittsburgh area. This goal is being realized slowly with the continuous provision of drinking water to Blawnox, Fox Chapel, Millvale, Reserve Township, portions of the Pennsylvania American Water System and intermittent provisions to a number of other neighboring communities.

WASTEWATER

Dealing with Water Pollution

By Uzair (Sam) Shamsi, PhD, PE

Wastewater engineering, a sub-discipline of civil engineering, involves conveyance and cleaning of wastewater (sewage) from residential, commercial, institutional and industrial customers. Wastewater collection and treatment is required for reasons of public health and safety to prevent discharge of untreated wastewater to water bodies and to minimize pollution of water bodies where treated wastewater is discharged. Civil engineers map out topographical and geographical features of land to determine the best means of wastewater collection. Civil engineers also study the flow rate (quantity) and characteristics (quality) of wastewater to design appropriate wastewater treatment plants. As such, civil engineers are responsible for planning, design, construction and sometimes operation of sewer systems and sewage treatment plants. This chapter presents a history of the Greater Pittsburgh region's wastewater collection and treatment system. The image here presents a timeline of Pittsburgh's regional wastewater history, which will be described in various sections of this chapter.

Early History

Water is life! Water is the most precious natural resource on the planet because humans, animals and plants cannot survive without it. According

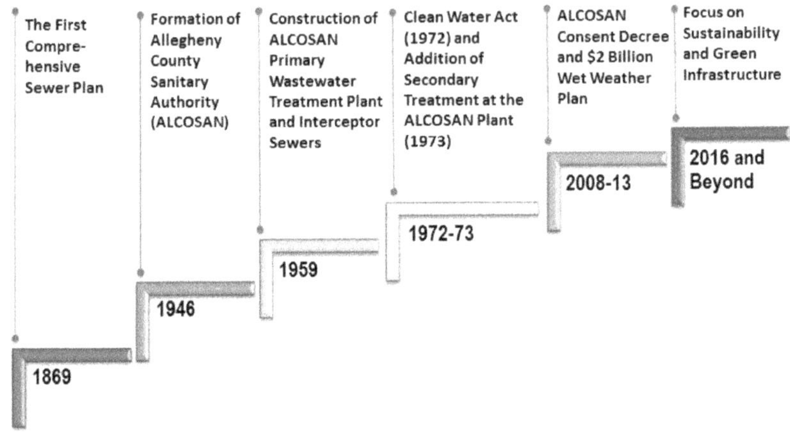

Greater Pittsburgh Wastewater History: A Journey through Time. A1 Applications, LLC.

to Pittsburgh Water and Sewer Authority (PWSA) website, the first documented effort to establish a public water system in Pittsburgh occurred in 1802, when the municipality had a population of about 1,600 persons. A history of Pittsburgh drinking water distribution and treatment systems is presented elsewhere.

From the early 1800s until around 1920, sewers in the city of Pittsburgh and surrounding communities were constructed to collect both wastewater and stormwater in a single pipe away from streets, businesses and homes and convey the combined flow directly to the rivers to reduce disease and flooding. Because the collection systems carried both stormwater and wastewater, they are called combined sewer systems. As early as 1930, the Pennsylvania Sanitary Water Board (PSWB) sought to compel Pittsburgh to submit a plan for a comprehensive sewage system. In December 1937, Pittsburgh mayor Cornelius Scully convened a meeting of Allegheny County municipalities to discuss possible collective action. The onset of World War II, however, delayed any action on sewage treatment. According to the 3 Rivers Wet Weather website, in June 1945, the PSWB issued the long-awaited orders to the City of Pittsburgh, 101 nearby municipalities and more than 90 Allegheny County industries to cease discharging untreated wastes into state waterways.

The image here shows an 1869 map of Allegheny City that accompanied the first comprehensive sewer plan report for the city (City of Allegheny,

1869). Allegheny City, now Pittsburgh's North Side, was a separate city from 1840 to 1907. Allegheny City was annexed by the City of Pittsburgh in 1907. The sewer master plan references private sewers already built, indicating that some city sewers predate the water system, which is unusual in most cities. The plan also proposed using the route of the Pennsylvania Canal, abandoned in 1864, for a sewer line. Evidence of this sewer was discovered when the canal locks were excavated for I-279. The Historic American Engineering Record report for the sewer is available in collections at the Library of Congress.

At the turn of the twentieth century, Pittsburgh embarked on its largest infrastructure improvement campaign, building sewers, water lines, roads and power lines that created the city we know today. And over the past fifty years, numerous changes have taken place such that Pittsburgh, once known as the "Smoky City," is now recognized as a center for advanced technology and research. A major part of these remarkable changes is the transformation of the area's rivers and streams from open sewers to waterways that are safe for recreation and commerce.

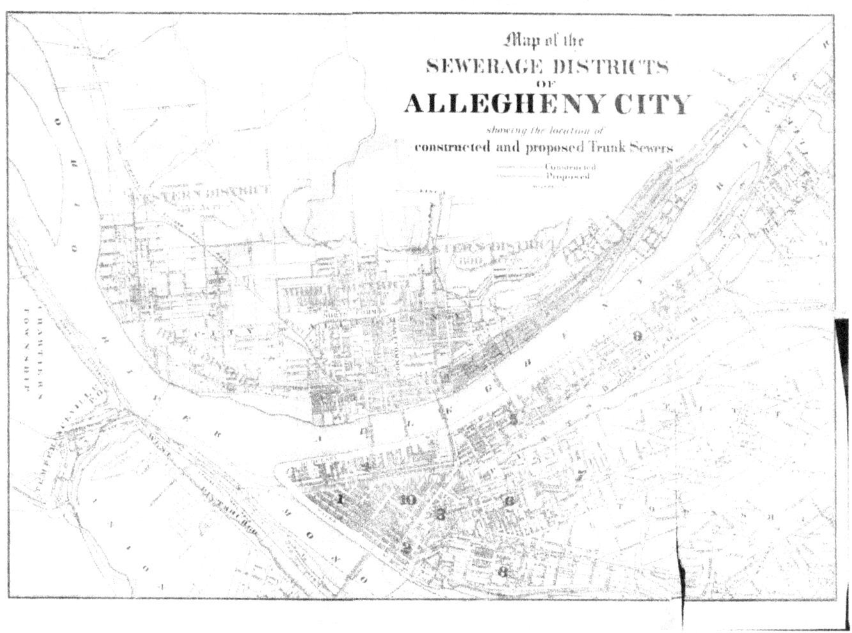

The First Comprehensive Sewer Plan Map of the Allegheny City, 1869. *Allegheny County.*

PWSA

The modern-day Pittsburgh Water and Sewer Authority (PWSA) was created in 1984. It merged with the Pittsburgh Water Department in 1995 and became the sole proprietor of the sewer system in 1999. PWSA owns and operates the wastewater collection system within the city of Pittsburgh, but it does not have a wastewater treatment plant. Wastewater treatment for the city and surrounding municipalities is provided by a regional wastewater utility called the Allegheny County Sanitary Authority (ALCOSAN).

ALCOSAN

In 1946, the Allegheny County Sanitary Authority (ALCOSAN) was formed to study the needs of the region and to develop and submit a treatment plan to Pennsylvania Sanitary Water Board. Along with the construction of a treatment plant, about ninety-two miles of very large pipes (some as large as twelve feet in diameter), called interceptors, were placed along the major rivers and streams in the 1950s. These interceptors were designed to receive wastewater from municipal sewer systems and "intercept," or redirect, the sewage to the ALCOSAN treatment plant, where, as required, it received primary treatment before reaching the waterways. Primary or physical/chemical treatment consists of temporarily holding the sewage in a sedimentation basin, where heavy solids can settle to the bottom while oil, grease and lighter solids float to the surface. The settled and floating materials are removed, and the remaining liquid may be discharged to receiving waters or subjected to secondary treatment. ALCOSAN's primary treatment plant became fully operative in 1959.

Located along the Ohio River on Pittsburgh's North Side, about three miles from the Point State Park, ALCOSAN as of 2017 provides wastewater treatment services to a population of 836,600 (2010 census) in eighty-three municipalities, including the city of Pittsburgh. ALCOSAN's fifty-nine-acre Woods Run treatment plant, one of the largest regional wastewater treatment facilities in the Ohio River Valley, processes up to 250 million gallons of wastewater daily. The map in the image here shows the ALCOSAN wastewater treatment plant location and service area boundary.

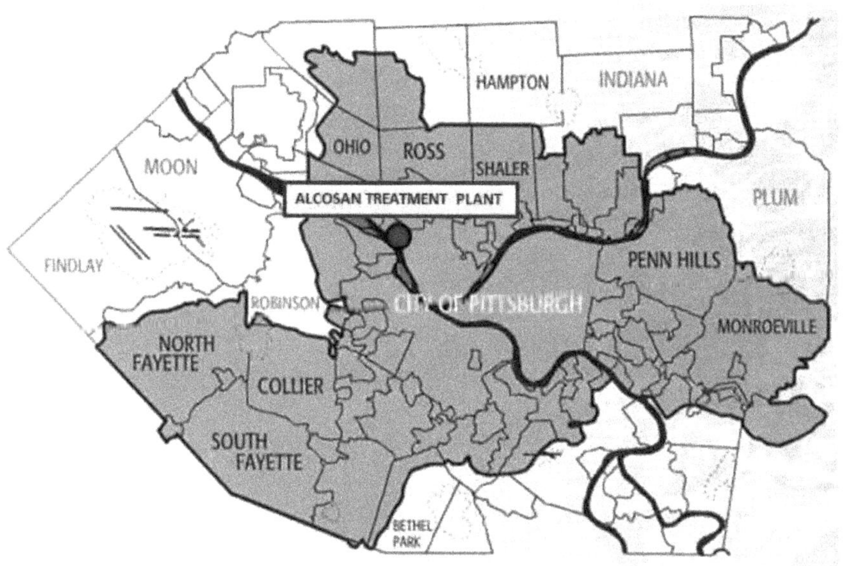

ALCOSAN wastewater treatment plant location and service area boundary. *A1 Applications, LLC.*

In the ALCOSAN system, each municipality or municipal authority owns, operates and maintains its municipal satellite collection system. Whether in a combined or separate sanitary collection system, pipes in the system carry sewage from many individual homes to a large trunk sewer. The trunk sewer then carries the wastewater from multiple municipal collection systems to ALCOSAN's interceptor sewer. The interceptors are a series of pipes that transport the wastewater on the final leg to the treatment plant. The interceptor system, buried up to 120 feet deep under the rivers, is sometimes referred to as the "deep tunnel system." About thirty miles of ALCOSAN interceptors are deep tunnel interceptors that extend along and cross under the Allegheny, Monongahela and Ohio Rivers, with concrete pipe grouted into rock bore tunnels. Originally, all the interceptor sewers along both the main rivers and tributary streams were designed as traditional open-trench construction (shallow-cut) sewers. However, the interceptor sewer design along the main rivers, navigable waterways under the jurisdictional authority of the United States Army Corps of Engineers (USACE), was subsequently changed to a deep tunnel configuration. This decision was made because construction permits for traditional trench sewers along navigable rivers would only be issued with the stipulation that the interceptors would be subject to lowering or removal upon order from the USACE.

The following subsections describe the history of ALCOSAN based on a 2013 article by ALCOSAN historian Michael Anthony.

The Problem

Before the nineteenth century, the narrow tract of land now occupied by the ALCOSAN wastewater treatment plant on the north side of the Ohio River opposite McKees Rocks was primarily known as a pass-through to points west. The coming of the Civil War in 1861 spurred massive industrialization in Northern cities. The industrialization of this area played a common yet integral role in Pittsburgh's early rise as the world's workshop. By staging their industries along the region's rivers, men like James Verner, Charles Schoen, Andrew Carnegie and Henry Clay Frick ensured convenient access to coal and other materials necessary to keep their factories and profits in motion. Rivers were viewed not as natural resources but as arteries to deliver natural resources and also discharge waste products as an integral part of the coal mining activities and the manufacturing processes of the glass, iron and steel industries that made Pittsburgh the "Iron City." As a result, little concern was afforded when waterways, once teeming with life, became lifeless streams of disposal for those same factories.

In the early 1900s, smoke billowing from factories blackened the midday sky and coated the city in tons of particulate matter. In addition, municipal and industrial waste, mine drainage and other pollutants led to poor water quality and the spread of disease. In 1907, Pittsburgh began sand filtration and chlorination of water supplies. At the same time, the city and hundreds of upstream communities continued to dump untreated sewage and industrial waste into the rivers. The image here shows an ALCOSAN photo circa 1940s, with sewage overflows into water. By the mid-1940s, less than 2 percent of the discharges into the Ohio River received any treatment at all, and the Monongahela River, void of aquatic life, ran red with acid mine drainage, mill effluent and other pollutants.

The election of Cornelius D. Scully as mayor of Pittsburgh in 1936 put a new emphasis on the environmental problems facing the city and the region. Scully was pressured by the newspapers to act in reversing the damage that years of industrial prosperity had wreaked on the condition of the city. He created the Commission for the Elimination of Smoke, opened new parks

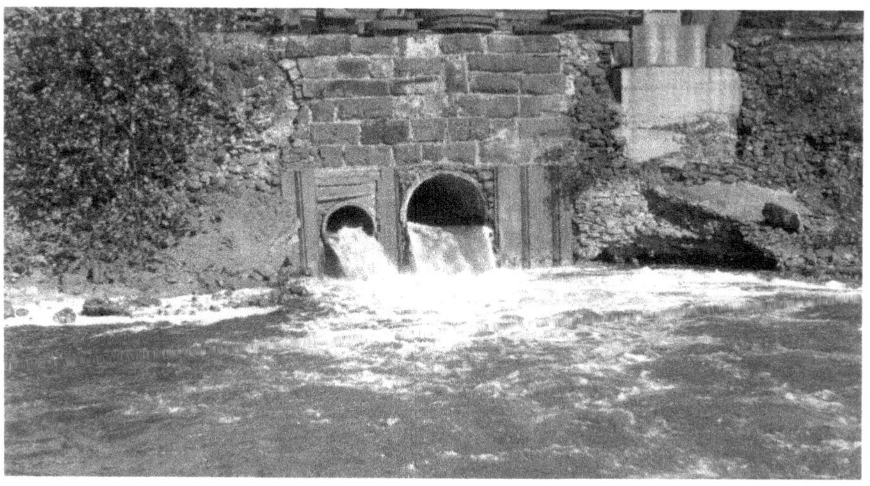

Discharge of untreated sewage in 1940s. *ALCOSAN.*

and concentrated on programs to provide the city with a cleaner water supply. With the coming of war in 1941, however, Scully was forced to put aside his campaign as the city's factories refitted to supply the war machine. The region produced 95 million tons of steel, 52 million shells and 11 million bombs to supply the Allied effort, but the pollution that resulted turned the rivers into cesspools and the day sky into night.

The Solution

As the war neared an end, civic leaders once again took up reversing years of environmental destruction in the region. Richard King Mellon, president of the Pittsburgh Regional Planning Association, generated support for a postwar planning committee to serve as a coordinating mechanism for regional transportation and environmental improvement efforts. The Allegheny Conference on Community Development was thus incorporated in 1944.

Forming a partnership with newly elected mayor David L. Lawrence, Mellon used the Allegheny Conference as a vehicle to promote what would be known as the "Pittsburgh Renaissance," a "growth coalition" of capital, labor and politics. The immediate goals of this powerful partnership included smoke abatement, flood control, renewal of the Golden Triangle business district and the establishment of a regional sanitation district.

In May 1945, two developments would move the county closer to addressing water quality issues. The Pennsylvania Municipal Authorities Act of 1945 provided for the incorporation of bodies with power to acquire, hold, construct, improve, maintain and operate, own and lease property to be devoted to public uses and revenues. These uses included transportation, bridges, tunnels, airports, sewer systems and sewage treatment works. Secondly, in the enforcement of PA Clean Streams Law of 1937, PSWB ordered 102 municipalities and 90 industries in Allegheny County to prepare preliminary plans and specifications for sewage treatment. The board further ordered cessation of sewage and industrial discharges by May 1947. At this time, raw sewage and industrial wastes flowed directly into the Pittsburgh waterways. Aquatic life and dissolved oxygen concentration in the Ohio, Monongahela and Allegheny Rivers were severely affected.

On March 5, 1946, the Allegheny County commissioners adopted a resolution creating ALCOSAN, with a plan to finance the agency through bond issues. Also in March, the authority was granted office space on the fifth floor of the City-County Building and use of the city's testing laboratory on Centre Avenue.

Planning and Design

By mid-1946, ALCOSAN had begun conducting sewer inspections and weir sampling to determine the extent of the region's sewage problems. This field work revealed previously unknown mileage, capacities and conditions of the county's 102 municipal sewer systems; 35 sewer locations were selected for preliminary sampling, which included the participation of 59 municipalities and 15 industrial sites.

Planning efforts continued through the first half of 1947, and by September 24, ALCOSAN had submitted a plan to the United States Army Corps of Engineers (USACE) to lay interceptor sewers along the Monongahela, Allegheny and Ohio Rivers. Preliminary sampling was completed in November 1947. In all, an average flow of 65 MGD from a population of about 678,000 was measured, sampled and analyzed to determine the properties of wastewater discharge from municipal and industrial sewers. On February 9, 1948, ALCOSAN released a plan recommending an $82 million regional wastewater treatment plant for Pittsburgh and the surrounding communities. The planned conveyance system included ninety-one miles of interceptor sewers and sixty-five miles of trunk sewers. The plan was approved by PSWB in 1948, and by June 1950, ALCOSAN had begun preliminary test borings in the area of the treatment plant site. The cores showed a variety of subsurface conditions, including river silt, ash, coal screenings, sand and building foundations remaining from old structures.

CONSTRUCTION

In 1951, ALCOSAN proceeded with planning for construction of the wastewater conveyance system and wastewater treatment by hiring Celli-Flynn of McKeesport as consulting architects for all ALCOSAN buildings and Michael Baker Jr. Inc. of Rochester to make soundings for eight interceptor river crossings. Plans and specifications for the treatment plant were completed by the consulting engineers Metcalf & Eddy in August 1953. The image here shows an architectural rendering of that treatment plant. Beginning in December 1955, ALCOSAN received bids for the first construction contracts. In all, $50 million worth of contract bids were opened through the month of December. In addition, all 343 property

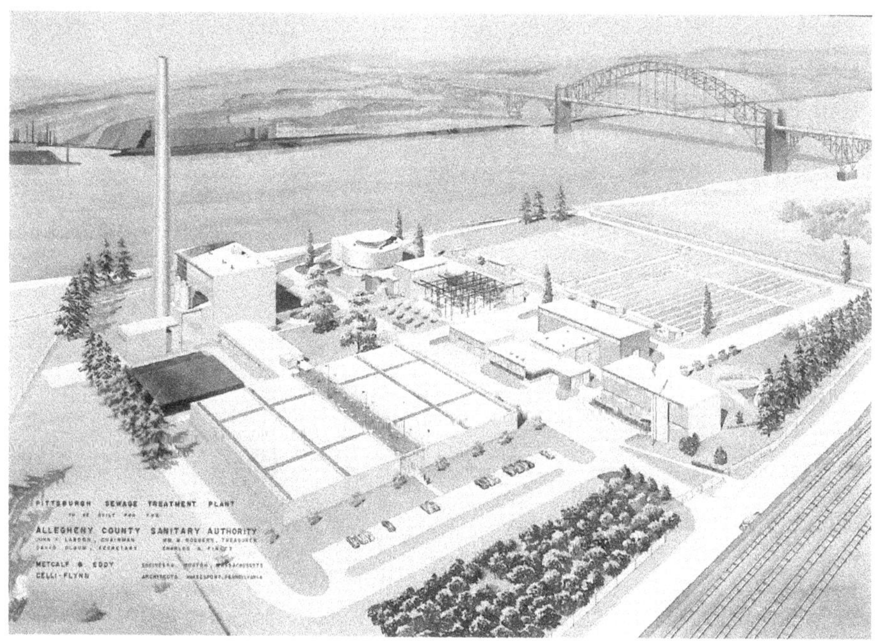

Architectural rendering of the ALCOSAN Primary Treatment Plant, constructed in 1959. *Celli-Flynn Brennan Architects.*

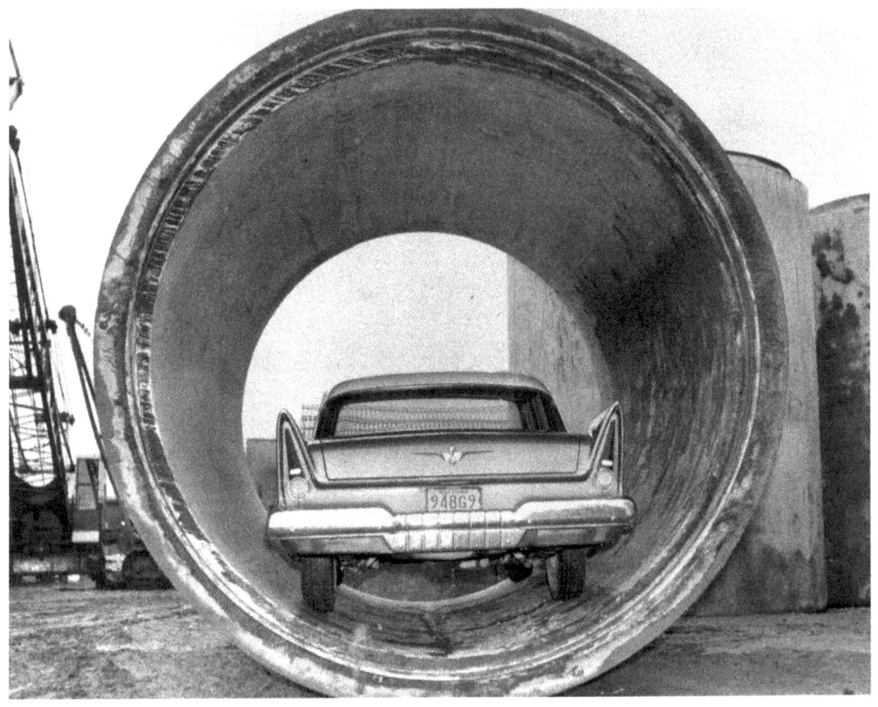

ALCOSAN interceptor sewer pipes, constructed in 1950s. *ALCOSAN.*

owners involved in required rights-of-way were contacted by year's end, with 26 properties expected to require condemnation proceedings.

Treatment plant construction began in March 1956. Contractors from Dravo Corporation began preparatory work for construction of the main interceptor, which ran along the main rivers. Workers began constructing concrete access shafts at Thirty-Sixth Street opposite Herr's Island and at Belmont Street just upstream of the West End Bridge. The images here show the large underground concrete pipes used for interceptor construction along the Ohio River and construction of an ALCOSAN deep tunnel interceptor.

In April 1957, Dravo Corporation completed construction of the river wall at the plant site, the first contract to be completed under the ALCOSAN plan. Construction of the treatment facilities continued through the winter of 1958 and into the spring of 1959. On April 30, bulkheads were removed from individual outfall connections, and the system was put into operation as a primary treatment plant. Initial operational difficulties included the formation of football-sized grease balls and odor from the plant chimney.

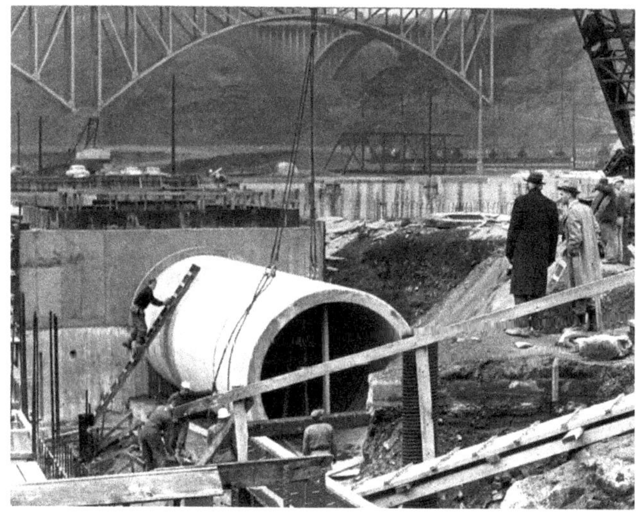

Sewer line installation near the Ohio River in 1957. *ALCOSAN; Weisberg, 2011.*

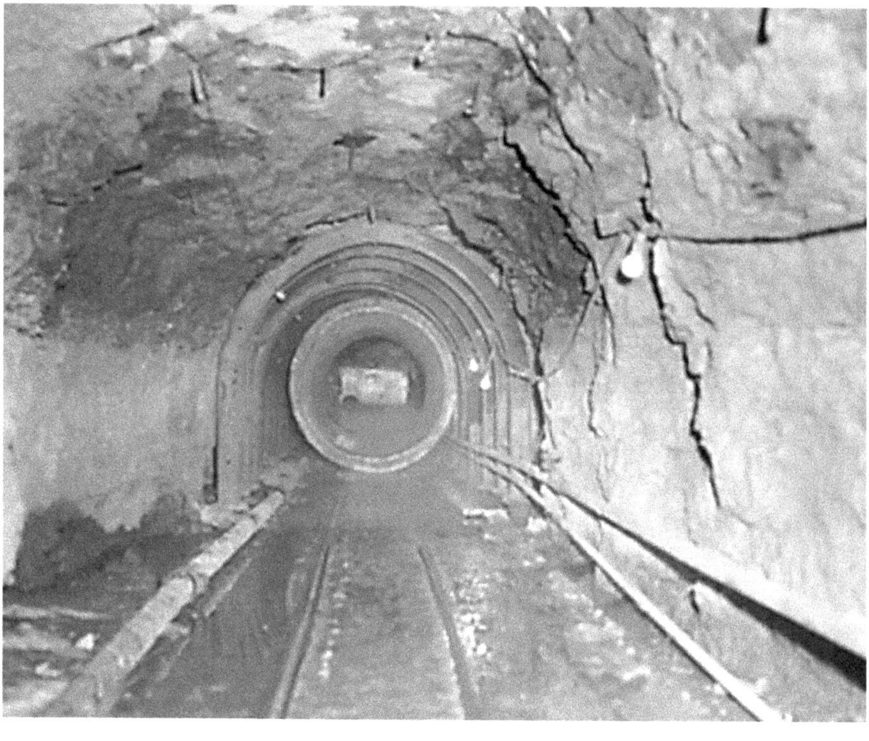

Construction of an ALCOSAN deep tunnel interceptor sewer. *ALCOSAN; ALCOSAN, 2012.*

As ALCOSAN executive director and chief engineer, Mr. John F. Laboon supervised the design and construction of the plant. Considered the father of ALCOSAN, he was an internationally famous sanitary engineer. In 1960, Laboon was named Engineer of the Year by the Pittsburgh Section of ASCE, and in 1969, he was elected an honorary member of ASCE. Speaking at a public hearing on May 14, 1958, regarding the discharge of wastes in the sewer system, Laboon stated that the Allegheny River would be fishable water again within six months of the system going into operation.

In 1960, ALCOSAN was nominated for the Outstanding Civil Engineering Achievement Award by ASCE. The recognition served as a fitting punctuation for the successful planning, design, construction and initial operation of ALCOSAN's collection and treatment system and would set an indicative tone for the authority's progression and expansion into the future.

The Federal Water Pollution Control Act of 1948 was the first major U.S. law to address water pollution. Growing public awareness and concern for controlling water pollution led to sweeping amendments in 1972. As amended in 1972, the law became commonly known as the Clean Water Act (CWA). The 1972 amendments established the basic structure for regulating pollutant discharges into the waters of the United States. CWA prohibited the discharge of pollution into waterways unless a permit had been secured. It also required secondary (biological) treatment at wastewater plants. ALCOSAN proactively started the design of secondary treatment processes in the late 1960s, and operation of the secondary treatment plant commenced in 1973.

In 1973, the Pittsburgh Section of ASCE recognized ALCOSAN with the Section's Civil Engineering Achievement Award for sanitary system design and construction.

CHALLENGES

Civil engineers faced challenges during the design of the ALCOSAN treatment plant and the interceptors related to geotechnical investigations and hydraulics, as these structures were being built for the first time to satisfy the regulatory mandates. The engineers did not have computers and modeling software at that time, so design calculations had to be done manually. The main contribution of civil engineers to wastewater control in Allegheny County was to design these complex hydraulics structures from scratch without existing handbooks and design manuals. Another challenge was political rather than technical. The commonwealth mandated wastewater treatment, but the elected representatives resisted, as a reflection of public resistance to pay the costs.

RECENT PAST (1992–2012)

By 1992, ALCOSAN had begun addressing the growing concern over sewer overflows and wet weather pollution control. In 1994, ALCOSAN started planning for permit requirements as required by the Clean Water Act and the EPA's Combined Sewer Overflow (CSO) Control Policy.

From 1995 to 1999, ALCOSAN worked with federal and state environmental regulatory agencies to negotiate a consent decree that would satisfy ALCOSAN's obligations under environmental law to comply with the Clean Water Act and U.S. EPA CSO Control Policy. The consent decree received final approval in January 2008. The decree required that ALCOSAN prepare and implement a Wet Weather Plan (WWP) to repair broken sewer lines, reduce inflow and infiltration, reduce the frequency and

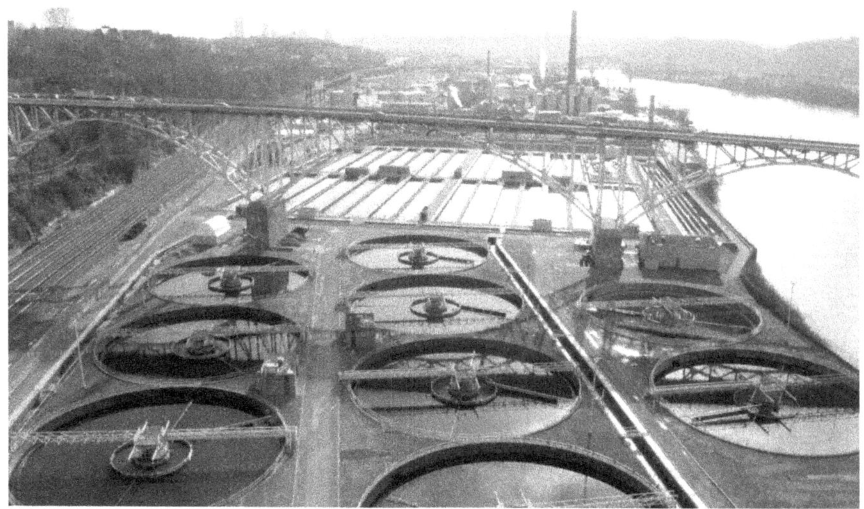

ALCOSAN's present wastewater treatment plant showing secondary clarifiers. *ALCOSAN.*

amount of CSOs and eliminate Sanitary Sewer Overflows (SSOs) by 2026. The WWP report was released by ALCOSAN in 2012.

From 2000 to 2012, ALCOSAN completed a $400 million capital improvement program, which addressed odor control, treatment capacity, solids handling and wet weather planning. The secondary treatment clarifiers are located at the bottom of the photo. The image here shows a recent photo of the ALCOSAN wastewater treatment plant.

PATH FORWARD: 2016 AND BEYOND

Pittsburgh owes its existence to the meanders and confluence of three great American rivers. The Allegheny, Monongahela and the Ohio Rivers are a point of pride and are integral to the city's identity. As the city continues its historic transition from a riverfront industrial superpower to an education and research mecca, the quality of our rivers and riverfronts is of paramount importance.

In 2016, ALCOSAN started design of Phase 1 of its Wet Weather Plan, which is considered to be the largest public works project in the region's history, through $2 billion in engineering and construction projects.

The first canon of the ASCE's 2014 Code of Ethics emphasizes sustainable development: Engineers shall hold paramount the safety, health and welfare of the public and shall strive to comply with the principles of sustainable development in the performance of their professional duties.

Green Infrastructure

The Pittsburgh wastewater community and civil engineers are now considering sustainable alternatives in addressing local and regional wet weather issues. Since 2015, the wastewater treatment emphasis in the Greater Pittsburgh region has shifted from conventional gray infrastructure to sustainable infrastructure. Gray infrastructure is brick, mortar and concrete construction such as pipes, tunnels and storage tanks. Because ALCOSAN wastewater includes both sewage and stormwater runoff, its volume can be reduced by reducing the stormwater component. When green infrastructure is used for reducing stormwater entering a sewer system, it is referred to as green stormwater infrastructure (GSI). As noted by Shamsi (2017),

GSI such as rain gardens, green roofs and porous pavement is considered sustainable because it uses natural processes such as infiltration and evaporation to capture stormwater runoff close to its source at distributed (decentralized) locations throughout a watershed. In some locations, GSI can be a cost-effective, sustainable and environmentally friendly way to manage the volume, rate and water quality of stormwater runoff entering the sewer system and waterways while providing additional benefits to communities. More than one hundred years ago, when combined sewers were constructed in Pittsburgh, they were perceived to be a cutting-edge gray infrastructure solution. Pittsburgh region is now spending billions of dollars to fix the CSO problems of that inadequate gray system. Likewise, GSI is not a panacea and should be planned, designed, constructed and maintained carefully for effective CSO control.

Pittsburgh is now riding the green wave. In 2016, ALCOSAN changed its logo to reflect its green infrastructure focus and launched a multimillion-dollar Green Revitalization of Our Waterways (GROW) grant program. The GROW program provides grants to green infrastructure and other source reduction projects for the eighty-three Allegheny County municipalities, including the city of Pittsburgh, that are served by ALCOSAN. The program has offered $19 million in grants for fifty-nine projects since January 2017.

In 2016, Pittsburgh Water and Sewer Authority (PWSA) completed a draft of a City-Wide Green First Plan that looks at ways to keep the Pittsburgh

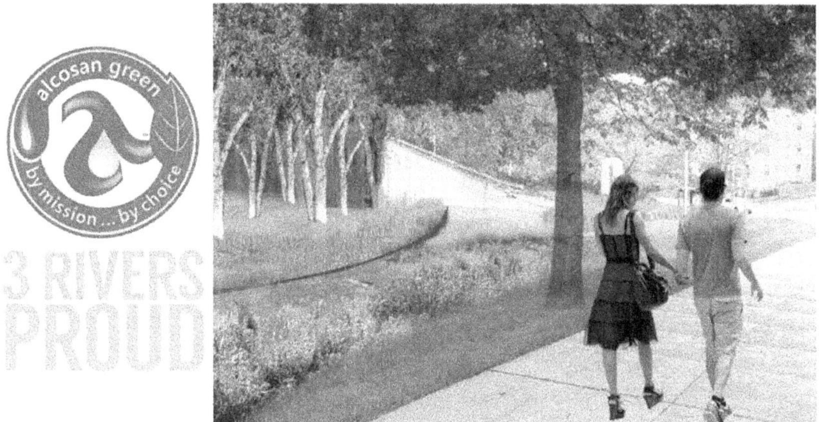

Pittsburgh Green Wave at ALCOSAN and PWSA. *ASCE.*

rivers clean while creating great community-focused infrastructure for a maturing city. The draft plan examines the existing stormwater conditions that will guide where green infrastructure will be installed to achieve the most cost-effective and beneficial results to the residents of Pittsburgh. PWSA expects to implement the recommendations of this plan by 2032 by achieving the goal of managing 1,835 acres of impervious surface using green infrastructure practices. The image here shows conceptual rendering for PWSA's GSI Park in the Upper Hill District neighborhood. It is currently scheduled for completion in the spring of 2018. The project will manage more than 1 million gallons of runoff.

Wastewater Infrastructure Report Card

Every four years, the ASCE Report Card for America's Infrastructure depicts the condition and performance of American infrastructure in the familiar form of a school report card—assigning letter grades based on the physical condition and needed investments for improvement. As shown in the image here, the 2017 Infrastructure Report Card grades the national wastewater infrastructure as a "D+." Although the current grade shows a slight improvement from the 2013 grade of D, it is essentially the same as in the first report card issued in 1998. To raise the grade, the 2017 infrastructure report suggests, among other things, renewed or enhanced federal and state aid and supporting green infrastructure.

In addition to national infrastructure, ASCE also grades the state infrastructure. The latest Pennsylvania Report Card was released in 2014. Unfortunately, at a D-, Pennsylvania's 2014 wastewater grade is below even the national wastewater grade, mostly due to relatively higher number of combined sewer overflows (CSOs). In fact, Pennsylvania has the highest number of CSOs of any state. The Pennsylvania wastewater infrastructure report indicates that aging wastewater management systems discharge billions of gallons of untreated sewage into Pennsylvania's surface waters each year. The commonwealth must invest $28 billion over the next twenty years to repair existing systems, meet clean water standards and build or expand existing systems to meet increasing demands. Improving CSO infrastructure could cost $20.8 billion based on applying reported costs from Pittsburgh, Philadelphia, and the City of Lancaster to the remaining 151 cities with CSO. While investment needs are estimated to cost eighty-seven times the cost of the

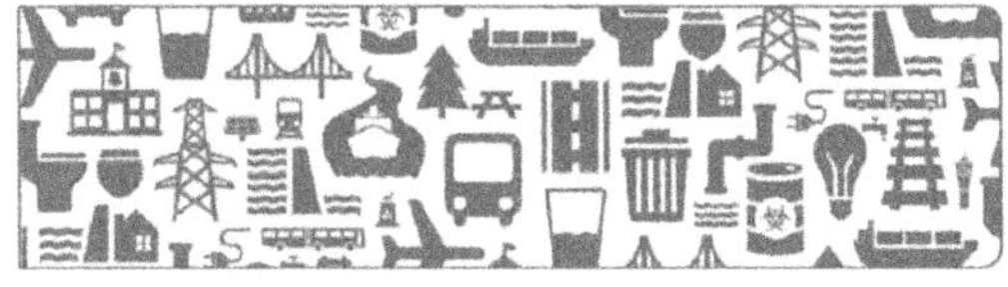

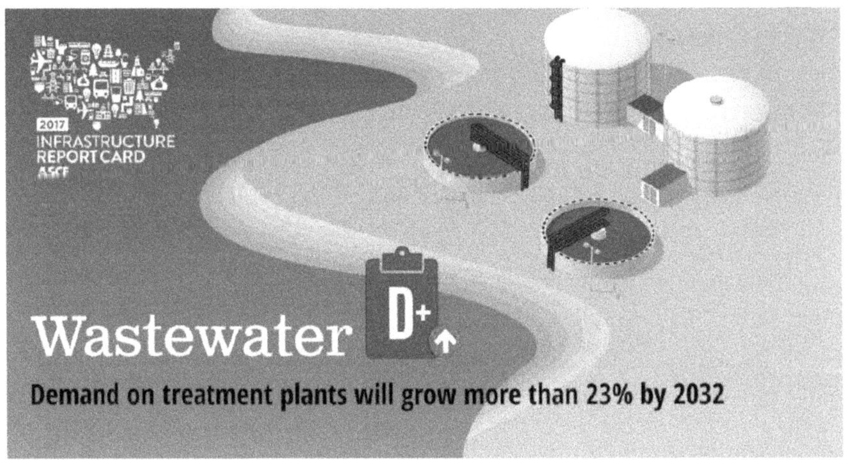

2017 ASCE Infrastructure Report Card.

Pittsburgh Penguin's CONSOL Energy Center, funding has decreased. The Pennsylvania Infrastructure Investment Authority's (PENNVEST) budget in 2013 for grant and loan awards for sewer projects is $335 million, less than 25 percent of the required annual investment. As noted by ASCE, in 2014 Pennsylvania's appropriation from the Federal Clean Water Act also decreased to $53 million.

Regarding hydraulic fracturing for oil and natural gas drilling and production, the 2014 Pennsylvania infrastructure report indicates that at the onset of the surge in unconventional drilling in 2008, Pennsylvania's infrastructure was inadequately prepared to deal with the unique challenges of this new drilling technique. This resulted in frac water disposal at wastewater treatment facilities not equipped to handle the high total dissolved solids (TDS) in the waste stream. On April 19, 2011, Pennsylvania Department of Environmental Protection (PADEP) issued a "Call to Action" letter to all gas drilling operators to cease, within thirty days, delivering this wastewater to facilities that had been accepting the water under special provisions of the commonwealth's regulations that exempted these facilities from TDS treatment requirements. Since this

Call to Action, ASCE in 2014 reported that the percentage of wastewater going to treatment facilities has decreased from 57 percent to 16 percent, and the amount of on-site reuse of frac water has increased from 31 percent to 74 percent.

Although ASCE does not grade local infrastructure, the Greater Pittsburgh wastewater grade is expected to be close to the state grade of D- due to high number of CSOs. This poor grade indicates a compelling need for reinvestment to maintain and upgrade the existing wastewater systems in the Pittsburgh region.

NAVIGATION AND FLOOD CONTROL ON THE THREE RIVERS

By Brian Greene, PhD, PG; Anton Krysa, PE; Werner Loehlein, PE; Stephen Stoltz, PE; and Patrick J. Sullivan Jr., PE

Introduction

This chapter deals with the history of navigation on Pittsburgh's three rivers and the history of past floods and efforts to mitigate future flooding of the city. In their natural, pre-1760 state, the Allegheny, Monongahela and Ohio Rivers (i.e., the "Three Rivers") were very dynamic, reacting to the forces of nature. For most of the year, the river levels were low, but these periods were punctuated by brief, swiftly rising levels with high velocities greatly hindering navigation and urban development. Civil engineers have long been at the heart of providing systems and structures that permit the rivers to serve as a major means of transportation in support of the industrial core of Pittsburgh. Initially, the area's rivers were a key means of transportation, but they were unreliable due to spring floods and summer low-water stages. In 1866, Congress authorized the Rivers and Harbors Act to seek a means to permit year-round, reliable navigation for commercial river towboats and barge traffic.

The act resulted in far-sighted civil engineers, including William Milnor Roberts and Colonel William Merrill, performing detailed surveys to develop a comprehensive plan for a slackwater canalization of the Ohio

River. Completed in 1869, the surveys offered indispensable engineering and hydrological data later used to plan navigation projects, as M.C. Robinson noted in his 1983 national waterways study. Completed in the late 1800s, Davis Island Lock and Dam (L/D) was built about five miles downstream from the Point of Pittsburgh and represented the first navigation project on the Ohio River. Following Davis Island L/D, a network of descending locks and dams made year-round navigation of bulk goods possible. In addition, many tributaries located upstream of Pittsburgh were dammed so that floodwaters could be stored for future planned release. The added benefits of the dams and reservoirs in the Pittsburgh's Ohio River drainage basin include water for public consumption, irrigation, recreation, reliable navigation and hydropower. The Three Rivers represent the lifeblood of Pittsburgh, both historically and in the present. The benefits of the system of locks and dams are immeasurable and clearly result in the most economical means to move bulk commodities throughout the region. There has been an ongoing investment in the repair and replacement of navigation locks of Pittsburgh, as well as improvements to key upstream flood-control dams. The term "flood control" has been replaced with "flood risk management" in recent years.

OVERVIEW OF DAMS IN PENNSYLVANIA

The Commonwealth of Pennsylvania has a variety of dams that vary in their construction materials, including earthen embankments, concrete gravity dams and combination dams. The most recent survey by the Pennsylvania Department of Environmental Protection, Division of Dam Safety and the American Association of State Dam Safety Officials indicates that as of 2015, there are 3,373 state-regulated dams located in the commonwealth. Existing dams, with their associated reservoirs, are used for multiple purposes: flood mitigation, navigation, hydropower, irrigation, water quality and recreation. Flood-control dams in Pennsylvania date back to the 1800s, although few have been built since 2000. The Pittsburgh District of the U.S. Army Corps of Engineers operates and maintains 23 locks and dams on the Allegheny, Monongahela and Ohio Rivers. The first navigation dams were built on the Monongahela River and were paid for by user tolls. Later, the Corps of Engineers took over the responsibility for the dams and locks to provide reliable navigation. Many of the existing locks and dams were built in the

1930s and are operating well beyond their estimated fifty-year service lives. The 2014 ASCE *Report Card on Pennsylvania's Infrastructure* grades dams low and indicates a compelling need for reinvestment to maintain these structures.

FLOOD-CONTROL DAMS

The Upper Ohio River Basin has seen its share of major floods since the construction of Fort Pitt in the 1760s. Since that time, the Greater Pittsburgh area has experienced many severe flooding incidents created by a variety of events. Beginning in March 1763, floodwaters inundated Fort Pitt. As Pittsburgh grew, so did the city's and region's experiences with overbank flooding. Downtown Pittsburgh, at the confluence of the Allegheny and Monongahela Rivers, flooded an average of twice per year. Overbank flooding was such an issue for the region that in 1907, the Pittsburgh Chamber of Commerce organized the Pittsburgh Flood Commission under the leadership of H.J. Heinz. In 1912, the commission published the so-called Heinz Report. The report detailed the impact of flooding in the region and outlined a system of upstream flood protection dams in the Allegheny, Monongahela and Beaver River Basins of the Upper Ohio River Valley to

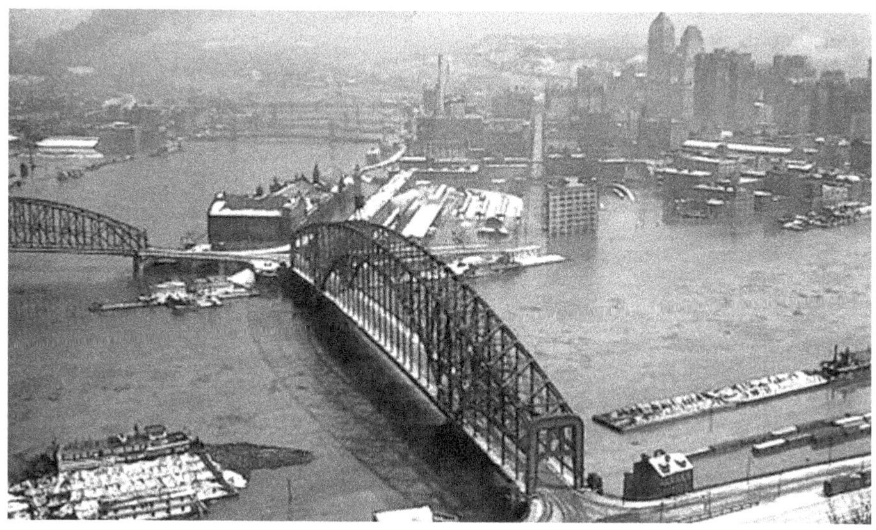

March 1936 flood in Pittsburgh, Pennsylvania. *From www.postgazette.com.*

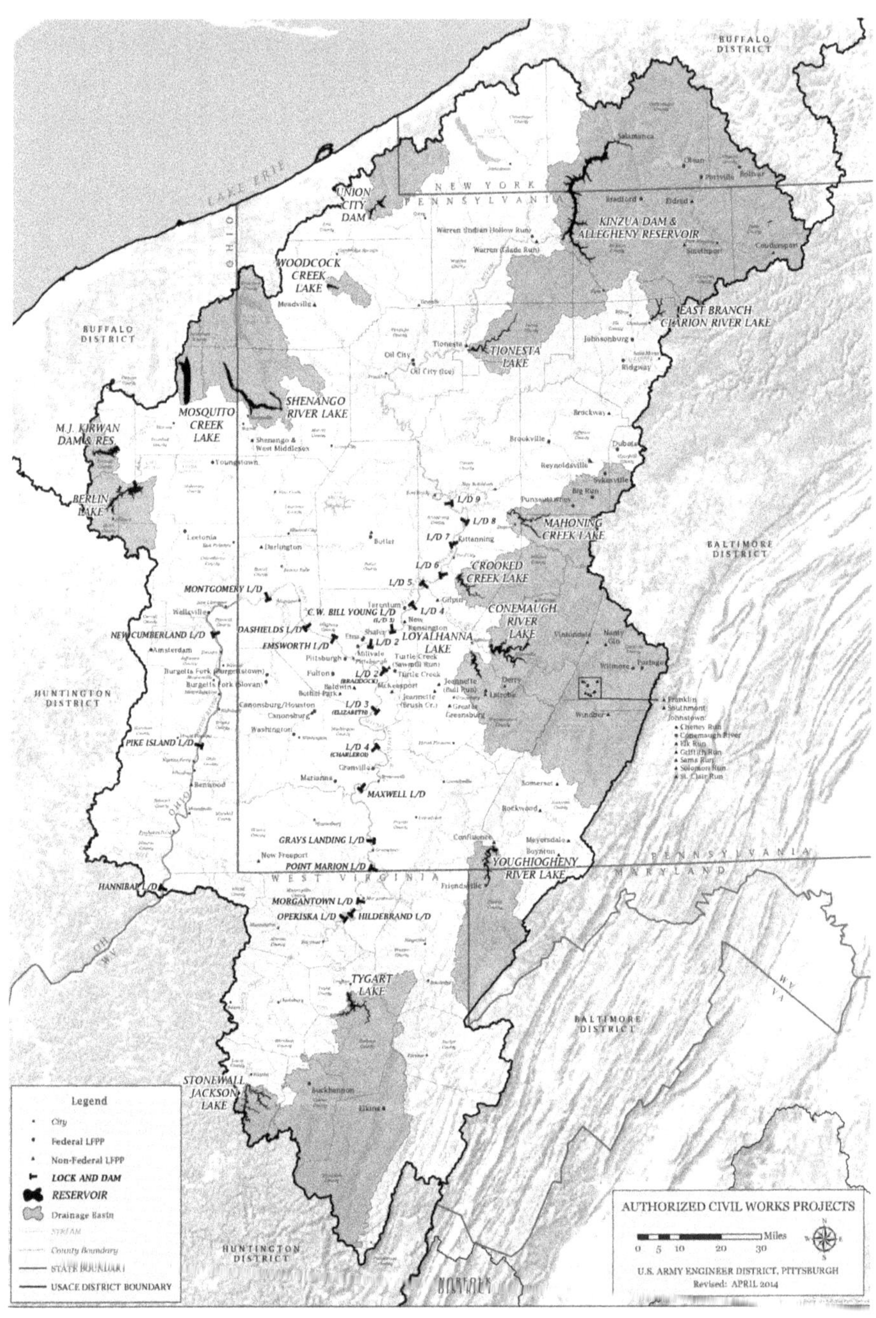

Federal flood damage reduction projects, Upper Ohio River Basin. *U.S. Army Corps of Engineers, Pittsburgh District.*

protect the residents from damaging floodwaters. Unfortunately, the plan failed to gather much federal support following the Great Flood of 1913 and through the 1920s.

It was not until the region and country experienced the severe droughts of the early 1930s, followed by the March 1936 St. Patrick's Day Flood, the largest flood of record in the Upper Ohio River Valley, that action was finally taken. This flood prompted the passage of the Flood Control Act of 1936 by Congress. Following record floods along the middle Ohio River in January 1937 and the lower Ohio River in March 1937, the 1936 act was amended with more projects and in 1938 funded the construction of most of flood protection projects east of the Mississippi River. The result in the Upper Ohio River Basin was a system that currently consists of sixteen federally built flood-control and multipurpose dams. This reservoir system has substantially reduced flood damages since the dams were constructed. For example, these projects combined to reduce the 1972 Hurricane Agnes flood by an estimated 12 feet at Pittsburgh. Without the upstream reservoirs, this flood would have been 2 feet higher than the record flood level recorded in March 1936, which crested at 46 feet. The January 1996 flood, which crested at 34.6 feet, was reduced by 10 feet at Pittsburgh—otherwise, it would have nearly equaled the flood elevations recorded during the March 1936 flood.

MULTIPURPOSE DAMS

Following passage of the Flood Control Act of 1936, several of the dams in the Upper Ohio Basin were authorized for design and construction. Two prominent Corps of Engineers dams were Youghiogheny Dam, completed in 1944 and located on the Youghiogheny River, a tributary of the Monongahela River, and Kinzua Dam, completed in 1965 and located on the main stem of the Allegheny River.

Youghiogheny Dam

Youghiogheny Dam is located on the Youghiogheny River upstream from Confluence, Pennsylvania. The dam is an earthen structure, 184 feet high and 1,610 feet long at its crest. The reservoir extends 16 miles into Western Maryland and has a normal surface area of about 4.4 square miles.

Boaters consider Youghiogheny River Lake, with channels up to half a mile wide, the best powerboat and water-skiing lake in southwestern Pennsylvania. The tail waters of the dam are some of the few in Pennsylvania that open for trout fishing year round and are stocked by the Pennsylvania Fish and Boat Commission on a regular basis throughout the spring and summer.

An interesting fact associated with the construction of the dam is that the former town of Somerfield, Pennsylvania, located about three miles from the dam crest, was abandoned, razed and inundated when the reservoir was filled. The town was formed in 1818 and existed until the dam was constructed in 1942. Every so often, during extremely low water levels, former sidewalks of the town and the old stone arch Great Crossings Bridge of the National Road, which was the original Route 40, will appear.

Kinzua Dam

Kinzua Dam, located 6 miles east of Warren, Pennsylvania, is one of the largest dams in the United States east of the Mississippi River and the only flood-control dam on the main stem of the Allegheny River. The dam is a 179-foot-high and 1,877-foot-long combination concrete gravity/embankment dam that impounds a reservoir having a total length of 24.2 miles at normal pool. The dam is located within the 500,000-acre Allegheny National Forest. The dam created Pennsylvania's second-deepest lake, the Allegheny Reservoir, also known as Kinzua Lake. The lake extends north, nearly to Salamanca, New York, which is within the Allegany Reservation of the Seneca Nation of New York. Federal condemnation of tribal lands to be flooded for the project displaced more than six hundred Seneca members and cost the reservation 10,000 acres. The relocation is still a contentious issue within the Seneca Nation.

In 1966, the Pittsburgh Section of ASCE bestowed its first Civil Engineering Achievement Award to the Kinzua Dam Project. The primary purpose of the Kinzua Dam and Reservoir project is flood mitigation, but it is also used for navigation, pollution abatement, recreation and hydropower, all which are carefully balanced to optimize the use of the available water. Immediately above the downstream side of the dam is the Seneca Pumped Storage Generating Station. The pumped storage facility has a circular reservoir located on the left hillside, well above the dam. The pumped storage hydroelectric power plant distributes electricity to the power grid across the region.

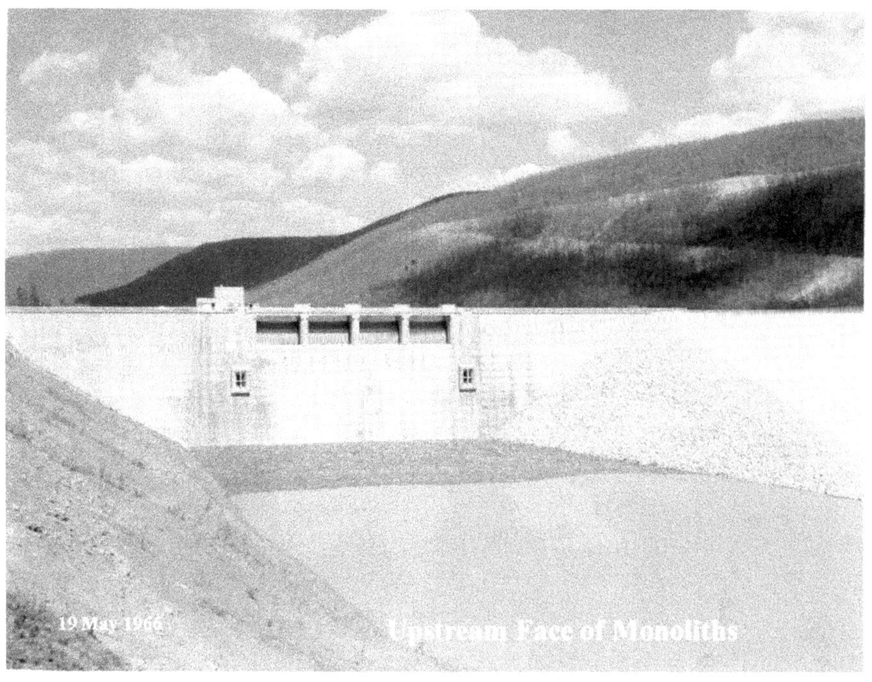

Photograph of Kinzua Dam soon after completion in 1966. *U.S. Army Corps of Engineers, Pittsburgh District.*

River Navigation Structures

Since the early settlement of Western Pennsylvania, the Allegheny, Monongahela and Ohio Rivers have served the region for basic transportation and shipment of goods and cargo using barges pushed by towboats. The amount of coal transported downriver from Pittsburgh by these tows greatly increased following the Civil War, according to Johnson's *Headwaters District*. The size of the tows/number of barges also grew with the amount of coal hauled against its increasing downriver demand. Due to the growing coal trade, the federal government began studying methods to produce a reliable navigation depth on the Ohio River. In 1866, Congress authorized the Rivers and Harbors Act, which launched a study to analyze a comprehensive plan for a slackwater canalization of the Ohio River. The study led to a determination that construction of an integrated system of locks and dams, each forming an upstream pool (defined as a slackwater lake, or a reach of artificially deepened river), was the best solution to meet the demands of the growing navigation industry. The increased storage capacity of each pool increased the amount of river water that could be managed by sequential release from each pool of a dam proceeding downriver.

DAVIS ISLAND LOCK AND DAM

The opening of the first lock and dam on the Ohio River at Davis Island in 1885 proved to be a significant technologic advance for the civil engineering profession at large. When completed, the Davis Island project incorporated the world's first rolling lock gate and, at 600 feet long and 110 feet wide, was the widest lock chamber ever built at the time of its construction in 1878–85. The Davis Island navigation project incorporated a wooden timber wicket dam almost 1,900 feet long. Wicket dams were composed of moveable slab sections that were hinged at the bottom and held upright by adjustable props. Davis Island served as a prototype for the subsequent

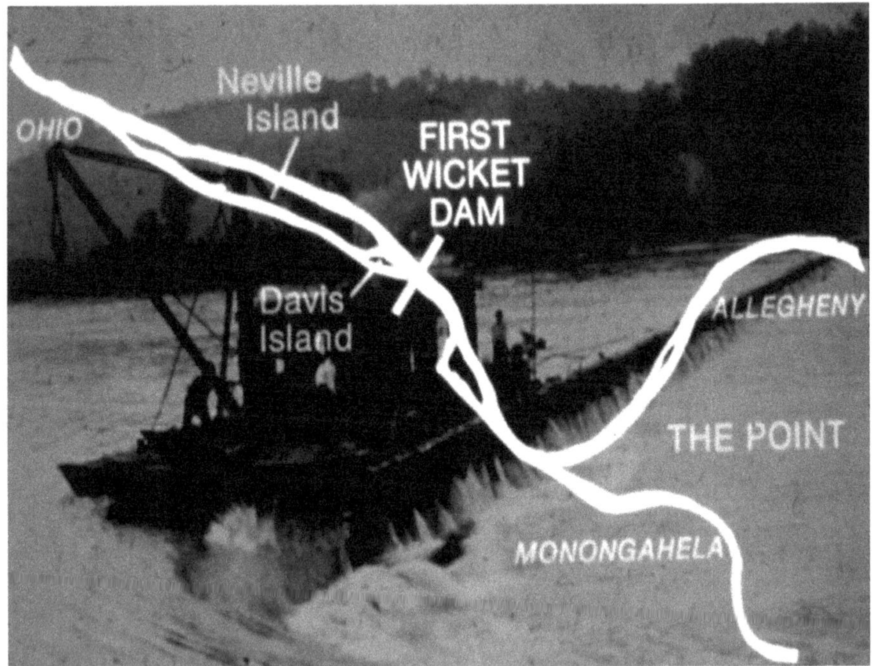

Map and photograph of Davis Island Lock and Dam. *U.S. Army Corps of Engineers, Pittsburgh District.*

fifty locks to be built on the Ohio River. Davis Island Lock and Dam was removed in 1922 and replaced with Emsworth Locks and Dam, located downstream.

Locks and Dams (1900 through 2000)

In 1910, the Rivers and Harbors Act was authorized by Congress, providing for the systematic construction of a system of locks and dams along the Ohio River. This project was completed in 1929 and produced fifty-one wooden wicket dams and typical lock chambers with dimensions of 600 feet long by 110 feet wide along the length of the river, starting at Pittsburgh. Wicket dams in the Pittsburgh region were the earliest structures to be replaced by mass concrete dams.

Taken together, the systems of locks and dams on the three rivers of the Pittsburgh region have been described as "rivers that are highways." Even today, they are the most efficient means to move bulk commodities such as coal and construction aggregates compared to rail or truck transport. Throughout the late nineteenth and early twentieth centuries, the Monongahela River has carried a greater tonnage of bulk commodities than any other inland river in America, as Johnson noted in *Headwaters District*. In comparison with the Ohio and Mississippi Rivers, the Monongahela River was called the "Little Giant" because of the tonnage transported on it annually. Moving coal mined in Pennsylvania and West Virginia to steel mills in the Western Pennsylvania towns upstream and downstream of Pittsburgh was especially important, especially to the war effort in the late 1930s and early 1940s.

During the 1940s, a shift from steam-propelled to diesel-powered towboats allowed for more barges/larger tows on the river. However, due to the size of the lock chambers, the tows had to be disassembled upstream, and a select number of barges were "locked" through the lock chambers in multiple lockages. Once in the downstream pool, the tow was then reassembled before continuing downstream. This functional inconvenience backed up river traffic and increased expenses for the river towboat industry. Even as modernization of locks in the lower Ohio River was initiated in the 1950s to handle the larger tows/more barges, the locks in the Pittsburgh region remained unchanged. In the upper Ohio River, nearest Pittsburgh, each river navigation dam, either a gated type or a simple concrete weir structure, has two parallel, adjoining lock chambers—

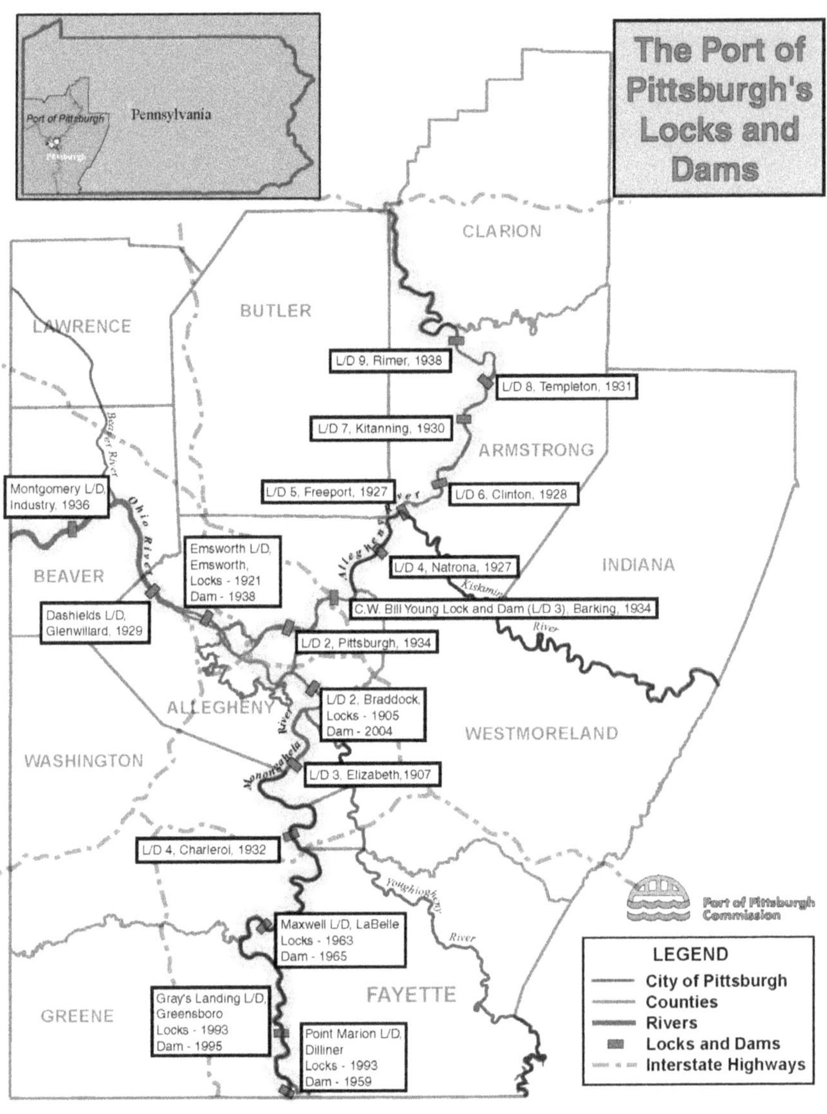

Map of USACE locks and dams on the Three Rivers. *Port of Pittsburgh Commission.*

one a 600-foot-long by 110-foot-wide main lock and the other a 360-foot-long by 56-foot-wide auxiliary lock.

The Pittsburgh District, Corps of Engineers, currently operates and maintains twenty-three locks and dams on the three rivers. This operation represents the largest number of navigation projects in any district of the Corps of Engineers, and it systematically provides a nine-foot minimum depth navigation "pool" depth. In the 1990s, a new locks and dam project was built on the Monongahela River. The project, Grays Landing Locks and Dam, located eighty-two river miles south of Pittsburgh, involved traditional cofferdam construction. Steel sheet piles were used to form a series of interconnecting coffer cells. Once completed, the inner cofferdam area was pumped dry. Excavation of alluvial sediments, removal of rock, preparation of the foundation and placement of concrete was then performed.

Point Marion Lock Cofferdam

In 1990, work began on a replacement lock chamber at Point Marion Lock and Dam, located on the Monongahela River about seventy-five miles south of Pittsburgh and one mile above the confluence of the Monongahela and Cheat Rivers. The new lock chamber measured 84 feet by 720 feet, eliminating the traffic bottleneck of the old smaller 56- by 360-foot lock chamber. A larger lock chamber avoided reconfiguring barges into smaller components to lock through and then returning the configuration back to the original series of interconnected barges before continuing downriver. This inefficient double lockage procedure added about an additional hour to a typical lockage of about a half hour. Plans called for the new lock to be constructed landward of the existing lock, which would be incorporated as part of the river arm of the cofferdam. An important requirement was that the existing lock had to remain open during construction to avoid shutting down all traffic in the river. This required extensive stabilization of the existing wall since the proposed excavation for the new lock typically was within 10 feet of the existing landwall and extended up to 13 feet below its foundation. The new upper approach was extended and broadened for a distance of nearly one mile, which required removal and disposal of approximately 1 million cubic yards of material excavated from the left bank.

Existing walls had been incorporated into cofferdams in the past. In 1961, an existing lock landwall was incorporated as part of a cofferdam at the Tennessee Valley Authority's General Joe Wheeler Lock and Dam, but the approach proved disastrous. The lock wall moved about thirty feet into the dewatered excavation, killing two people and suspending navigation on the Tennessee River for years until the lock was reconstructed. The cause of the failure was sliding of the existing lock wall on an undetected weak clay seam in the foundation rock.

Foundation explorations at Point Marion identified weak clay seams within the underlying rock. To avoid a sliding failure similar to that experienced at Wheeler Lock, 425 large-capacity post-tensioned rock anchors were installed in three rows to ensure the required stability of the existing land wall. The image here depicts a typical section through old lock wall showing rock anchor locations. Even more rock anchors were required for the coffercells making up the remaining portion of the cofferdam.

For the landwall proper, 139 vertical anchors were installed to prevent overturning. Two rows of 286 inclined anchors were placed to resist sliding of the landwall monoliths along the top, as well as within the underlying

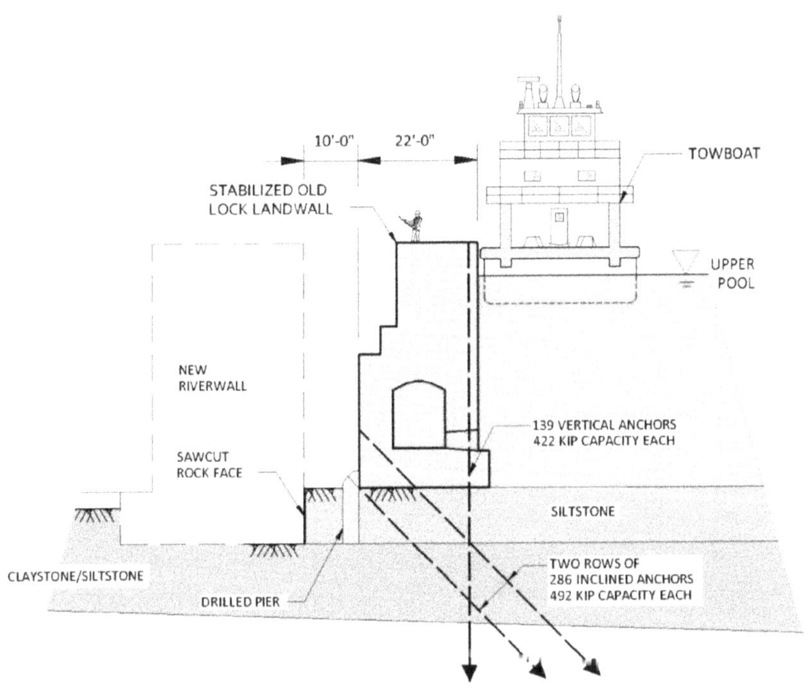

Typical section through old lock wall showing rock anchor locations. *Anton Krysa.*

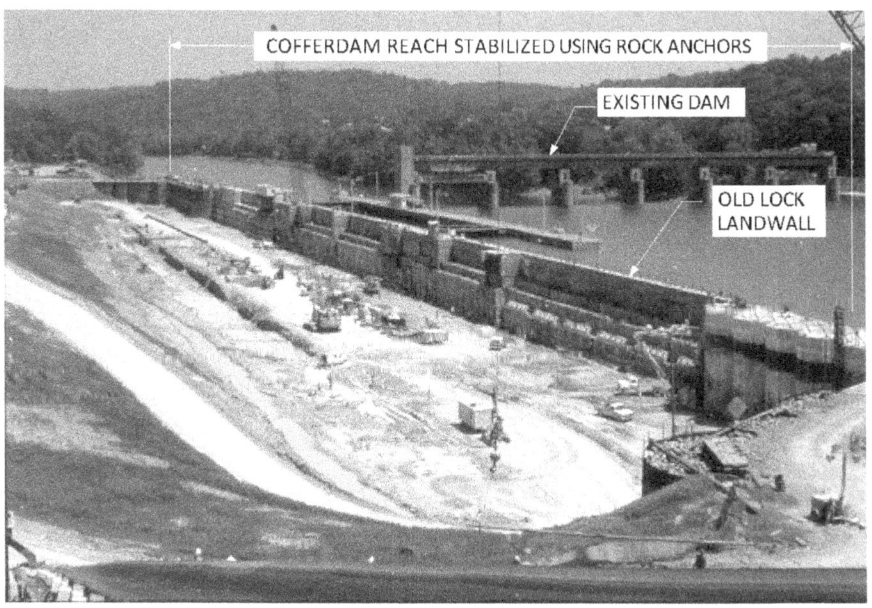

Construction phase with anchors installed and cofferdam dewatered. *U.S. Army Corps of Engineers, Pittsburgh District.*

weak rock. Excavation proceeded in stages and was closely linked to the installation and stressing of each row of anchors. An assortment of sensors linked to computers allowed real-time monitoring of the performance of the cofferdam throughout construction.

The image here is an aerial photograph taken during the construction phase of the project, with anchors installed and cofferdam dewatered. Even with the extensive stabilization measures, the response of the existing lock walls to the removal of the supporting backfill material was noticeable. The instrumentation proved to be invaluable in allowing quick modifications to the construction.

The Point Marion Lock Cofferdam Project was the recipient of the 1993 Civil Engineering Achievement Award by the Pittsburgh Section of ASCE. The new lock at Point Marion improved navigation on the Monongahela River and extended the project life of this important structure. The new larger lock chamber provided by the new construction resulted in more efficient lockages, thus eliminating a bottleneck to commercial barge traffic in this section of the river.

BRADDOCK DAM: THE FIRST FLOAT-IN DAM

Braddock Dam (Dam No. 2), located twelve miles upstream from Pittsburgh on the Monongahela River, was put into operation in 1906, and a pair of lock chambers was added in 1953. The land chamber is 110 feet wide by 720 feet long, and the river chamber is 56 feet wide by 360 feet long. By the late 1990s, replacement of the nearly one-hundred-year-old Braddock Dam had become necessary because as a fixed weir structure, the level of the upstream pool could not be regulated above the crest elevation, and locks were too small to permit long tows to pass through. To overcome these deficiencies, planning commenced for a replacement dam. Taking lessons learned from projects in Europe and Japan, the Corps of Engineers decided to use for the first time in the United States the innovative "in-the-wet" methods to expedite the construction schedule, improve construction quality control and reduce cost, among other reasons.

Construction of the new Braddock Dam consisted of two reinforced concrete shell segments set on eighty-nine drilled shafts founded in bedrock. The new gated structure was built about five hundred feet upstream of the almost one-hundred-year-old fixed crest dam that it replaced. Having a gated dam permitted control of the upper pool elevation and made river navigation more efficient. Braddock Dam introduced a new type of in-river construction that did not employ the use of cofferdams, which represented a first for dam construction worldwide. This project employed the most recent innovative construction techniques and was a major departure from the proven method of dam construction within a dewatered cofferdam that had been used for decades. The replacement Braddock Dam employed "float-in" or "in-the-wet" construction. The project began in 1999 and was completed in 2004. It was the first time in the history of an inland navigation system that a precast concrete dam had been floated into place.

As opposed to traditional "in-the-dry" methods of cofferdam construction, the "in-the-wet" method involved foundation preparation and construction of drilled shaft foundations at the site, while two dam segments, composed of a combination of precast concrete panels and conventional concrete that would be the visible above water portion of the dam, were fabricated at an offsite casting basin located downstream of Pittsburgh. While the dam segments were being assembled, eighty-nine reinforced concrete drilled shafts were constructed within the footprint of the dam. Each shaft was seventy-eight inches in diameter and forty feet long, which included a fifteen-to twenty-foot-long drilled rock socket. About 20 percent of the drilled shafts were affixed with circular-form, hydraulic flat jacks at the top of the shaft to level the segments of the dam once they were aligned and placed over the shafts. Once the drilled shafts were completed, the two precast concrete dam segments were separately floated upriver to an outfitting area (located upstream of Braddock Locks and Dam), passing through three locks (Dashields and Emsworth Locks on the Ohio River and Braddock Locks on the Monongahela River) to the location of the new dam site, as noted by Edwardo, Karaffa and Greene.

Dam Segment 1 was a 11,600-ton, 330-foot- by 104-foot-wide concrete section of the dam. The size of the dam segment allowed it to be towed and "locked" through the Dashields, Emsworth and Braddock Locks. The segment was lowered onto the drilled shaft foundations by filling the structure with water and sinking it. The segment-shaft connections were grouted underwater, and the interior of the segment was filled with tremie concrete to displace the water. A neat cement grout was used to fill the 1-foot void that remained between the base of the dam and a pre-placed graded gravel base under the footprint of the dam after the segment was submerged. As part of the foundation preparation, steel sheet piles were driven to rock at both the upstream and downstream limits of the dam segments to serve as

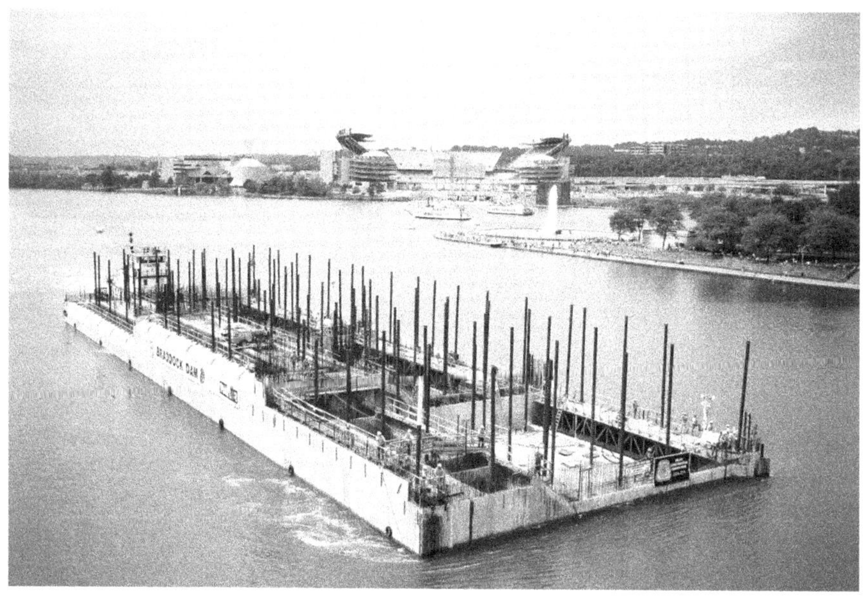

Braddock Dam Segment 1 being towed toward the Point of Pittsburgh. *U.S. Army Corps of Engineers, Pittsburgh District.*

an additional barrier to prevent seepage under the dam. Dam Segment 2, measuring 265 feet by 104 feet and weighing 9,000 tons, was installed in the same manner as Segment 1. There was a cellular closure section that connected Segment 2 to the left abutment of the dam.

To complete the Braddock Dam project, the existing one-hundred-year-old fixed crest dam, located about six hundred feet downstream, was completely removed to the riverbed, and the demolished concrete was used to create underwater simulated reefs to promote fish habitat. Another environmental aspect of the project involved the riverside disposal of material dredged from the footprint of the new dam that was deemed suitable for disposal. Some 400,000 cubic yards of dredged material provided cover for the restoration of a nearby Brownfield site that had been an abandoned steel mill property.

The Braddock Dam Project was recognized in 2004 when selected as the Civil Engineering Project of the Year Award by the Pittsburgh Section of ASCE.

CURRENT IMPROVEMENT ACTIVITIES: LOWER MON PROJECT

Braddock Locks and Dam (or L/D 2); Locks and Dam 3, in Elizabeth, Pennsylvania; and Charleroi Locks and Dam (or L/D 4), in Charleroi, Pennsylvania, are all located on the Monongahela River. They are the three oldest locks currently operating navigation facilities on the Monongahela River in the Pittsburgh District, Army Corps of Engineers. Former Locks and Dam No. 1 was located in Pittsburgh but no longer exists. These locks experience the highest volume of commercial traffic on the entire Monongahela River Navigation System. The pools created by these locks provide industrial and municipal water to local users and are popular with recreational boaters.

As described in the previous section, the Lower Mon Project recently replaced the nearly one-hundred-year-old fixed-crest dam at Braddock Locks and Dam with a gated dam, and in the future, it will involve removal of Locks and Dam 3 in Elizabeth, Pennsylvania, and with the construction of two new 720-foot-long by 84-foot-wide lock chambers at Charleroi Locks located in Monessen, Pennsylvania. The removal of Locks and Dam 3 will create a single pool, between Braddock and Elizabeth, and having a newer gated dam at Braddock Locks and Dam will permit the pool to rise a nominal

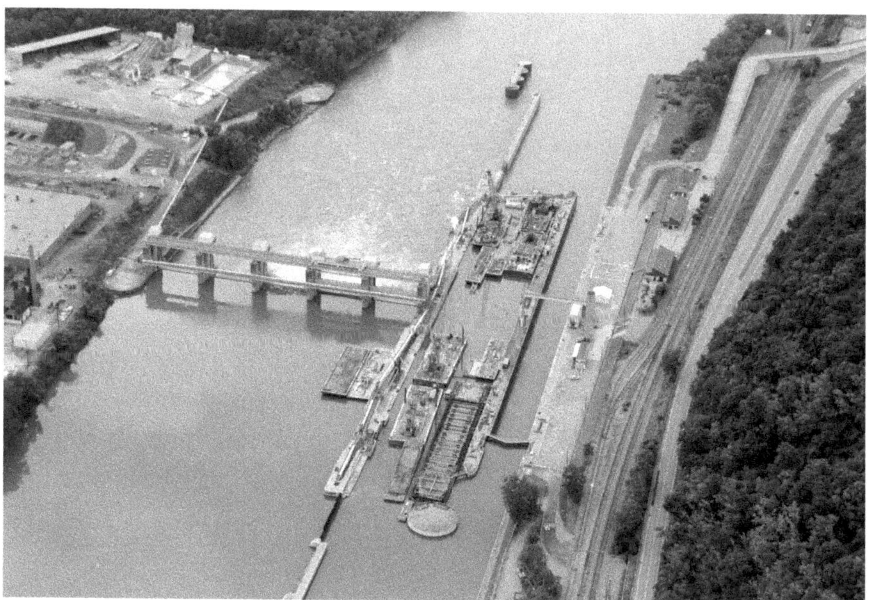

Photograph of current new Charleroi Locks construction. *U.S. Army Corps of Engineers, Pittsburgh District.*

5 feet within this reach of the river. With Locks and Dam 3 removed, from Elizabeth to Charleroi, the river pool will drop a nominal 3.2 feet. Even though familiar river/pool levels will change, there will be no increase in flooding events along the Monongahela River.

Current work at the new Charleroi Locks employs innovative construction features such as precast, post-tensioned box beams founded on drilled shaft piers for the upper guard wall and precast concrete wall panels supported by drilled shafts for the lower guard wall. The new river wall is a combination of cast-in-place monoliths constructed within internally braced cofferboxes and tremie placed concrete monoliths in a non-cofferbox wall constructed in-the-wet using reusable forming system founded on drilled shafts and an emptying basin composed of seven precast segments lifted and placed in-the-wet on concrete pedestals. The new middle wall will be composed of cast-in-place monoliths constructed in internally braced cofferboxes founded on drilled shafts and innovative through-the-sill filling and emptying system located in the upper sill of the new chamber.

FUTURE NAVIGATION IMPROVEMENTS: UPPER OHIO PROJECT

The Upper Ohio Navigation Study (October 2014, revised October 2016) recommends Congressional authorization of the National Economic Development (NED) plan for improving the upper Ohio River Navigation System. The navigation structures in this reach include Emsworth, Dashields and Montgomery Locks and Dams. Emsworth, Dashields and Montgomery, all constructed before 1936, are the first three locks and dams on the Ohio River downstream from Pittsburgh. Montgomery Locks and Dam is located thirty-two miles downstream from Pittsburgh, with the locks near Monaca, Pennsylvania. These facilities have the oldest and smallest lock chambers in the entire Ohio River Navigation System. Built before use of air-entrained concrete, all three lock structures have experienced severe concrete deterioration and are nearing the end of their service lives. The study report recommends construction of one new 110-foot-wide by 600-foot-long lock chamber at each facility, in the footprint of the existing 56- by 360-foot auxiliary lock chambers.

The wider replacement lock chambers will necessitate removal of one gate bay at Emsworth Main Channel Dam and at the Montgomery Dam. At the fixed-crest Dashields Dam, the recommended plan includes shortening the fixed-crest dam and installing one hydraulically operated gate and appurtenant facilities. The recommended new lock will be constructed using in-the-wet construction methods, including a combination of fixed and floating approach walls and a through-the-sill filling and emptying system. The total project cost for all three new chambers is approximately $2.3 billion (October 2014 cost level). The recommended plan's incremental benefit to cost ratio is approximately 4.3:1. This study determined the best plan for maintaining efficient and reliable navigation on the Upper Ohio River over a fifty-year period. The navigation project improvements will maximize economic development benefits consistent with protecting the environment. The three locks and dam facilities were constructed in the 1920s and 1930s, and their reliability exceeds what was the projected service life of all three projects; none of the structures meets modern design criteria. At each navigation structure, there is deteriorated structural concrete and antiquated operating systems.

However, early design efforts are underway to plan for the replacement of the three navigation projects. Foundation explorations at Montgomery

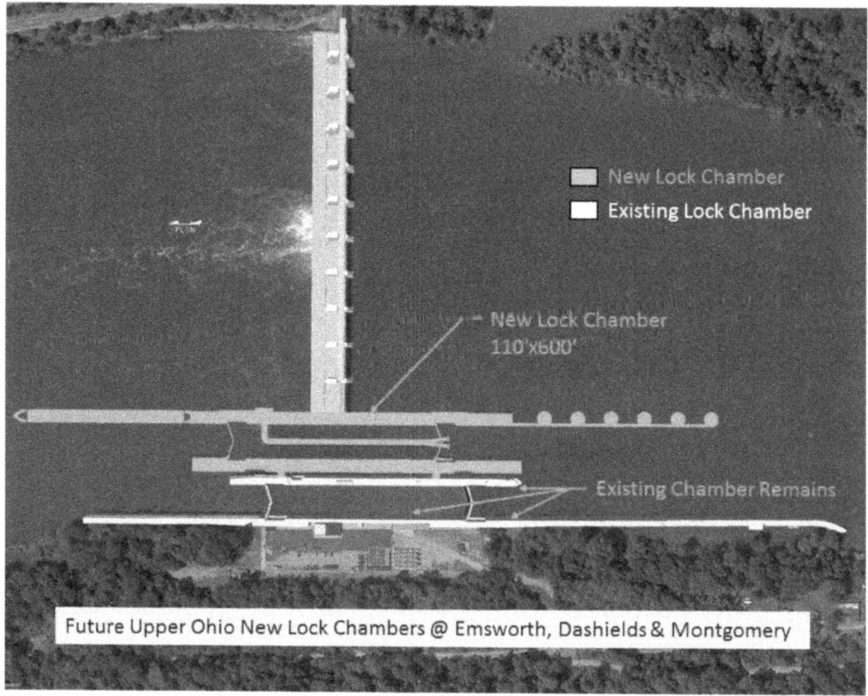

Future Upper Ohio new locks project (rendering). *U.S. Army Corps of Engineers, Pittsburgh District.*

Locks and Dam were initiated in March 2018, which is an important initial design step in the overall Upper Ohio Navigation Study.

With the Lower Monongahela Project being brought to completion in 2024, if efficiently funded, and with the Upper Ohio Navigation Study leading to future improvements of the three navigation projects located downstream of Pittsburgh, the region will realize needed infrastructure upgrades.

BUILDINGS

By John F. Oyler, PhD, PE

The partnership between architects and civil (structural) engineers has evolved in recent years, paralleling the evolution of technology for tall buildings. Historically, small buildings were the province of architects, with an emphasis on aesthetic features. But understanding construction materials and the methods of using them has been the province of engineers, based on their educational training and application in professional practice. With the advent of "skyscrapers," it became obvious that a thorough comprehension of the way gravity and horizontal (primarily wind) loads are transferred from their point of application to the foundation was essential to the design of a functioning structure. To many observers, the importance of the "engineer" part of the architect/engineer team has surpassed that of the "architect" for tall buildings.

The world's first skyscraper was constructed in 1885 in Chicago—the Home Insurance Building. Ten stories and 138 feet high, it was designed by William Le Baron Jenney, an engineer and classmate of Gustave Eiffel at École Centrale Paris. Jenney was born in 1832 in Massachusetts and served as an engineering officer under Generals Sherman and Grant. After the war, he established a firm in Chicago specializing in urban planning and the design of commercial buildings. Several of the future leaders of the "Chicago School" of architecture, including Louis Sullivan and Daniel Burnham, served apprenticeships in his firm.

Although the structure was originally conceived as a wrought-iron structure, Andrew Carnegie persuaded Jenney to utilize "an exotic new material," steel, in the Home Insurance Building. The success of the building obviously influenced the design of Carnegie's new headquarters building in Pittsburgh. The Carnegie Steel Building, constructed in 1895, was Pittsburgh's first steel-framed skyscraper and one of the earliest buildings of this type anywhere in the world. Its architect—the firm of Longfellow, Alden & Harlow—is credited with its conception. It is an early example of the "Chicago School" architecture, heavily influenced by Jenney. At thirteen stories and two hundred feet, it was taller than any other structure in the city except for the granite masonry tower of H.H. Richardson's magnificent Allegheny County Courthouse. The building served as the headquarters for Andrew Carnegie's steel company and later for the United States Steel Company. Located at 428–38 Fifth Avenue, it was demolished in 1952 to permit expansion of Kaufmann's Department Store.

The Park Building (with its Beaux-Arts façade), constructed in 1896, still stands at 351 Fifth Avenue. Fifteen stories and 199 feet tall, it was constructed by industrialists David and William Park and was the first building in Pittsburgh with automatic elevators. Its design is credited to architect George B. Post.

When constructed in 1902 at 437 Grant Street, the Frick Building became Pittsburgh's tallest at twenty floors. Ten years later, when Grant's Hill was removed to facilitate traffic on Grant Street, its basement became its ground floor; consequently, it is now classified as a twenty-one-story building, 330 feet tall. Either designation would have delighted Henry Clay Frick, whose only requirement for the building, located across the street from the thirteen-story headquarters of his rival Andrew Carnegie, was that it be tall enough to keep Carnegie always in Frick's shadow. The architect/engineer for the Frick Building was Daniel Burnham, who would later design the Pennsylvania Railroad's Union Station in 1902 and the Henry W. Oliver Building in 1910. His technical training had come during his employment as a draftsman for Jenney after failing admissions examinations for Harvard and Yale.

The site on which the Frick Building was constructed had been the location of St. Peter's Episcopal Church. Frick had the church carefully disassembled and moved to Oakland, where it was rebuilt at the corner of Forbes Avenue and Craft Street, an interesting decision by a man vilified as a greedy robber baron. Years later, Carlow University demolished the church and constructed an academic building on the site.

The Penn Rose Building, located between Sixteenth and Seventeenth Streets on Penn Avenue, in the Strip District, is believed to be the first all-

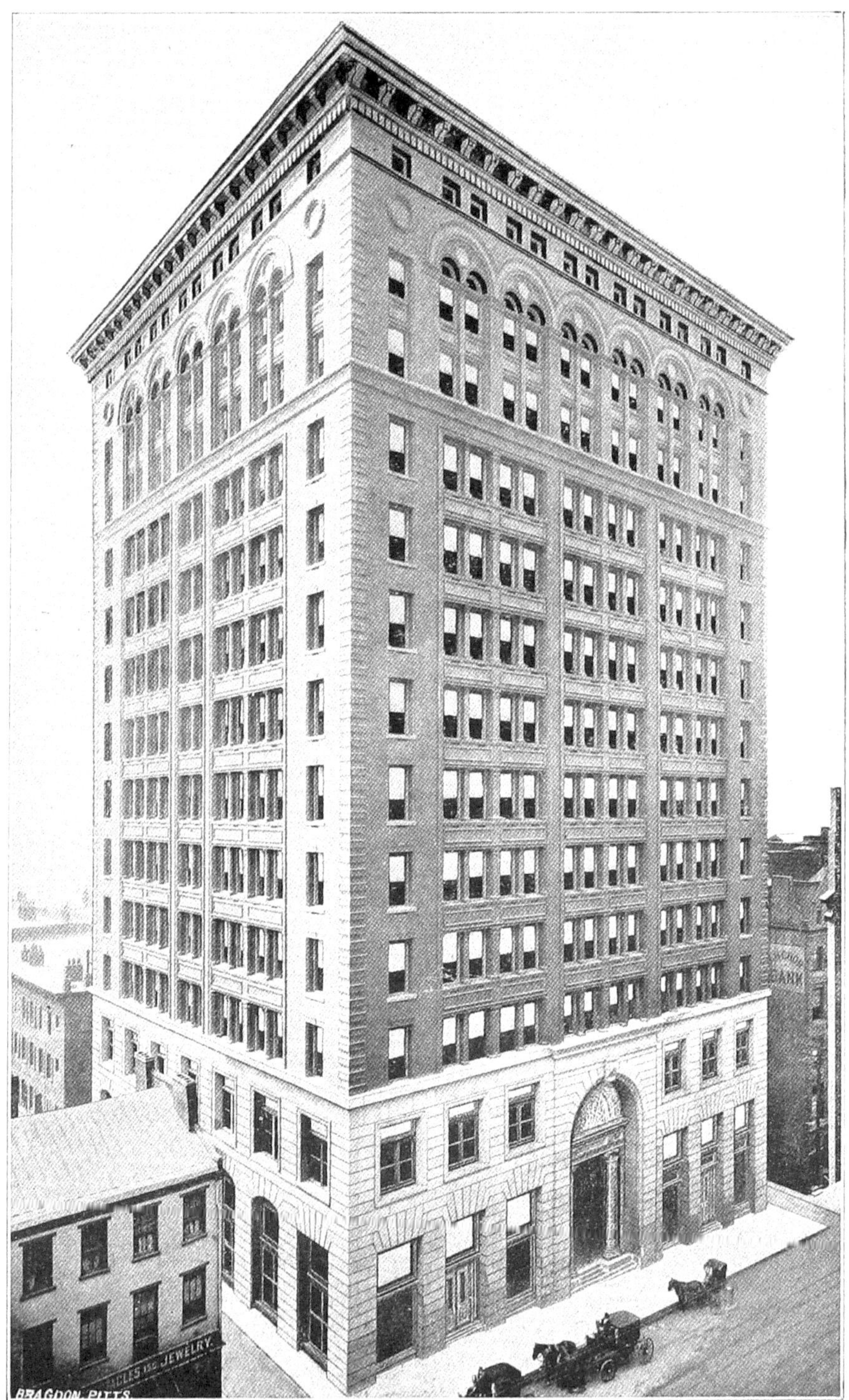
JEWELRY.
BRAGDON, PITTS.

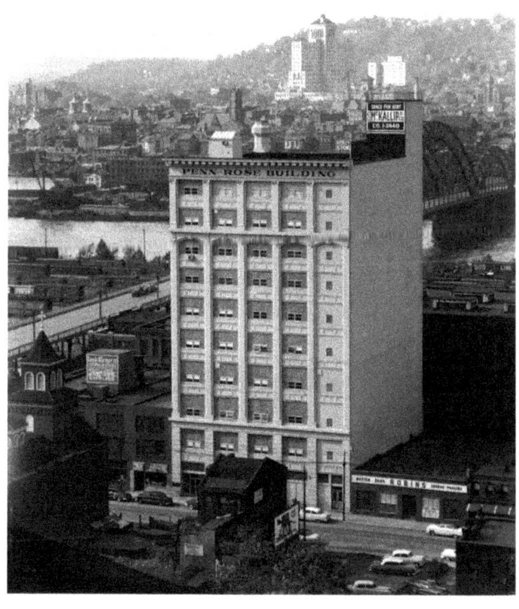

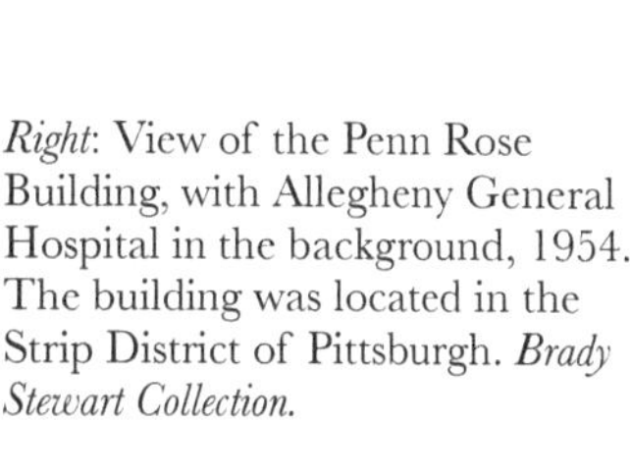

Right: View of the Penn Rose Building, with Allegheny General Hospital in the background, 1954. The building was located in the Strip District of Pittsburgh. *Brady Stewart Collection.*

Opposite: View of the Carnegie Building in 1905 by photographer John Bragdon. *Wikimedia Commons.*

concrete building in Pittsburgh. Built in 1906, it is ten stories tall and is currently being repurposed as a mixed-use/residential facility. Originally known as the Pennsylvania Chocolate Company Building, it was owned by S.S. Marvin and designed by a Philadelphia architectural firm, Ballinger and Perrot.

The distinction of being Pittsburgh's tallest building passed from the Frick Building to the Farmers Deposit National Bank Building in 1910. Designed by architects Arlen & Harlow, it rose twenty-seven stories and 344 feet. Located at 500 Wood Street, it was acquired by Rockwell International Corporation in the mid-1960s and gained national fame when artist Judy Penzer painted a mural fifteen stories high on one face depicting Pittsburgh sports heroes Roberto Clemente, Bill Mazeroski, Jack Lambert, Joe Greene and Mario Lemieux. The building was demolished in 1997.

In 1912, the Henry Oliver Building at 535 Smithfield Street became the tallest structure in the city. Designed by Daniel Burnham, its twenty-five stories and height of 347 feet provided him the opportunity to regain his status as designer of the tallest building in the city. The steel-framed structure is clad with stone and terra cotta. The Oliver Building reigned as "top dog" until 1928, when the First National Bank Building, twenty-six stories and 387 feet high, was completed and became the city's tallest, a title it held

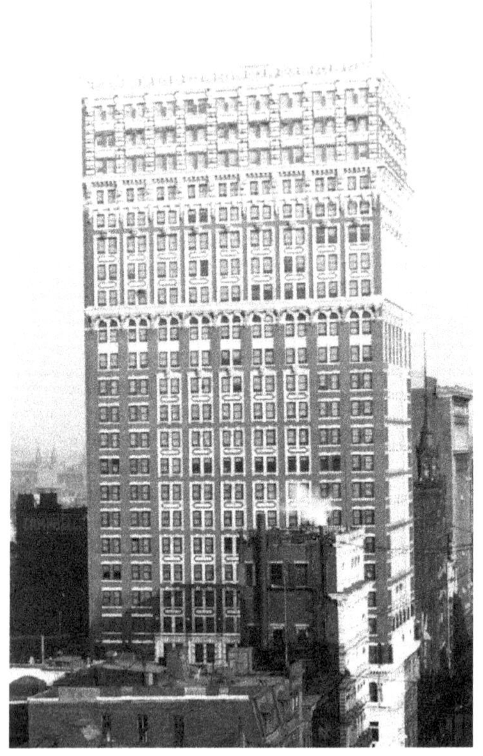

View of the new Farmer's Bank building from the roof of the Empire Building. The building was completed in 1903 and had twenty-four stories. It was demolished in 1997. *Brady Stewart Collection.*

for only one year. It was located at 511 Wood Street. Actually, the original First National Bank Building, an eight-story structure, had been constructed in 1908 by the James L. Stuart Company, a predecessor of Mellon-Stuart. Daniel Burnham was responsible for designing the additional eighteen stories, which were constructed by Thompson, Jarret & Company, one of the first construction firms to build skyscrapers on a national basis.

The Grant Building was completed in 1929. Its forty stories towered over 310 Grant Street and provided an antenna for broadcasts by pioneer radio station KDKA. Henry Hornbostel and Eric Fisher Wood are the architects of record. Dwight P. Robinson & Company was responsible for its construction. The Grant Building surrendered its claim of tallest building to the Cathedral of Learning the next year.

In 1908, the University of Pittsburgh hired architect Henry Hornbostel to develop a plan for its new forty-three-acre campus in Oakland. The resulting "Acropolis Plan" was a series of three-story Classical Revival buildings along the hillside, facing southeast toward Forbes and Fifth Avenues. In 1920, after five buildings had been constructed, the new

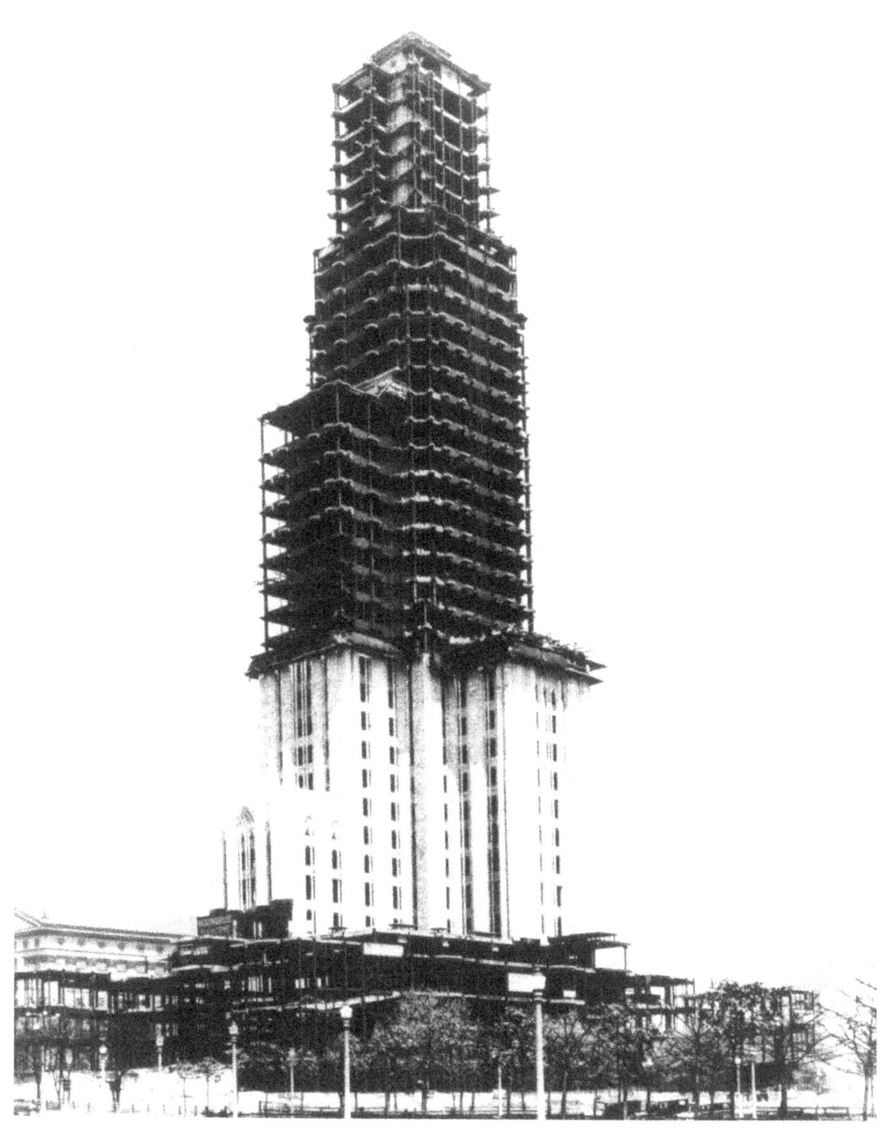

The steel framing of the Cathedral of Learning, 1930. *University of Pittsburgh Archives.*

chancellor, John Bowman, had a different vision. He envisioned a tall building, "a symbol of the life that Pittsburgh through the years had wanted to live." He persuaded Andrew and Richard Mellon to purchase a fourteen-acre site in Oakland, Frick Acres, for its location. They suggested that their nephew, architect Edward P. Mellon, be retained to design the new campus. His concept was an interlocking labyrinth of six-story buildings along the four sides of the large block, with a skyscraper tower at one end. Chancellor Bowman thanked Mellon for his scheme, paid his retainer and then hired Gothic Revival architect Charles Klauder to conceive the tower, which quickly became known as the Cathedral of Learning. Klauder managed to combine the concept of the modern skyscraper with the principles of Gothic architecture. It indeed became a place where "[t]hey shall find wisdom here and faith—in steel and stone, in character and thought."

Structural design of the cathedral was done by Homer S. Balcom, better known as the structural designer of the Empire State Building. Construction was performed by the Stone & Webster Engineering Company under the responsibility of Edward F. Blakeslee. The same firm also was responsible for design and construction of nearby Pitt Stadium. When the last girder was placed and the United States flag was hoisted at the top of the steel structure in 1929, it was the tallest building in the city. Although the first classes, in engineering drafting, were held in February 1931, the cathedral's construction phase was not considered complete until June 1937.

At 582 feet high and forty-four stories, the Art Deco Gulf Building, at 707 Grant Street, was the tallest building in Pittsburgh when it was opened in 1932. The McClintic-Marshall Construction Company served as structural engineer, and Mellon-Stuart functioned as general contractor. The architects were Trowbridge & Livingston, with Edward P. Mellon assisting. The building is best noted for the changes in lighting of its pyramidal top to denote changes in the weather.

The Mellon-Stuart Company, now a subsidiary of Michael Baker International, was created in 1917 by the merger of the James L. Stuart Company and the Robert Grace Contracting Company, a firm founded by Thomas A. Mellon to provide general contracting services to the railroad industry. In addition to the Gulf Building, Mellon-Stuart also constructed the nearby 475-foot-tall, thirty-four-story Koppers Building.

In 1888, Charles D. Marshall and Howard McClintic graduated from Lehigh University with degrees in civil engineering. With three other associates, they formed the Shiffler Bridge Company, later part of the American Bridge Company. With financial help from Andrew Mellon,

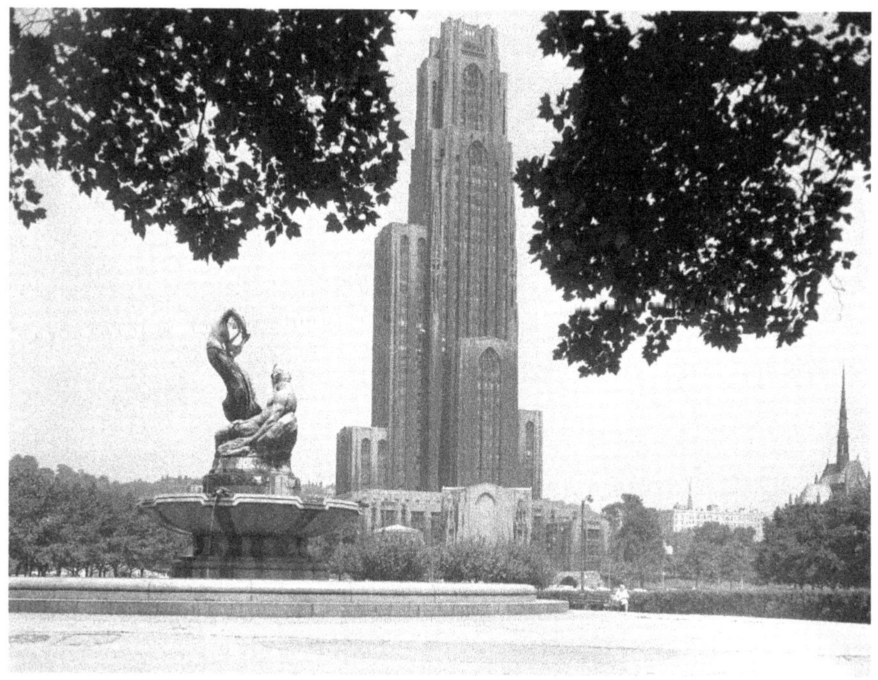

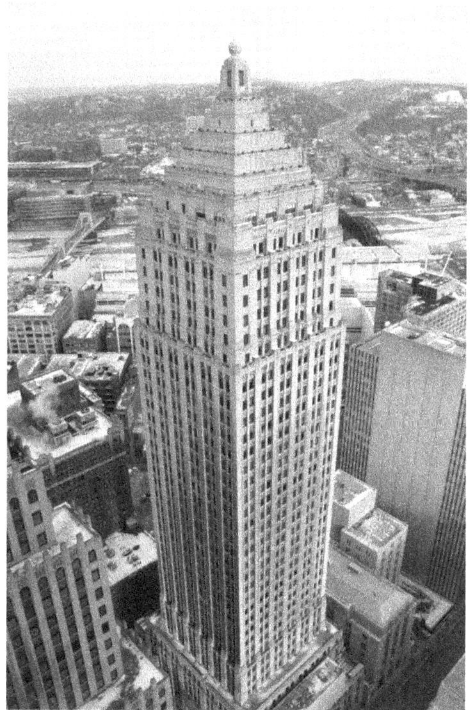

Above: The forty-two-story Cathedral of Learning is the tallest educational building in the Western Hemisphere. The 2,000-room and 2,529-window building was completed in 1937. View from the University of Pittsburgh Cathedral of Learning from Schenley Park, Oakland section of Pittsburgh, 1952. *From http://brooklineconnection.com/history/Facts/Cathedral.html.*

Left: Gulf Tower, from US Steel Tower, photographed by Derek Jensen, 2007. *Brady Stewart Collection.*

the pair then organized the McClintic-Marshall Construction Company, which by 1930 was the largest independent steel manufacturer in the country. In addition to the Gulf Building, their accomplishments include the Ambassador Bridge in Detroit, the longest span in the world at the time; the George Washington Bridge, which then became the longest span in the world; one half of the floors in the Empire State Building; and the lock gates for the Panama Canal.

The Aluminum Corporation of America moved into its new Pittsburgh headquarters in the thirty-story, 410-foot-tall Alcoa Building at 425 Sixth Avenue in 1953. Designed by architect Harrison & Abramovitz, it was the first major building in the world with an all-aluminum façade. The George A. Fuller Company served as general contractor.

In 1960, IBM decided to build a thirteen-story office building in Pittsburgh at 60 Boulevard of the Allies. The building is now known as the United Steelworkers building. The architectural firm selected, Curtis and Davis, had no experience with tall buildings; it turned to Worthington, Skilling, Helle, and Jackson for engineering support. John Skilling proposed a new concept, which he called a "framed tube." The design was based on carrying all the vertical and horizontal loads in the external faces, leaving the interior column free. Skilling proposed designing the external frames as lattice trusses, much like the Ithiel Town trusses in covered bridges a century earlier. All the members were oriented diagonally, connected to one another to form a series of diamonds. It is believed this was the first major building to be designed without either internal framing or an independent concrete core handling transverse loads.

Responsibility for the design of this unique building was assigned to the firm's New York office, managed by Leslie Robertson. Because of the multiple redundancy of the lattice truss, he elected to utilize Hardy Cross moment distribution to analyze it. He assembled a team of twenty analysts, each operating a mechanical desk calculator, to perform the many calculations required for the numerous iterations on which this method is based. In addition, because the lattice truss required all members to have roughly the same size, Robertson decided to take advantage of different strength steels, another novel concept for building design. Eventually, five different grades of steel were used, color coded to minimize confusion during construction. U.S. Steel supplied the steel, and American Bridge erected it. U.S. Steel was so pleased with the design that it was a foregone conclusion that Robertson would be selected to design its new corporate center in Pittsburgh.

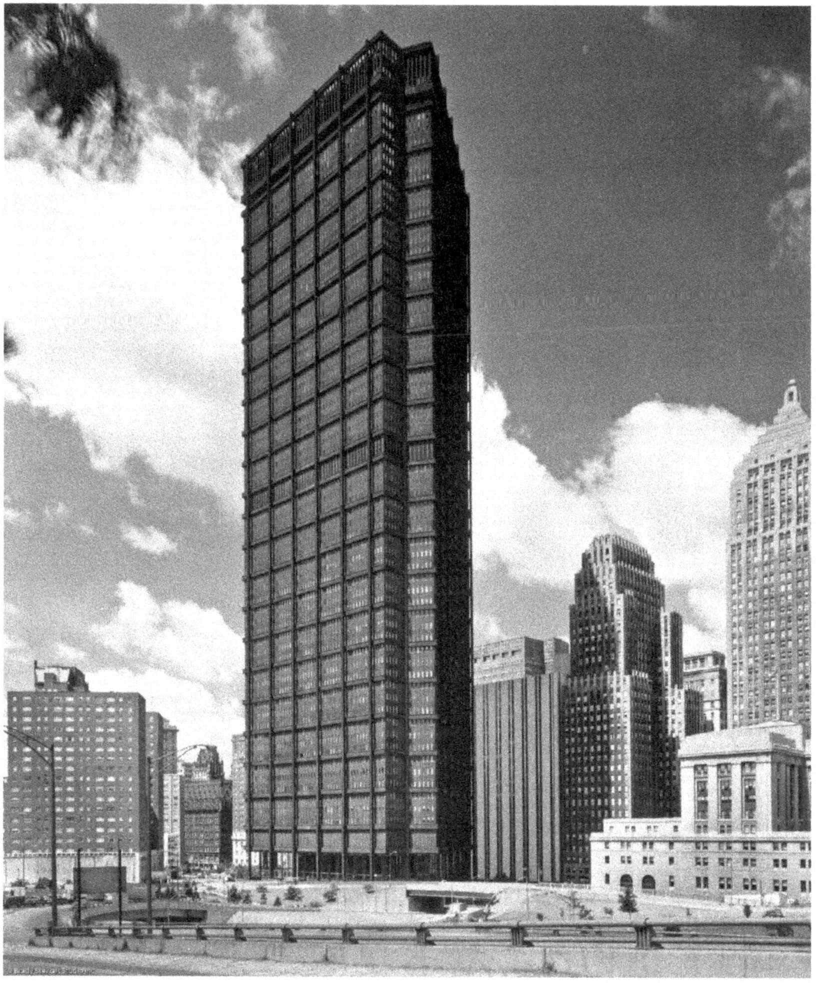

View of the new U.S. Steel Building, 1971. Completed in 1970, the U.S. Steel Building is the largest skyscraper in Pittsburgh and the fourth largest in Pennsylvania at sixty-four floors. *Brady Stewart Collection.*

The U.S. Steel Building, located at 600 Grant Street, was a remarkable engineering achievement when it was completed in 1971. At that time, it was the tallest building in the world outside New York and Chicago at sixty-four stories and 841 feet. It has a triangular footprint echoing downtown Pittsburgh's Golden Triangle, with indented corners to provide additional corner offices. Each of the floors and the roof has an area of 36,500 square feet, giving it the distinction of having the largest roof at its height of any building in the world.

The structural design for the building was by Leslie E. Robertson Associates. In an effort to demonstrate the practical aspects of Cor-Ten, a new weathering constructional steel formulated to resist corrosion despite remaining unpainted, the massive columns were exposed on the exterior of the building. The result was a distinctive dark-brown oxide coating that required minimum maintenance. In addition, the hollow columns were filled with water and a rust inhibitor to provide fire protection.

Between the design of the IBM Building and the U.S. Steel Building, Robertson's major project was the design of the Twin Towers at the World Trade Center. By that time, his office had acquired its first computer, an IBM 1620, and the programming language STRESS (Structural Engineering System Solver). STRESS was developed at MIT by Dr. Steven Fenves while on a postdoctoral engagement there before returning to his alma mater, the University of Illinois, and joining the faculty there. Dr. Fenves came to Carnegie Mellon University in 1971, eventually becoming head of its Department of Civil Engineering and being elected to the National Academy of Engineering in 1976. The inspiration for STRESS was the success of COGO (Coordinate Geometry), a data conversion program used by surveyors to produce digital maps, developed earlier at MIT. STRESS eventually evolved into STRUDL (Structural Design Language), a basic platform for structural design and finite element analysis. When the STRESS package became generally available, an active users group immediately began to develop specialized versions of it. Like Robertson and his colleagues in New York, two young structural engineers employed by Pittsburgh's Dravo Corporation, Richard Harig and David Heindel, developed DravoSTRESS, a powerful package customized for the analysis of complex bulk material–handling machines and heavy-duty industrial mill buildings.

Several notable tall buildings have been erected in Pittsburgh since construction of the U.S. Steel Building. One Oxford Centre, 300 Grant Street, opened in 1983. It has forty-five stories and towers 615 feet high. The same year, the BNY Mellon Building, 500 Grant Street, was completed. Originally intended to house the headquarters of the Dravo Corporation, it is the second-tallest building in the city at 725 feet, with fifty-four stories. Wilson Becket and Associates was the architect and Turner Construction the general contractor.

In 1984, Philip Johnson's magnificent PPG Place was opened. Its Neo-Gothic design was influenced by the Allegheny County Courthouse and the Cathedral of Learning. Bounded by Wood Street, Forbes Avenue, Stanwix Street and the Boulevard of the Allies, the complex includes six towers, the tallest of which,

One PPG Place, has forty stories reaching a height of 635 feet. The complex contains more than 1 million square feet of PPG Solarban windows, an effective demonstration of the owner's primary product. Leslie E. Robertson Associates performed the structural engineering for the complex, which was constructed by a joint venture of Mellon-Stuart and Blount Brothers.

Located at the corner of Fifth and Liberty Avenues, Fifth Avenue Place, completed in 1988, was originally intended to have a height of 616 feet, but zoning restrictions limited it to thirty-one stories. The architect, Stubbins Associates, responded to the restriction by incorporating a long, slender mast protruding from a quartered pyramidal roof, producing a design evoking memories of superhero comic books. Mellon-Stuart served as general contractor for the building.

Completed in 2015, the thirty-three-story Tower at PNC Plaza, 300 Fifth Avenue, is credited with being one of the "greenest" tall buildings ever built. Among the sustainable attributes that won it a LEED Platinum rating are an operable double-skin façade and an innovative solar chimney in its core that together enable the building to operate at "net-zero" energy 30 percent of the time. Also inherent in its design are an onsite gray water reusage system and a large sloping roof that serves as a solar collector. The tower was constructed by P.J. Dick, with Buro Happold Pittsburgh providing the structural engineering.

Pittsburgh has been the home to numerous impressive sports stadia, including three incarnations of Exposition Park on the North Side from 1879 to 1915, Forbes Field from 1909 to 1969, the previously mentioned Pitt Stadium, Three Rivers Stadium from 1970 to 2001, Heinz Field from 2001 to present and PNC Park from 2001 to present. Forbes Field was designed by architect Charles Leavitt and constructed by the Nicola Building Company. The home of the Pittsburgh Pirates, it was located on seven acres of land near the Carnegie Library adjacent to Schenley Park in the Oakland section of Pittsburgh. Remnants of the ballpark still stand, including a section of the brick outfield fence near where Bill Mazeroski hit a celebrated home run to win the 1960 World Series.

The architects for Three Rivers Stadium were Deeter, Richy Sipple and Michael Baker Jr. Osborn Engineering provided the structural engineering. A joint venture of Huber, Hunt & Nichols and Mascaro Corporation performed the construction. A unique characteristic of this multipurpose stadium was its ability to move large portions of the grandstand to accommodate the different layouts required for baseball and football. The system of trucks and hoists used to move the grandstands was designed and installed by the Engineering Works Division of Dravo Corporation. The stadium was imploded in 2001 and converted to parking for the Pittsburgh Pirates at PNC Park and Pittsburgh Steelers and University of Pittsburgh Panther football games at Heinz Field. Heinz Field was designed by architects HOK Sports and WTW Architects, with structural engineering by Bliss & Nyitray Inc. A joint venture of Hunt Construction Group and the Mascaro Corporation built the stadium. HOK Sports and L.D. Astorino & Associates served as architects for PNC Park, with the Thornton-Tomasetti Group providing structural engineering and Dick Corporation performing construction of the facility.

Completed in 1961, the Civic Arena was a remarkable engineering and architectural achievement, the first major sports venue in the world with a retractable roof. Covering 170,000 square feet, the roof consisted of eight

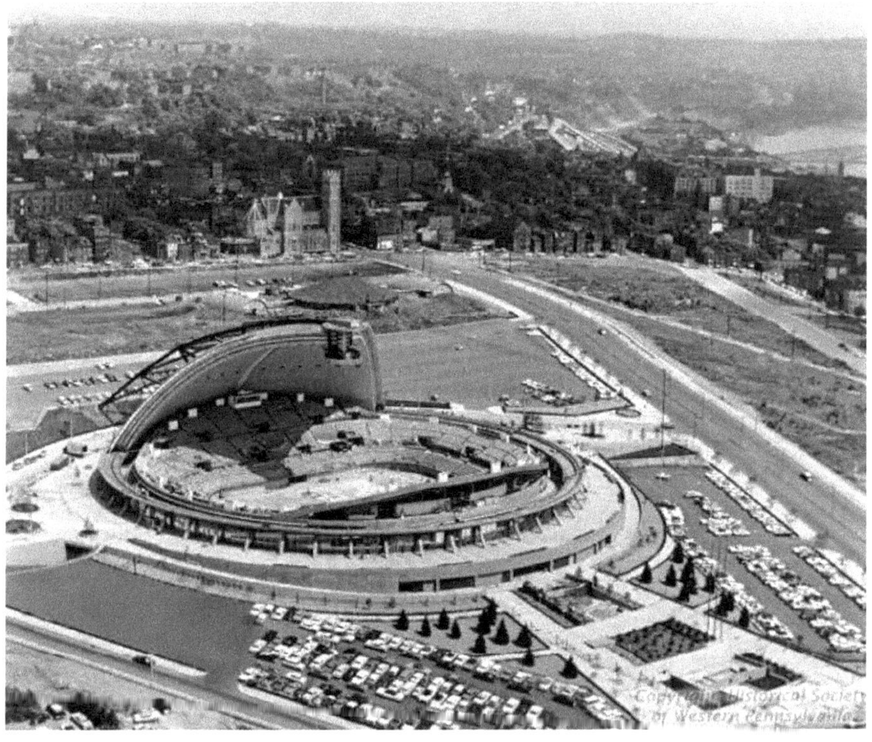

The Civic Arena, originally the Civic Auditorium and later renamed Mellon Arena, was built in 1961. The arena, which covered 170,000 square feet, had the first retractable roof ever on a major sports venue in the world. It was constructed with just shy of three thousand tons of steel manufactured in Pittsburgh. *From http://brooklineconnection.com/history/Facts/Cathedral.html.*

overlapping leaves, each supported on powered trucks running on a 417-foot-diameter track at the roof's base and a universal pivot joint 109 feet above the center of the track. The pivot was supported by a massive tripod space frame cantilevered from one side.

The architect for the Civic Arena was Mitchell & Richey; Amman & Whitney designed the dome. The trucks were designed and supplied by Heyl and Patterson. Dick Corporation executed the foundation and reinforced concrete portion of the project. American Bridge erected the dome, utilizing a pair of custom-designed pie-shaped rolling steel scaffolds. Constructed initially as a venue for Pittsburgh's Civic Light Opera, the arena quickly established a reputation as a home for the National Hockey League Pittsburgh Penguins, with the obvious nickname "the Igloo." The last time the roof was opened was in 1995, for a musical concert. In 2010, the Penguins moved to a new, larger venue in nearby CONSOL Energy Center (now known as PPG Paints Arena). Despite passionate opposition by historical preservationists, the arena was demolished two years later.

No discussion of civil engineering achievements in Western Pennsylvania would be complete without mention of George Washington Gale Ferris Jr. and his observation wheel. Ferris was a well-established civil engineer and bridge builder in 1891 when he learned that Daniel Burnham, by now the director of works of the World Columbian Exposition, had issued a challenge to American engineers to design and build a signature monument for the upcoming World's Fair in Chicago "that would surpass the Eiffel Tower."

A civil engineering graduate of Rensselaer Polytechnic Institute, Ferris had spent five years building railroads and bridges for a variety of employers before moving to Pittsburgh in 1886 and establishing G.W.G. Ferris & Company, Inspecting Engineers. He then diversified by forming Ferris, Kaufman and Company to design and build major bridges across the Ohio River at Wheeling and Cincinnati. Ferris's response to the fair promoters' challenge was an impressive effort to surpass Eiffel: a large observation wheel with thirty-six cars, each capable of holding sixty people. For fifty cents, a fairgoer was treated to a twenty-minute trip around two revolutions of the wheel's 864-foot circumference, including one uninterrupted nine-minute revolution. William F. Gronau, Ferris's partner and fellow RPI alumnus, is credited with responsibility for the detailed design of the wheel, while Ferris concentrated on business aspects. After its rousing success in Chicago, the wheel later became a showpiece at the Louisiana Purchase Exposition in St. Louis in 1903. It was eventually scrapped in 1906.

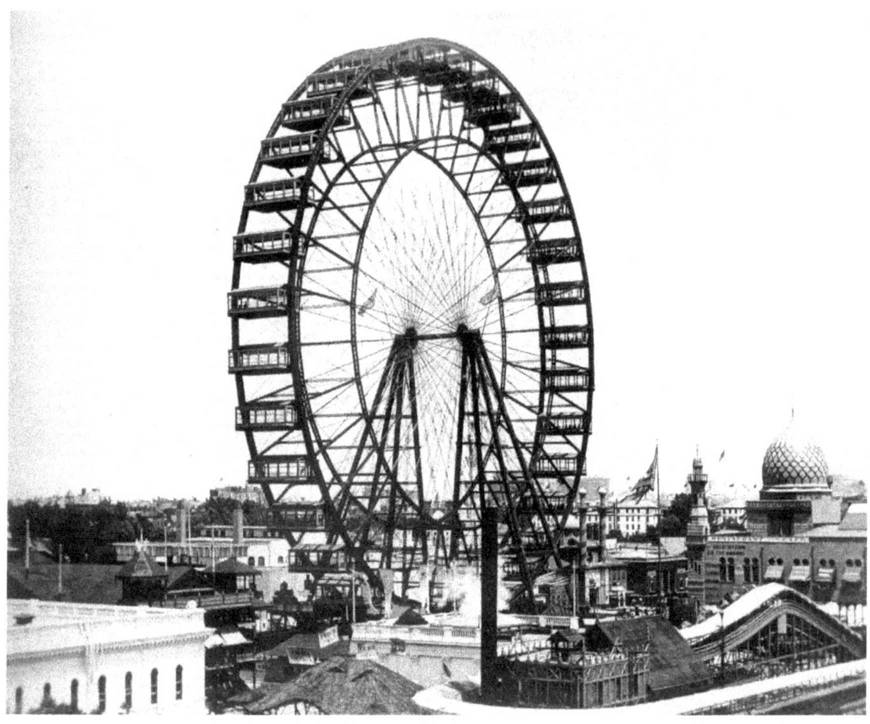

Ferris wheel exposition, 1893. *Historic Photos of the Chicago World's Fair; text and captions by Russell Lewis, obtained from https://jcallahanphotoshop.wordpress.com/tag/chicago-worlds-fair.*

Although some of the buildings discussed in this chapter are no longer in existence, those that remain are an important part of the civil engineering heritage of this region. It is appropriate that the contribution of the civil engineers who designed and constructed them be remembered and their legacy be shared with future generations of civil engineers.

Epilogue

A MOMENT IN TIME

By N. Catherine Bazán-Arias, PhD, PE

It's the spring of 2018. For more than a year, our authors have strived to take the readers on a journey of our region's and city's civil engineering history. This was an ambitious endeavor: Pittsburgh's resilience and innovation must be experienced; each version of Pittsburgh's story has been unique to the witness. Because their work could not be exhaustive, the authors aimed to entice the readers to learn more—experience more—beyond the covers of this publication.

In a parallel timeline one hundred years ago, the ASCE Pittsburgh Association—present-day ASCE Pittsburgh Section—was founded. The Section's inaugural officers and members aimed to provide a platform for civil engineers to gather; exchange ideas; transfer knowledge; encourage academic formation, research and applied knowledge; and thus optimize their work to best serve the public. From its inception, this platform extended to the public including students, researchers, teachers and other professionals.

It's now time to look forward. What will the next one hundred years bring for civil engineering in Pittsburgh? And how will ASCE's Pittsburgh Section support civil engineers in the future?

A significant part of the answer to this question lies in our exponential advancement in technology in the past few decades. Unprecedented, groundbreaking progress in nanotechnology, construction materials, construction techniques, modeling and reliability techniques—to name a few fields—has exponentially advanced and enhanced the role of civil engineers in our communities. Another part of the answer lies in recent natural extreme events that today affect significant numbers of people. Lastly, the growth of our population—and thus the increased density of residents in our region—is demanding new ways to address maintenance of our infrastructure and financial support of new capital projects.

The Pittsburgh Section has exalted, and will continue to exalt, civil engineers who promote innovative approaches to our professions. The Section advocates that these "thinkers" and "doers" are the bridge between great ideas and feasible solutions—all for society's benefit. A recent achievement recognized at our Section's Award Banquet is a project team that pioneered the use of a Diverging Diamond Interchange (DDI) in Pennsylvania. This new interchange design improves pedestrian and traffic safety by minimizing conflict points and shortening pedestrian crossing lengths, among other benefits. Another garlanded team of engineers implemented state-of-the-art design practices and re-created a landmark structure at the entrance to one of Pittsburgh's most historic parks. Innovative design concepts allowed the steel arch and floor system of the replacement bridge to be erected during a one-weekend closure of the underlying interstate by erecting sub-assemblies prior to installation. As a final example, yet another group of civil engineers used a creative and innovative approach to meeting the "Triple Bottom Line" by sustainably improving environmental, economic and social conditions for bicyclists in the city of Pittsburgh. Civil engineers provided a design to reduce the number of conflict points to improve safety, reclaimed green space and updated bicycle lanes, including Pittsburgh's first implementation of two-stage, left-turn boxes for bicycles.

These awards highlight some recent civil engineering achievements in Pittsburgh and its surrounding regions. But the future lies with developing technology to open even more doors to new implementations. Our local academic and research institutions are working on making our built—and yet to be built—environment more operationally efficient and robust through research on the use of information and communication technologies; sustainable engineering; high-performance buildings; life-cycle assessment; risk management; and industrial ecology, among many other growing areas.

What will the next one hundred years bring for civil engineering in Pittsburgh? Perhaps construction methods, materials and equipment that can address project needs using a fraction of the resources these presently take; materials that heal and learn to better adjust to changing climate and loading; tele-transportation to the newly developed Moon City…the sky may no longer be the limit!

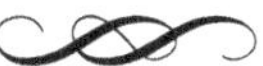

We can only tentatively predict what the future holds, but we're certain that civil engineers will continue to address society's needs in technically sound and culturally thoughtful ways. In devoting dedication, commitment and passion to this publication, we do so as a testimonial for our profession and our communities. We trust you will share this work with all those who will benefit and ideally carry their own contributions to our region and city's infrastructure. We trust the future generations of civil engineers that will follow us will create their own legacy and become part of the sturdy backbone and intricate web that will allow Pittsburgh and its environs to thrive for centuries to come. Our best wishes remain with you so that someday the story you witness and share with others can also be reflected in the prosperity of our city and our region. In Pittsburgh, we trust that the ASCE Section will continue to strengthen and grow as we have seen in the last century. Further, we entrust future members to remain engaged with our region, our city and our Section and steward civil engineering and carry it through 2118 and beyond.

BIBLIOGRAPHY

Prologue

American Society of Civil Engineers. "About ASCE." http://www.asce.org/about_asce.

———. "About Civil Engineering." http://www.asce.org/about_civil_engineering.

The Brookline Connection. "Short History of the Evolution of Coal Hill (Mount Washington)." http://www.brooklineconnection.com/history/Facts/CoalHill.html.

The Free Library. "The Testimony of William Hunter Dammond: The First African American Graduate of the University of Pittsburgh." *Journal of Pan African Studies* (2007). https://www.thefreelibrary.com/The+testimony+of+William+Hunter+Dammond%3a+the+first+African+American...-a0192353372.

Maier, Em. "225: Through Decades and Change Cathedral Endures, Develops." *Pitt News*, October 12, 2012. https://pittnews.com/article/13284/archives/225-through-decades-and-change-cathedral-endures-develops.

Meadowcroft Rockshelter and Historic Village. http://www.heinzhistorycenter.org/meadowcroft.

Palucka, Tim, and Sherie Mershon. *The Engineers' Society of Western Pennsylvania: Celebrating 125 Years of Engineering*. Tarentum, PA: Word Association Publishers, 2006.

Pennsylvania's Borders

The American Society of Civil Engineers. "The Mason-Dixon Line National Historic Civil Engineering Landmark, 1978." http://www.asce.org/project/mason-dixon-line.

The Internet Archive. "Fitzherbert's Book of Husbandry." http://www.archive.org/details/bookofhusbandryOOfitzuoft.

Linklater, Andro. *Measuring America*. New York: Walker & Company, 2002.

Pennsylvania Historical & Museum Commission. "Pennsylvania Charter to William Penn—March 4, 1681" http://www.phmc.state.pa.us/portal/communities/documents/1681-1776/pennsylvania-charter.html.

Sipe, C. Hale. *The Indian Chiefs of Pennsylvania*. Lewisburg, PA: Wennawoods Publishing, 1927.

Stevens, Sylvester K., Ralph W. Cordier and Florence O. Benjamin. *Exploring Pennsylvania*. New York: Harcourt, Brace & World Inc., 1953.

Whitman, Benjamin. *Nelson's Biographical Dictionary and Historical Reference Book of Erie County, Pennsylvania.* Erie, PA: S.B. Nelson, 1896. The Internet Archive. https://archive.org/details/nelsonsbiographi00whit.

Canals

Baumgardner, Mahlon J., and Floyd G. Hoenstine. *The Allegheny Old Portage Railroad, 1834–1854: Building, Operation and Travel between Hollidaysburg and Johnstown Pennsylvania*. N.p.: Pennsylvania Society Sons of the American Revolution, 1952.

Bornstein, Peter L. *Wedding of the Waters: The Erie Canal and the Making of a Great Nation*. New York: W.W. Norton & Company, 2005.

Corkan, A.M., AB. "The Beaver and Erie Canal." Washington and Jefferson College, for Master of Arts in Graduate School of University of Pittsburgh. Available at Pennsylvania Department, Carnegie Library of Pittsburgh, qr 386.C81.

Harris, Robert. *Canals and Their Architecture*. New York: Frederick A. Praeger, Publishers, 1969.

Jacobs, Harry A. *The Juniata Canal and Old Portage Railroad*. Hollidaysburg, PA: Blair County Historical Society, 1941. Reprint, 1969.

Johnson, George W. *History of the Development of Transportation in Lawrence County*. New Castle, PA, 1916.

Kapsch, Robert J. *Over the Alleghenies: Early Canals and Railroads of Pennsylvania.* Morgantown: West Virginia University Press, 2013.

McCullough, Robert, and Walter Leuba. *The Pennsylvania Main Line Canal.* York, PA: American Canal and Transportation Center, 1973.

Pennsylvania Board of Canal Commissioners' Records, Bureau of Land Records. Pennsylvania Historical and Museum Commission, Pennsylvania State Archives, Harrisburg, Pennsylvania.

Pennsylvania Main Line Canal, Juniata and Western Divisions. Special Study, National Park Service, 1993.

Roberts, Solomon W., Civil Engineer. *Reminiscences of the First Railroad Over the Allegheny Mountain.* N.p., 1878.

Shank, William H. *The Amazing Pennsylvania Canals.* York, PA: Historical Society of York County, 1965.

Sylvester Welch's Report on the Allegheny Portage Railroad, 1833. Gettysburg, PA: Thomas Publications, 1988.

Railroads

Aitken, David W. *The Little Saw Mill Run Railroad: Its Life and Legacy.* Chicora, PA: Mechling Bookbindery and Bookbinders Workshop, 2017.

Herron, James T. "Canonsburg's Prosperity Arrived by Railroad." *Jefferson College Times*, March, 2000. Jefferson College Historical Society.

Oyler, John F. "The Beginnings of the Chartiers Valley Railroad." Bridgeville Area Historical Society, February 16, 2017. http://www.bridgevillehistory.org/oyler-2017-02-16.html.

———. "The Pittsburgh and Castle Shannon Railroad." Bridgeville Area Historical Society, April 17, 2017. http://www.bridgevillehistory.org/oyler-2017-04-17.html.

Schaeffer, Gene P. *Montour Railroad.* N.p.: Silver Brook Junction Publishing Company, 1996.

Walton, Walter F. "Pittsburgh Southern Railroad, West Virginia Aspirations that Came to Naught." Three Rivers Narrow Gauge Historical Society, March 1990.

———. "The South Pennsylvania Railroad, or The Railroad that Might Have Been." History and Heritage Committee, Pittsburgh Section, the American Society of Civil Engineers, 1984.

Roads and Highways

Bigelow, Edward. "Let's Learn from the Past." *Pittsburgh Post-Gazette*, December 9, 2017. http://www.post-gazette.com/life/lifestyle/2009/07/16/Let-s-Learn-From-the-Past-Edward-Bigelow/stories/200907160401.

Bridges and Tunnels of Allegheny County and Pittsburgh, PA. "Bigelow Boulevard, Pittsburgh, PA." http://pghbridges.com/articles/fieldnote_bigelowblvd.htm.

Brookline Connection. "The Boulevard of the Allies." December 9, 2017. http://www.brooklineconnection.com/history/Facts/BlvdAllies.html.

Bruckart, Aaron T. "Tour Highlights History of Butler Plank Road." *Pittsburgh Tribune-Review*, November 15, 2007. http://triblive.com/x/pittsburghtrib/news/pittsburgh/s_537946.html.

Dakelman, Mitchell E., and Neal A. Schorr. *The Pennsylvania Turnpike*. Charleston, SC: Arcadia Publishing, 2004.

Fort Necessity National Battlefield. "The National Road." National Park Service. https://www.nps.gov/fone/learn/historyculture/nationalroad.htm.

Jones, Penelope R. *The Story of the Pennsylvania Turnpike*. Mechanisburg, PA: Camelot Farms, 1950.

Lincoln Highway Association. "Lincoln Highway Info." https://www.lincolnhighwayassoc.org/info.

Olmsted, Fredrick Law. *Pittsburgh, Main Thoroughfares and the Down Town District*. Report to the Pittsburgh Civil Commission, 1911.

Pennsylvania Highways. "I-79." December 29, 2017. http://www.pahighways.com/interstates/I79.html.

———. "I-376." December 29, 2017. http://www.pahighways.com/interstates/I376.html.

———. "I-279." December 29, 2017. http://www.pahighways.com/interstates/I279.html.

———. "US 30." http://www.pahighways.com/us/US30.html.

———. "US 22." http://www.pahighways.com/us/US22.html.

Pittsburgh Art Places. http://www.pittsburghartplaces.org/accounts/view/290.

Preston, David L. *Braddock's Defeat*. New York: Oxford University Press, 2015.

Shank, William H., PE. *Indian Trails to Super Highways*. York, PA: American Canal & Transportation Center, 1988.

Verona Historical Society. "Stone Pylons." December 9, 2017. http://www.veronahistory.org/stone-pylons.html.

Wallace, Paul A. *Indian Paths of Pennsylvania*. Harrisburg: Pennsylvania Historical and Museum Commission, 1965.

Bridges

Baughn, James, et al. bridgehunter.com.

bridgemapper.com.

Cridlebaugh, Bruce. Bridges and Tunnels of Allegheny County and Pittsburgh, Pennsylvania. www.pghbridges.com.

DeLony, Eric. *Landmark American Bridges*. New York: American Society of Civil Engineers, Bullfinch Press, 1993.

Gangewere, Robert J. *The Bridges of Pittsburgh and Allegheny County*. Pittsburgh, PA: Carnegie Library of Pittsburgh, 2001.

Gies, Joseph. *Bridges and Men*. New York: Grosset & Dunlap, Universal Library, 1963.

Historic American Buildings Survey/Historic American Engineering Record/Historic American Landscapes Survey. Library of Congress. http://www.loc.gov/pictures/collection/hh.

Holth, Nathan, et al. historicbridges.org.

Hopkins, H.J. *A Span of Bridges: An Illustrated History*. United Kingdom: David & Charles, 1970.

Jackson, Donald C. *Great American Bridges and Dams.* New York: John Wiley & Sons Inc., 1988.

Kidney, Walter C. *Pittsburgh's Bridges Architecture and Engineering*. Pittsburgh, PA: Pittsburgh History & Landmarks Foundation, 1999.

Leech, Thomas, and Linda Kaplan. *Bridges…Pittsburgh at the Point: A Journey through History*. Tarentum, PA: Word Association Publishers, 2016.

Mack, Elizabeth B. *The Architecture of Bridges*. New York: Museum of Modern Art, 1949.

Pennsylvania Department of Internal Affairs. *Historic Highway Bridges in Pennsylvania*. Harrisburg, PA, 1986.

White, Joseph. *The Bridges of Pittsburgh*. Pittsburgh. PA: Cramer Printing, 1928.

Wilson, Todd, and Helen Wilson. *Images of America: Pittsburgh's Bridges*. Charleston, SC: Arcadia Publishing, 2015.

Public Transportation

Aupperlee, Aaron. "Former CMU Professor to Lead Uber Self-Driving Car Efforts in Pittsburgh." TribLIVE, April 28, 2017. http://triblive.com/local/allegheny/12243801-74/former-cmu-professor-to-lead-uber-self-driving-car-efforts-in-pittsburgh.

———. "Uber Users Can Get a Driverless Car in Pittsburgh." TribLIVE, September 19, 2016. http://triblive.com/news/allegheny/11105274-74/uber-driving-self.

Birdsong, Shelly. "Pittsburgh & Castle Shannon Railroad." *Historic American Engineering Record*, PA-410 (n.d.): 13–14.

Bowman, Lee. "Riders Bid Farewell to 'Parkway Limited.'" *Pittsburgh Press*, November 14, 1981, sec. A.

GTECH Strategies. "Preserving a Piece of Pittsburgh's Incline History." October 24, 2016. https://gtechstrategies.org/preserving-piece-pittsburghs-incline-history.

Johnstown Inclined Plane. "History." June 18, 2017. https://www.inclinedplane.org/history.

Official Site of the Duquesne Incline. "About the Incline." June 18, 2017. http://www.duquesneincline.org/index.php?page=about-the-incline.

Pennsylvania Transportation. Mansfield: Pennsylvania Historical Association, 1968.

Pennsylvania Trolley Museum. "Early Days & Formative Years." November 21, 2013. https://pa-trolley.org/ptm-quick-history/early-days-formative-years.

Pittsburgh Commercial Gazette. "On the Hill-Tops." May 10, 1884.

Pittsburgh Highways. "Martin Luther King Jr. East Busway." August 5, 2017. http://pittsburgh.pahighways.com/busways/ebusway.htm.

———. "South Busway." August 5, 2017. http://pittsburgh.pahighways.com/busways/sbusway.html.

———. "West Busway/Wabash HOV Facility." August 5, 2017. http://pittsburgh.pahighways.com/busways/wbusway.html.

Pittsburgh Post-Gazette. "Celebrating City of Pittsburgh's Firsts in Transportation." January 14, 2018. http://www.post-gazette.com/local/south/2009/07/30/Celebrating-city-of-Pittsburgh-s-firsts-in-transportation/stories/200907300244.

———. "History of the Overbrook Line." August 20, 2017. http://old.post-gazette.com/regionstate/20000413TimeLine9.asp.

Pittsburgh Press. "Twentieth Century Progress Dooms Vehicle Incline Built Before Autos Replaced Hansoms and Victorias." October 11, 1935.

Port Authority of Allegheny County. June 18, 2017. http://www.portauthority.org/paac/schedulesmaps/inclines.aspx.

Proceedings of the Engineers' Society of Western Pennsylvania 31 (1915): 932. Pittsburgh, Pennsylvania.

Regan, Bob, and Jeff Wingard. *Pittsburgh Steps: The Story of the City's Public Stairways*. Guilford, CT: Globe Pequot, 2015.

Springirth, Kenneth C. *Pittsburgh Streamlined Trolleys*. Charleston, SC: Arcadia Publishing, 2006.

Wired. "How Pittsburgh Birthed the Age of the Self-Driving Car." June 3, 2017. https://www.wired.com/2016/08/pittsburgh-birthed-age-self-driving-car.

Airports and Aviation

Butler, R.O. *Had a Good Time: Stories from American Postcards*. N.p.: Recorded Books Inc., Grove/Atlantic Inc., 2007.

Eversmeyer, M. *Pittsburgh, 1900–1945*. Charleston, SC: Arcadia Publishing, 2009.

Freeman, P., and T. Freeman. Abandoned and Little Known Airfields. http://www.airfields-freeman.com.

Kambic, T. "Bettis: The Field that Brought Airmail to Pittsburgh." *The Progress* (July 1976).

Montanzez, V. "History Lesson: Amelia Earhart Crash Landing in Pittsburgh." *Pittsburgh Magazine* (2015).

Ohara Township History. http://www.ohara.pa.us/history.asp.

OX5 Aviation Pioneers. "Pittsburgh Aviation History." 2015. http://ox5.org/wp-content/uploads/PGH-B.pdf.

Oyler, J. Bridgeville Remembered. The Bridgeville Area Historical Society. http://bridgevillehistory.org.

Prevenslik, N. "Airport's Past, Present, Future Detailed in Hardbound History." TribLive, 2012. http://triblive.com/x/blairsvilledispatch/s_52256.html.

Trimble, W.F. *High Frontier: A History of Aeronautics in Pennsylvania*. Pittsburgh, PA: University of Pittsburgh Press, 1982.

Drinking Water

Baldwin, Leland D. *Pittsburgh: The Story of a City, 1750–1865*. Pittsburgh: University of Pittsburgh Press, 1937.

The Pittsburgh Water & Sewer Authority. "PGH2O History." http://www.pgh2o.com/history.

Report of the Filtration Commission of the City of Pittsburgh, Pennsylvania. January 1899.

Wastewater

ALCOSAN. "About Us." November 2017. www.alcosan.org.

———. "Wet Weather Plan" (draft), July 2012.

American Society of Civil Engineers (ASCE). *Infrastructure Report Card*, 2017.

———. *Report Card for Pennsylvania's Infrastructure*, 2014.

Anthony, M. "From Pork House to Project Z: An Early History of the Allegheny County Sanitary Authority." *Pittsburgh Engineer Magazine* (Winter 2013).

City of Allegheny. *Report of the City Engineer to the Sewerage Commission on a Proper System of Sewers for the City of Allegheny*. Pittsburgh, PA: printed by Order of Councils by W.G. Johnson & Company, 1869.

Pittsburgh Water and Sewer Authority (PWSA). "The Green First Plan: A City-Wide Green Infrastructure Assessment" (draft). Pittsburgh, PA, 2016.

———. "History." November 2017. www.pgh2o.com/history.

Shamsi, U.M. "Green First Approach for Wet Weather Programs." *Journal of Water Management Modeling* (2017). https://www.chijournal.org.

3RWW. "History." November 2017. www.3riverswetweather.org.

Weisberg, D. "Taming the Water." Public Source, November 2, 2011. www.publicsource.org.

Navigation and Flood Control on the Three Rivers

Edwardo, H., W. Karaffa and B.H. Greene. "First Floating Dam." *Military Engineer*, no. 617 (2002): 61–62.

Johnson, L.R. *The Davis Island Lock and Dam, 1870–1922*. Prepared for the U.S. Army Corps of Engineers, 1985.

———. *The Headwaters District: A History of the Pittsburgh District, U.S. Army Corps of Engineers*. Prepared for the U.S. Army Corps of Engineers, 1978.

Robinson, M.C. *History of Navigation in the Ohio River Basin*. National Waterways Study, U.S. Army Engineer Waterways Support Center, Institute of Water Resources, 1983.

USACE Upper Ohio Navigation Study, Pennsylvania: Final Feasibility Report and Integrated Environmental Impact Statement. October 2014, revised October 2016.

Buildings

Brown, Mark McCullough. "The Cathedral of Learning: Concept, Design, and Construction." Henry Clay Frick Fine Arts Building, University of Pittsburgh, 1987.

Fedele, John. "The Cathedral of Learning: A History." *Pitt Chronicle*, March 12, 2007.

Hatch, Sybil E., and Tyler S. Sprague. *We Had to Be Dreamers*. Seattle, WA: Magnusson Klemencic Associates Inc., 2016.

Helvenston, H. Rey. "Retractable Dome for Pittsburgh's Auditorium." *American Society of Civil Engineers* (June 1961).

Van Trump, James D., and Arthur P. Ziegler. *Landmark Architecture of Allegheny County, Pennsylvania*. Pittsburgh, PA: Pittsburgh History and Landmarks Foundation, 1967.

Weingardt, Richard G. "Circles in the Sky: The Life and Times of George Ferris." *American Society of Civil Engineers* (2009).

———. "Homer Gage Balcom and the Empire State Building." *American Society of Civil Engineers* (April 2011).

Epilogue

Carnegie Mellon University. "Research at CEE." https://www.cmu.edu/cee/research/index.html.

Diverging Diamond Interchange. "History." https://divergingdiamond.com/history.

Swanson School of Engineering—CEE Faculty Research Areas. http://www.engineering.pitt.edu/Departments/Civil-Environmental/_Content/Research/CEE-Faculty-Research-Areas.

ABOUT THE AUTHORS

N. Catherine Bazán-Arias, PhD, PE, D.GE, PMP, F.ASCE, is a senior engineer with DiGioia, Gray & Associates and the chair of the ASCE Pittsburgh Section's 100th Anniversary Task Committee. She has served as president of the Pittsburgh Section and as at-large director of the ASCE National Board of Direction. In 2015, the Engineers' Society of Western Pennsylvania bestowed its Engineer of the Year Award on Cathy.

Gregory F. Scott, PE, is currently serving on the Environmental Water Resources Institute (EWRI) Governing Board. He served two terms as a Region 2 ASCE governor from 2006 until 2012 representing civil engineers from Pennsylvania, Delaware, Maryland and the District of Columbia. He is the lead author of our "Pennsylvania's Borders" and "Drinking Water" chapters.

Jodi Klebick is the public relations representative for the ASCE Pittsburgh Section. Formerly president of Klebick & Company, Jodi served as president of the Board of Pittsburgh Urban Magnet Project and as co-founder of the International Silk Screen Asian Festival. She is a past winner of the National Association of Women Business Owners' "Make the Connection" award.

David L. Wright, PE, PLS, is a project manager with Allegheny County Public Works Department, handling right-of-way acquisition and trail development. He is a former chair of the ASCE Pittsburgh Section's History and Heritage Committee and director for Pennsylvania Canal Society and Canal Society of Ohio.

John F. Oyler, PhD, PE, has recently completed twenty-five years as an associate professor in the Civil and Environmental Engineering Department at the University of Pittsburgh, a career preceded by thirty-eight years as an engineer and engineering manager for the Dravo Corporation. He has an intense interest in local history and functions as the historian for the Bridgeville Area Historical Society.

Jason M. Machuga, PE, is a transportation engineer working in Pittsburgh. He coauthored the "Roads and Highways" and "Public Transportation" chapters.

Carrie Machuga is a public involvement specialist working in Pittsburgh. She coauthored the "Roads and Highways" and "Public Transportation" chapters.

Todd Wilson, MBA, PE, is an award-winning transportation engineer currently serving as the ASCE Pittsburgh Section's History and Heritage chair. He wrote the "Bridges" chapter and performed Pittsburgh's bridge count. Todd has traveled to all fifty states and twenty countries researching and photographing bridges, and he previously coauthored Arcadia Publishing's *Images of America: Pittsburgh's Bridges*.

Patrick Mulvihill, DEd, teaches undergraduate and graduate courses as an assistant professor of management in the Rowland School of Business at Point Park University. Mulvihill was also an academic information analyst at Point Park and a part-time instructor for both the School of Business and Department of Criminal Justice and Intelligence Studies. He authored the "Airports and Aviation" chapter.

Rachel Rampa currently serves as the assistant communications manager at the Pittsburgh Water and Sewer Authority (PWSA). Rachel brings her seventeen years of marketing and communications experience to PWSA and is also the collections manager at Brew: The Museum of Beer in Pittsburgh. She coauthored the "Drinking Water" chapter.

Uzair (Sam) Shamsi, PhD, PE, F.ASCE, D.WRE, is a member of the Board of Directors for the ASCE Pittsburgh Section, SPEO and La Roche College. Sam is also the current Continuing Education Committee chair for the Pittsburgh Section and authored the "Wastewater" chapter.

Brian H. Greene, PhD, PG, completed a thirty-two-year career with the U.S. Army Corps of Engineers, Pittsburgh District, and currently works for Gannett Fleming Inc. He has been chairperson of the AEG Dams Committee since 2008 and been involved with foundations of dams for forty years. Brian has published more than twenty-five technical papers.

Anton H. Krysa, PE, is a retired structural engineer with the U.S. Army Corps of Engineers with thirty-five years of experience in the design of navigational and flood-control structures in the Pittsburgh District. He was often called on to design specialized post-tensioned anchors to extend the service life of aging facilities.

Werner C. Loehlein, PE, M.ASCE, is a retired supervisory hydraulic engineer from the U.S. Army Corps of Engineers, Pittsburgh District, where he spent forty-four years. He is currently an adjunct professor at the University of Pittsburgh. Werner is a former ASCE Pittsburgh Section president and has published twenty-six technical papers.

Stephen Stoltz, PE, is the chief of the Navigation Design Branch within the Engineering & Construction Division of the U.S. Army Corps of Engineers, Pittsburgh District. He specializes in engineering management of complex inland navigation design projects. Stephen served as treasurer of the ASCE Pittsburgh Section's Structures Technical Group.

Patrick J. Sullivan Jr., PE, M.ASCE, is a principal with Civil & Environmental Consultants Inc. in Pittsburgh and has more than thirty-three years of experience in water resources, civil, environmental and geotechnical engineering. He served as president of the ASCE Pittsburgh Section in 2016–17 and is licensed in eight states.

Visit us at
www.historypress.net

www.ingramcontent.com/pod-product-compliance
Lightning Source LLC
LaVergne TN
LVHW052336100826
845147LV00020B/1080

* 9 7 8 1 6 2 5 8 5 9 6 9 3 *